English Heart, Hindi Heartland

FLASHPOINTS

The series solicits books that consider literature beyond strictly national and disciplinary frameworks, distinguished both by their historical grounding and their theoretical and conceptual strength. We seek studies that engage theory without losing touch with history and work historically without falling into uncritical positivism. FlashPoints aims for a broad audience within the humanities and the social sciences concerned with moments of cultural emergence and transformation. In a Benjaminian mode, FlashPoints is interested in how literature contributes to forming new constellations of culture and history and in how such formations function critically and politically in the present. Available online at http://repositories.cdlib.org/ucpress.

1. *On Pain of Speech: Fantasies of the First Order and the Literary Rant,* by Dina Al-Kassim
2. *Moses and Multiculturalism,* by Barbara Johnson, with a foreword by Barbara Rietveld
3. *The Cosmic Time of Empire: Modern Britain and World Literature,* by Adam Barrows
4. *Poetry in Pieces: César Vallejo and Lyric Modernity,* by Michelle Clayton
5. *Disarming Words: Empire and the Seductions of Translation in Egypt,* by Shaden M. Tageldin
6. *Wings for Our Courage: Gender, Erudition, and Republican Thought,* by Stephanie H. Jed
7. *The Cultural Return,* by Susan Hegeman
8. *English Heart, Hindi Heartland: The Political Life of Literature in India,* by Rashmi Sadana

English Heart, Hindi Heartland

The Political Life of Literature in India

Rashmi Sadana

UNIVERSITY OF CALIFORNIA PRESS
Berkeley · Los Angeles · London

THIS BOOK IS MADE POSSIBLE BY A COLLABORATIVE GRANT FROM THE ANDREW W. MELLON FOUNDATION.

University of California Press, one of the most distinguished university presses in the United States, enriches lives around the world by advancing scholarship in the humanities, social sciences, and natural sciences. Its activities are supported by the UC Press Foundation and by philanthropic contributions from individuals and institutions. For more information, visit www.ucpress.edu.

University of California Press
Berkeley and Los Angeles, California

University of California Press, Ltd.
London, England

Library of Congress Cataloging-in-Publication Data

Sadana, Rashmi.
English Heart, Hindi Heartland: The Political Life of Literature in India / Rashmi Sadana.
p. cm.—(FlashPoints ; 8)
Includes bibliographical references and index.
ISBN 978-0-520-26957-6 (pbk. : alk. paper)
1. Indic literature (English)—20th century—History and criticism. 2. Publishers and publishing—India—History—20th century. 3. Book industries and trade—India—History—20th century. 4. Politics and literature—India—History—20th century. 5. Postcolonialism in literature. 6. Postcolonialism—India. I. Title.
PR9489.6.S26 2012
820.9'954090051—dc23

2011026588

Manufactured in the United States of America
21 20 19 18 17 16 15 14 13 12
10 9 8 7 6 5 4 3 2 1

In keeping with a commitment to support environmentally responsible and sustainable printing practices, UC Press has printed this book on 50-pound Enterprise, a 30% post-consumer-waste, recycled, deinked fiber that is processed chlorine-free. It is acid-free and meets all ANSI/NISO (Z 39.48) requirements.

For my parents and my sister

Contents

Acknowledgments

This book is about the politics of language in India's literary field. Several key figures in that field—the publisher Ravi Dayal, the writer Nirmal Verma, the literary scholar Meenakshi Mukherjee—passed away before it was published. I am grateful to them and to all those represented in these pages who shared their experiences and insights with me.

The support for the original research for this book came from Foreign Language and Area Studies fellowships, a Society of Women Geographers' Fellowship, a Robert E. Lowie Grant, and two Humanities Research Grants from the University of California, Berkeley, where I was a graduate student in anthropology. Lawrence Cohen, my advisor at Berkeley, has been with this project from beginning to end, and his support, in too many ways to recount, has been tremendous. Vasudha Dalmia has been a true mentor to me, and I must have consulted her on every aspect of this book and its publication. I can't thank her enough. At Berkeley, I was also inspired and challenged by Stefania Pandolfo, Aihwa Ong, Raka Ray, Gene Irschick, Tom Metcalf, Sharon Kaufman, Michael Watts, Trinh Minh Ha, and Usha Jain. I first began to form some of the intellectual questions I had about Indian modernity when I took Sudipta Kaviraj's politics seminar at the School of Oriental and African Studies, and I was fortunate to be able to study with him again when he came to Berkeley as a visiting scholar. It was my good luck that Ram Guha was also a visiting scholar around this time and taught a brilliant course on Gandhi.

The period of revision and further research was made possible when I was a National Science Foundation–funded postdoctoral fellow at Columbia University, in the Department of Anthropology, from 2003 to 2006, and then by a second postdoctoral fellowship in the Committee on Global Thought in 2006–7. I thank Nick Dirks, Sherry Ortner, Brink Messick, Kate Wittenberg, Partha Chatterjee, and Akeel Bilgrami for providing the intellectual support and institutional space that made my time there so productive and enjoyable. In New York, I was also fortunate to receive encouragement and valuable feedback for this project from Robert Young and Rajeswari Sunder Rajan.

My revisions were helped along with the excellent comments I received from audiences when I was invited to present work at the Mellon Humanities Workshop at Stanford University, the South Asia Colloquium in Anthropology at Yale University, the Department of English at New York University, the Departments of History and Asian Languages and Cultures at the University of Michigan at Ann Arbor, the Department of Anthropology at the London School of Economics, the Women's Studies Programme at Jawaharlal Nehru University, the Centre for Contemporary Theory in Baroda, and at Sarai / the Centre for the Study of Developing Societies in Delhi.

Teaching in India for the past two years has been a wonderful experience and has deepened my understanding of the issues of place and language that are central to this book. I thank my students, as well as V. R. Muraleedharan and Chella Rajan of the Indian Institute of Technology (IIT) Madras and Amrit Srinivasan of IIT Delhi for making it possible. The Sahitya Akademi was one of my research sites, but it also became a place where I sat and wrote. I thank the staff of the library there and especially S. Padmanabham.

I feel lucky to be part of the FlashPoints series and am grateful to the editorial board for its enthusiastic support of the manuscript from the start. Special thanks go to Ali Behdad of FlashPoints and Lynne Withey of UC Press for expertly shepherding the manuscript through. I also thank my two anonymous reviewers for their excellent suggestions for revision. I was thrilled to have Rukun Advani on board as the publisher of the book in India, and credit goes to him for coming up with the book's title. Portions of this book originally appeared in earlier versions in the following journals: "Two Tales of the City: The Place of English and the Limits of Postcolonial Critique," in *Interventions;* and

"A Suitable Text for a Vegetarian Audience: Questions of Authenticity and the Politics of Translation," in *Public Culture*.

The continual support of family and friends has strengthened and, in many cases, made possible this work. I thank Promilla Mathur, Veena Naregal, Sunila and Pramod Sharma, Sonia Palitana, Raj and Indra Chugh and families, who over the years in their respective homes created a base for me in Delhi, Mumbai, and Pune, one that was then happily fortified by Harini Narayanan, Gautam Mody, and Alli Roshini in Delhi and Padma and R.I. Narayanan in Chennai. Veena Sadana, Suren Sadana, Ritu Sadana, Jacques Bury, Jacques-Kabir Bury, and Gitanjali Bury have given unstinting support everywhere and through it all. Meanwhile, Ambika delights as we anticipate which language her first words will be in.

My co-conspirators, Falu Bakrania, Ritu Birla, Diana Blank, Anindita Chakrabarty, Batya Elul, Ilana Feldman, Paul Frymer, Rachel Heiman, Poonam Joshi, Mani Lambert, Scott Morrison, Gustav Peebles, Renee Rubin Ross, Neil Safier, Shalini Satkunandanan, Miriam Ticktin, and Ananya Vajpeyi read drafts, showed by example, and much else; Vivek Narayanan did all the above and brought the essential perspective that had been missing for too long.

Prologue

The Slush Pile

In the mid-1990s, working as a part-time editorial assistant at Granta in London, I was, for a very short time, in charge of the slush pile. The pile consisted mostly of short stories that had been sent in to the magazine; they came unsolicited and without representation by a literary agent. The submissions largely came from the United States and Britain but also from places like Bangladesh, Canada, India, Kenya, Nigeria, and Singapore—together sometimes referred to as the British Commonwealth or, lately, the Anglophone world. I found myself reading stamps and return addresses as carefully as the stories and concluded that they made a story of their own.

I read solicited manuscripts, too, most of which came from first-time American and British writers, all of whom had agents. But it is the slush pile I was most impressed by, the collective bulk of it, lying in stacks that lined one side of the office. On several Saturdays I was asked to come in to read through it, that immovable feast. I was given few formal instructions about what to do, but I knew I was supposed to make the pile smaller, if for no other reason than to create room for the new submissions that were continually streaming in. Someone gave me a stack of little mimeographed rejection slips. It was assumed that if I came across a gem I would pass it on to the editor. Unfortunately, on the few Saturdays I worked on the slush pile, that never happened, but the experience gave me a different way to think about the nature of what is often called "postcolonial literature."

As I sifted through the pile and read through the stories, it became apparent just how different these writers' relationships to the English language were. The pile offered an array of Englishes, but it also offered an array of literary representations from vastly different societies. It seemed too simple to think of this literary democracy that was the slush pile as evidence of a vibrant Commonwealth or Anglophone world of letters. Instead, I started to think about what was behind some of this English, such as the other languages in its midst, and the realms of literary production in different parts of the world. In the case of India, whose cultural and political history I had been studying at the School of Oriental and African Studies (SOAS), English was just one of more than a dozen important literary languages with long histories of their own, including Hindi, Urdu, Tamil, Marathi, Malayalam, and Bengali, to name a hefty handful.

In those days, from the Granta office in Islington, I used to take the tube from Angel station; two stops later, Russell Square, and a short walk over to SOAS. Between trendy Islington and stately Russell Square, I would change from the Northern Line to the Piccadilly Line at King's Cross Station, surely one of the world's most impressive confluences of people, nationalities, and languages. Where, I wondered, did literature begin? In a place? In a language? Over that year, I started to see in concrete terms how publishing was about the politics of language and location.

I also saw in the offerings of the slush pile a politics of desire. It made me consider what literature was before agents and publication, before texts are made great and become known. I became increasingly curious about the writers of these submissions themselves and how they might live in a non-English milieu or a multilingual one, yet write in English, and sometimes desire to be published abroad. Did their stories *have* to be told in English? Or was it just that the desire to be published internationally was very strong? Was what I was seeing in the slush pile the old Naipaulian quest, writers desperate to connect to a bigger, wider, better literary world, writers whose very sense of self and being in the world depended on it? Was it not possible to be a writer at home? Or was the very meaning of writing in English still, after years of supposed independence, to aim for London?

Some of these questions have been at the center of postcolonial studies for many years. Its central paradigm—indigenous resistance to colonial domination and, in literary terms, of "writing back to empire"—has necessarily and productively emphasized "the postcolonial" as a conversation between Europe and its others. It has largely been the story of how writers of colonized or formerly colonized nations reappropriated European colonial languages—English, French, Spanish, and Portuguese—as a form of political resistance and cultural critique. This paradigm forged new understandings of the nature of knowledge, culture, and power in diverse colonial and postcolonial contexts. It also became a way to begin to understand the neocolonial world in which we live.[1]

Yet the premise of the postcolonial critique has been that the traffic in ideas moves from the centers to the peripheries and back again. I believe this premise, based as it is on a single model of resistance, limits our understanding of how colonial languages become indigenized and begin to create their own circuits of knowledge and power. Part of the problem with the postcolonial paradigm is that it has become so linked with issues of migration and transnationalism that the focus has remained on and in many respects has strengthened an East-West dialectic. What, I wondered, had happened and was happening to English in India after colonization? How and why did it sustain itself as an Indian language, and to what extent was it part of Indian cultural life? These questions are pertinent not only to the story of English in India, but to the disparate processes of the globalization of English happening around the world.

I became convinced that I would not find the answers only by reading and analyzing Indian English texts or by comparing them to other bodies of literature. The texts mattered, but so, I started to believe, did the place from which the writing emerged. For one, I needed more tools that would enable me to see—literally—the ground of literature. As a result, I turned to anthropology as a way to question the role of language in colonial discourse, the relationship between history and ethnography, and eventually between language and textual production.[2] I realized that rather than only study literature, I needed to immerse myself in the larger world of the production of literature in India.

CHAPTER I

Reading Delhi and Beyond

THE PAVEMENT BOOKSELLER

I ask a pavement bookseller what he has for sale, and he replies, "Only best-sellers." I have little interest in best-sellers, but that is about to change. "What makes a book a best-seller?" I ask matter-of-factly. He points to *Difficult Daughters,* the first novel by the Delhi-based writer Manju Kapur. To me this novel is serious literary fiction, and I am happy to hear that it is also selling well. A paperback copy of the book is lying face up on the ground with other novels, magazines, travel guides, and histories about India. Whether for tourists or locals, in Delhi the roadside compulsion to define India is strong.

We are in Kamla Nagar market in north Delhi, near Delhi University. The bookshops here on Bungalow Road mostly sell English-language textbooks. Students appear with lists and leave with books, the ones they have to have, the ones they can't get online. One shop in the row sells spiritual texts and guides; it has the most floor space and the fewest customers. The pavements are reserved for best-sellers. Some are re-bound photocopies selling for half the price of the published versions. The print is faded, but you can still read it.

The pavement bookseller explains to me in Hindi that when Amitabh Bachchan asked who the author of *Difficult Daughters* was, as a trivia question on *Kaun Banega Crorepati?* (Who Wants to Be a Millionaire?), the novel started to sell.[1] What became a best-seller certainly also had to do with the perennial best-seller status of the Bachchan brand. If the "Big B" was mentioning the novel and asking who its author was, surely it was worth knowing who she was and perhaps even buying what she had written.

A few years later when I told Kapur about my encounter, she smiled incredulously and said, "Really?" At that time the paperback version of her fourth novel, *Home* (2006), was just coming out, and she was a bit dismayed by the cover. It was being published by Random House India, one of the new MNCs (multinational corporations) on the block that had launched its Indian venture with Kapur's novel. The hardcover features a curtained window on the facade of a house with a telephone wire crossing the foreground, all overlaid in mustard hues. I told Kapur how I thought the image perfectly captured the essence of the novel, since the reader gets to pull aside that curtain and witness the intimate lives of a joint family in an everyday Delhi milieu, the old neighborhood of Karol Bagh. She smiled and nodded and said, "But Rashmi, you're an academic so you *see* that."

Now it was my turn to be dismayed. I said, "But I'm a reader first! It appealed to me naturally!"

She then sighed and explained that she wanted her novel to be seen as serious literature but that her editor thought the book could be both serious and more popular, that is, reach a wider audience. The paperback version had a shinier look: its cover featured a blurred figure of a woman in a colorful sari with a large bunch of keys tied to her waist, as is the custom of the female head of household in the kind of joint family being depicted in the novel; another woman looms in the background, suggesting intrigue and potential conflict. Kapur was happy to have more readers, but she was also hoping the new cover would not diminish the seriousness of the work.

We returned to Amitabh Bachchan, and Kapur told me she had been at home watching the show with her family the night the question was asked. She seemed amused by it, even if reluctant to associate her works with a distinctly nonliterary media hype.

Star TV's *Kaun Banega Crorepati?* was the most popular Hindi television show at the time and became the vehicle by which Amitabh Bachchan reclaimed his number one superstar status. That the show was in Hindi but also offered up elements of Indian English culture was no surprise, as the worlds of Hindi and English constantly overlap. Moreover, print and electronic media worlds, especially in the nation's "metros," or urban centers, have become increasingly multilingual; Hindi newspapers feature advertisements in Hindi and English;

Hindi radio, especially stations geared to younger audiences, is peppered with English phrases and words; and popular Hindi romantic comedies feature titles such as *Jab We Met* (When We Met) and *Love Aaj Kal* (Love These Days), with Hindi dialogue spliced with English to match.

However, this "mixing" (*Hinglish,* as it is sometimes called) is evidence not merely of greater linguistic facility among India's cultural consumers; many, in fact, argue that the quality of spoken English in India is becoming worse, not better, as the number of people who know English increases. On the one hand, the urban middle classes have come to define their own identities partly through their association with the English language; English has become more integral to middle-class identity in the past few decades and has led to the rise of a sizable middle-class readership for English-language publications. On the other hand, the desire for the language is greatly expanding as more people further down the class and caste hierarchies see the possibility of adding it, in some form, to their social profiles. What has changed for everyone is that the things people feel they should or have to know—cultural information, trends, and trivia—are crossing the linguistic divide like never before.

On another pavement, in south Delhi, the drama heightens as younger "booksellers" step down onto the asphalt, selling their wares to the calibrated interludes of stop-and-go traffic. They sell paperbacks and glossy magazines, as well as balloons, roses, tissue boxes, and kitchen towels. The scene is replayed throughout the day and into the evening at any major "cutting," or intersection. An insistent boy carrying a stack of books will try to sell you a copy of Kiran Desai's *The Inheritance of Loss* as you sit in an auto rickshaw or car (as opposed to if you're riding a bicycle or on the bus).[2] He will also have Amartya Sen's *The Argumentative Indian* on offer, Jhumpa Lahiri's *The Interpreter of Maladies,* and perhaps Khushwant Singh's *Train to Pakistan.*[3] These are some of the emblems of Indian English culture, sold alongside international best-sellers by authors such as John Grisham, Paulo Coelho, and Dan Brown.

The boy, it turns out, gives most of his money to his parents, and with the encouragement of a local nongovernmental organization is learning the Hindi alphabet on some afternoons under the flyover. It is sometimes hard to know what the "serious" literature is in this scenario: the boy's life circumstance or the book in his hand?

In Delhi, as elsewhere, the two continually go together, but here what separates the boy from the book and the motorized world of

Indian English cultural production and consumption it represents is not merely the money to buy the book, but a private English-medium education that makes his chances of gaining fluency in English and entrance to the jobs and access to the cultural emblems of that world practically nonexistent. The legendary social divides in Indian society—of caste, class, gender, religion, and, perhaps most significant, urban versus rural belonging—work in tandem with linguistic divides. To speak of urban elites is to refer to the class of people (the rich, the upper middle class, and many sectors of the middle classes, who also tend to be upper caste) who are educated from primary school onward with English as their medium of instruction. The rest of India, about 80 percent of Indians have, until recently, tended to be educated in government schools that may teach English as a subject but whose medium of instruction is in one of the thirteen other official state languages. The boy may well be represented in the books that he sells, but he probably won't ever read them.[4]

It is this disjuncture—between the language on the ground, of daily life, and literary representation—that is most relevant to the place and role of Indian fiction in English. And it is in fact what raises the stakes of literary debate in the Indian context. English is part of the social scene, but the bulk of conversations and sentiments of fictional characters would in reality take place not in English but in one or more of the other Indian languages. More important, this disjuncture is indicative of a larger schism in Indian society that has to do not only with language as it is spoken but with the disparate thought-worlds and hierarchies of language that saturate everyday life. The linguistic divide is sometimes quite stark, especially where poverty and the lack of access to education mark its parameters. However, in many respects the divide is even more insidious for those who "know" English but have not had the opportunity to master it.

This divide came into relief in the tragic real-life story of Brajesh Kumar, a Hindi-educated twenty-two-year-old who came to Noida (a middle-class extension of Delhi's urban sprawl) and entered the world of English higher education to study engineering at a technical college. Kumar was from Jaunpur, a small city in Uttar Pradesh (the largest state in India and part of the Hindi heartland), and though he studied English as one of his subjects until the tenth standard, his medium of instruction was Hindi. In his suicide note he wrote that he had felt undue pressure from his English-language courses and did not want to burden his parents with the costs of English coaching to help him prepare better. This disturbing story, covered in the Hindi and English print media, highlights the long-standing divide between students who come from English-medium backgrounds and those who come from "vernacular" ones.[5]

Several months after Kumar's suicide, the weekly news magazine *Outlook* ran a cover story calling this aspect of the linguistic gap the "English speaking curse."[6] The story describes the mad rush among the middle and lower classes to get some kind of English any way they can, amid a sea of unqualified teachers at the primary and secondary levels, where funding for English-language instruction is extremely limited. Four months earlier, in the same magazine, the same reporter had written another story, "Jab They Met," about how English words and ideas were increasingly being featured in small Hindi magazines and newspapers published in the heart of the "Hindi belt," the state of Uttar Pradesh, in cities such as Lucknow, Kanpur, Meerut, Agra, and Varanasi.[7] It spoke of how young people wanted to "get into the mode" of English. The aim of editors in such a mixing of the languages was to reach "aspirational readers"—defined as people aged eighteen to thirty-five who wanted to live their lives partly in English and be part of the consumer revolution—and to use the English language "especially for descriptions of modular kitchens, cutlery, electronic gadgetry, career options and college festivals."[8]

Of course, there is nothing contradictory about English being both the language of aspiration and a curse for those not in a position to master it. The issue is not merely one of who speaks English and who does not, but is more substantially about a cultural divide based on the kinds of English that people learn, speak, and write, depending on their access to different levels and kinds of education. As one writer explained it to me, "One was learning English, talking English, but a large part of our consciousness was something else. There was a strange contradiction, which always had to be negotiated."[9] In these milieus knowing English is not a question of language fluency alone but says much about one's exposure to different worlds and values. This familiarity with and exposure to English resides alongside the mother tongues, hence English is at the heart of many social changes, yet exists within the reality and idea of the Hindi heartland. More and more Indians know and aspire to learn English, but the language marks a social, economic, and at times cultural divide that most are unable to cross.

THE PLACE OF ENGLISH

This book is an account of postcolonial literary production, centering on the relationship between language politics—what languages mean and represent—and the literary field. Its premise is that English has taken on a more contentious *and* more varied role in Indian society than it did during the period of British colonial rule, which formally ended in 1947. After independence, I argue, colonial binaries withered away, as English became a mediator between other Indian languages. English often takes on the role of mediator because of its seeming neutrality, a position that has a logic and new politics of its own. Politically, English becomes less polarizing even as it remains a clear marker—a dividing line really—of certain kinds of elite privilege. Knowing English fluently provides innumerable social and economic advantages, but—and this is key—it always exists alongside Hindi or other Indian languages. I contend that it is the qualities that different languages impart, at times manifesting themselves as veritable ideologies relating to caste, class, gender, and other social and political identities, that become important in a multilingual context, qualities that highlight or detract from various aspects of the identity of an individual, an institution, a community, or even a state.[10] Even for those who do not know English—the vast majority—it is a symbol of what is attainable by Indians in India, and this belief or aspiration is not confined to urban consumers or to the upper-middle-class intelligentsia. It is for this reason that an inquiry into the English language in India can never only be a story of numbers or of discernible public spheres. Most crucially, since English in Indian society is no longer a language of colonization, it must be viewed in the context of other Indian languages in order to grasp the profound effects of linguistic identity on modern Indian life. It is not enough to say that English is a language of privilege, which it is, among other things. English is also a language of globalization, but this fact alone does not tell us very much without delving into the specificities of place, history, and present circumstance. To this end, the process of reading Delhi and beyond highlights the place of English in the multilingual literary consciousness, the work it does as mediator in India's linguistic landscape, and its complex and hierarchical social positioning vis-à-vis other Indian languages, especially Hindi. What I find remarkable is not that Indians write, publish, and critique in the language of the former colonizer but that they do so in an English that has been infused with the social and political consequences of its own indigenization.

It is in this respect that literature, and specifically what might be called an *anthropology of literature*—one that outlines the literary field, delves into its production, and analyzes its individuals and institutions ethnographically—can allow us to understand the complexity of English and its relationship to other Indian languages and sensibilities in India today. In regard to "anthropology of literature," Arjun Appadurai likens the role of fiction to myth, and hence as being part of "the conceptual repertoire of contemporary societies." He goes on to link fictional content with social mores when he writes, "Readers of novels and poems can be moved to intense action (as with *The Satanic Verses* of Salman Rushdie) and their authors often contribute to the construction of social and moral maps for their readers."[11] I would take this assertion much further to say that the world of literary production shows not only how authors, readers, and texts but also how the entire nexus of literary producers and discourse create a social and moral framework that at once reflects and interrogates cultural norms. In this regard, I draw on Pierre Bourdieu's notion of the literary field; however, I build on it to include the social and political dynamics central to a field composed of multilingual literary production.[12] The multilingual is not a mere feature of the literary landscape, but rather it redefines and makes more complex the very notion of a literary field. My approach, therefore, dwells on the connections between place, language, and textual production in order to show what language comes to stand for in people's lives and in society more generally.[13]

By "literary production," I do not mean the actual putting together of paper and print, but I do mean the producers of literature, be they writers, editors, translators, or publishers. I also mean booksellers, readers, critics, and others who create meaning in and around texts once they are in the public domain. To write about these figures, connected directly and indirectly to the production of literary texts and the social life of those texts, is to do more than contextualize or even historicize the literary text at hand. By combining textual and ethnographic analysis, this book critically evaluates the problem and promise of the chasm between social reality and literary representation. It mines the paradoxes within this chasm. Thus, literary production is not only about the creation of literary texts but also about the production of social identities and the differences between them. It is in this sense that the anthropology of literature, in the way I have developed it, offers a new analytical frame.

In my approach, literature and novels in particular are significant both as works of the imagination and as cultural emblems that travel across regional and national borders carrying an array of meanings and significations.[14] These meanings and significations reveal the moral uses and dimensions of language. Thus, my engagement with English in India is also an engagement with English in the world, that is to say, how English mediates a set of social and linguistic hierarchies not only in India but also globally. This project is, in many respects, a response to the phenomenon of Indian fiction in English that has swept the English-reading public and its marketplace around the globe since the 1980s. This phenomenon has been mostly celebrated outside India; within India the response has been more ambivalent and varied, largely because of the homegrown politics of language that frame this international attention. The broadest aim of this book is to understand how this debate looks from the Indian side and to delve into the social factors and historical circumstances that have shaped it.

Literary fiction is a modern artistic and cultural form, replete with social values and symbolic meanings. I contend that these values and meanings created in turn generate their own social reality and that this reality has become central to debates about what is deemed culturally and linguistically authentic. I present different aspects of the authenticity question in the chapters that follow, showing it to be an elastic, ever-changing set of principles, one that drives debate and action forward in unlikely ways. A principal aim of this book is to show how the idea of cultural authenticity is a political variable—rather than a cultural truth—that comes into play depending on particular social and literary circumstances. These circumstances most often hinge on issues of caste, class, and gender—that is to say, markers of identity formation that have been central to the shifting, unstable articulation of modern Indian selves. English, and the way it is positioned among the other Indian languages, does not represent a fixed pole but rather serves to change political and literary alliances among classes and castes, often in surprising ways.

WRITING IN ENGLISH

Many Indian novelists who write in English about Indian social realities have written or spoken about how in one way or another they cross the linguistic divides of society by literally translating conversations in their heads as they write dialogue. This is not to say that they regret writing in English or believe they are less Indian or lesser writers for doing so. Yet the seeds of cultural debate—essentially about the relationship between literature and society—are planted here. It is not, however, that authors writing in other Indian languages represent monolingual worlds in their novels either. Where there is Hindi, for instance, and its numerous dialects, there might be Punjabi and Bengali too. Yet the literary divide among these languages—social, cultural, and linguistic—would certainly be smaller. There are more similarities between Bengali and Hindi or Hindi and Punjabi than there are between English and any of these languages. North Indian languages share Sanskrit and Persian-based vocabularies, a fact that distinguishes them as a whole from English. And even though the north Indian languages are also "modern" languages in that their grammatical and lexical standardizations were formalized in the eighteenth and nineteenth centuries, they have been existing in dialect form alongside one another for much longer; there is a shared social history among and between these languages to which English is a latecomer. English exists in a distinct temporal reality in the Indian context, as well as a distinct spatial reality, as it belongs neither to any particular region nor to any "indigenous" Indian cultural tradition. As in much of the world, literary culture—a record of society's practices, histories, and ways of being—has been part and parcel of defining particular nations and the cultures therein. For English, which has long symbolized modernity, its shifting lines of exclusivity create a situation whereby it commands popular recognition as a sign and symbol while largely being an instrument of the elite.

The Indian-English writer Shashi Deshpande, who comes from a Kannada-speaking background and has lived in various multilingual settings in India, puts it this way: "The truth is, that while a great number of people do speak English, it is yet a language that many of the characters we write of will not only *not* be speaking, it is one they will not be *able* to speak."[15]

Deshpande's comment captures a central paradox of writing about India in English: the question of the linguistic authenticity of fictional characters themselves. All writing and art for that matter is a representation of reality, even when the language of the text matches the language of the street. English is certainly part of India's social reality; it has filtered in to the most common and basic level of everyday communication, often in the form of phrases, slogans, idiomatic expressions, and advertisements. Yet English is not a sustained presence in most people's lives, and even those for whom it is are surrounded by non-English worlds. As a result, English can at times seem like it is everywhere and nowhere.[16]

Deshpande, who has grappled with incessant querying by others as to not just *why* she works in English, but *how she can,* writes: "The point is, that, not only was English not born in this soil, it has not grown through the daily use of all classes of people or developed layers like a pearl through years of its association with a particular people."[17]

However, this is only the beginning of the story. Despite Deshpande's assessment of linguistic authenticity, or perhaps because of it, she eloquently defends her use of English in the making of her literary prose and resents being marginalized for it, as she and others often are by the regional literary establishments. In an essay in which she both defines and rejects the notion of being a marginal writer, she writes of the circumscribed quality of her English, of its place in her life but also in the lives of her readers: "I began writing in English, not because I 'chose' to, but because it was the only language I could express myself in, the only language I really read. Yet, I had two other languages at home, languages I spoke and lived my daily life in. Living in a small town in a middle-class family, life was, in fact, lived mainly in Kannada; English came into the picture only for certain purposes and at certain times. . . . My readers were people who read English, but lived their personal and emotional lives, like I did, in their own languages."[18]

Although she writes in English, Deshpande draws on different linguistic realities to create her literary world. She is also informed by the thought-worlds of those languages and that knowledge, and those realities become part of her literary fiction. What is also significant for Deshpande is that her audience is chiefly based in India. Hers is not a Western-based readership but one composed of fellow Indians who have a relationship to the English language similar to hers. Some would say she is less successful because she is not known abroad, while others claim she has a more organic and grounded relationship to things Indian, even though she writes in English.

It is often these gradations of alleged insider- and outsider-ness that animate Indian cultural debates. An Indian author may write in English, but then, what is her perceived proximity to other languages, and by implication, to other social worlds and ways of thinking? Whether a writer has a "foreign" audience often becomes yet another part of the debate over a text's—and often an author's—cultural authenticity.

If one has a non-Indian audience, there is sometimes an assumption that one must be writing "further away" from Indian social worlds and concerns. When is one an "Indian" writer, and when does one become an NRI (nonresident Indian) or "foreigner"? The latter term, in popular parlance, connotes someone whose interests, and not only geographic location, may no longer "favor" India.

It should come as no surprise in a world of grossly uneven development that there is a moral dimension and sensitivity to how "India" is portrayed.[19] It is in these circumstances where the English language is at once seen as the language of the world literary stage and as a language that has over time come to represent complex, multilingual social worlds. It is no longer a question whether English is an Indian language; what is at issue is the moral dimension of its use and position.

THE REALITY OF FICTION

In fall 2008 I attended a book club meeting at the Habitat Centre in Delhi. Built by an array of corporations, the Habitat Centre is a major cultural venue for the city's elite. It is a vast, airy space near the India Islamic Cultural Centre, the Ford Foundation, UNICEF, the India International Centre, and other venues linking Indian cultural worlds to those abroad. Auto rickshaw—the ubiquitous three-wheel "scooter"—drivers tend to know it only as *"vah badi lal imarat Lodhi Road par"* (that big red building on Lodhi Road). That night at the book club meeting, Aravind Adiga's *The White Tiger* was being discussed. The novel had won the Man Booker Prize the previous month, and Adiga had publicly dedicated his prize "to the people of New Delhi."[20]

The novel was heralded by some critics and derided by others for its recounting of the stark social divides between rich and poor and one poor man's growing resentment of his place in this schema. Adiga is a Chennai-born Indian who was brought up partly in Australia and educated at Oxford and Columbia, details that inevitably became part of his "cultural cache" or, depending on his reviewer, evidence of his "foreignness."

That evening at the book club meeting, about twenty-five people, ranging in age from mid-thirties to mid-seventies, gathered to discuss the novel. After introductions over tea and biscuits in the foyer, we moved to a small auditorium and sat in clusters in the front center section. The two leaders of the group, an older man with short white hair and a woman in her late forties, sat up front facing the small group.

They began by reading from Amitava Kumar's review of the novel that had appeared earlier that week in the English daily *The Hindu*. Kumar criticizes the novel for grossly misrepresenting the realities of everyday life and speech—not because it was written in English but because Adiga's style distances the first-person narrator from the harsh realities of what he sees and describes. Kumar essentially argues that the real people behind Adiga's novel—the underclass that he is heralded for having represented—are in fact disrespected. The book club leaders raised some general questions for the group to consider: To what extent was Adiga's perspective that of an insider or outsider? Was his vision of the "underbelly" of Delhi life authentic or inauthentic? Was Adiga's novel, as Kumar had stated in his review, merely a "cynical anthropology"?[21]

About a third of the group had read the novel, and others said they were planning to, but everyone seemed to have an opinion. The hosts then alternated reading from parts of the beginning of the novel to give the flavor of the text. Written as a series of long letters from the protagonist, Balram Halwai, to the Chinese premier, Wen Jiabao, they explained, the novel begins:

> Mr Premier,
>
> Sir.
>
> Neither you nor I speak English, but there are some things that can be said only in English.
>
> My ex-employer the late Mr. Ashok's ex-wife, Pinky Madam, taught me one of these things; and at 11:32 P.M. today, which was about ten minutes ago, when the lady on All India Radio announced, 'Premier Jiabao is coming to Bangalore next week', I said that thing at once.
>
> In fact, each time when great men like you visit our country I say it. Not that I have anything against great men. In my way, sir, I consider myself one of your kind. But whenever I see our prime minister and his distinguished sidekicks drive to the airport in black cars and get out and do *namastes* before you in front of a TV camera and tell you about how moral and saintly India is, I have to say that thing in English.

They continued for a few pages and then came to another section:

> I am talking of a place in India, at least a third of the country, a fertile place, full of rice fields and wheat fields and ponds in the middle of those fields choked with lotuses and water lilies, and water buffaloes wading through the ponds and chewing on the lotuses and lilies. Those who live in this place call it the Darkness. Please understand, Your Excellency, that India is two countries in one: an India of Light, and an India of Darkness. The ocean brings light to my country. Every place on the map of India near the ocean is well-off. But the river brings darkness to India—the black river.[22]

For some, Adiga's style and portrait of Indian social realities was a timely unveiling of the real social divides in India, a counter to the "India Shining" slogan of the past decade that has trumpeted the roaring GDP and the rising disposable incomes of well-employed urbanites. Others saw the book as a crass diatribe based on Adiga's widely reported journalistic forays into "village India" when he was a reporter for *Time* magazine. Some said that his use of English did not convey the pain of the oppressed but mocked them by making them sound like American teenagers. Were his perceptions in fact "researched" and based on "truth," or were they a "foreigner's" view of what one expected "India" to look like?

In what is essentially an amoral morality tale, the servant-driver Balram eventually kills his rich employer, absconds with a bag of cash, and starts anew as an entrepreneur in Bangalore. He is never caught, nor does he feel remorse, he tells us, even with the knowledge that his extended family in his village would have surely been killed as punishment for his own deed.

The crux of the book club debate that evening—for it turned into a debate—was whether the novel revealed something true about the perpetual state of unease between the haves and have-nots in Delhi or whether it was merely sensationalistic. And if it was sensationalistic, as three quarters of the people in attendance seemed to think, why did it win the Booker?

The younger host asked, "Did the Western mind enjoy the sensationalism of an emerging nation? This award was given by a Western agency after all."

The white-haired man posed another leading question when he suggested we compare *The White Tiger* to other Booker Prize–winning novels the club had read, such as J.M. Coetzee's *Disgrace* and Yann Martel's *The Life of Pi*. "What is the literary merit of this book?" He asked. He went on to compare Adiga's novel to another Indian novel that had been short-listed the same year, Amitav Ghosh's *Sea of Poppies*. "Ghosh is a researched writer," he announced, as if that somehow answered his earlier question. Several people raised their hands, and a lively discussion ensued. One woman started to explain that ever since moving to Delhi she had felt under threat and spoke of how her home had been burgled twice, coinciding with the marriage of each of her daughters. "This book struck a chord with me; this is how it is here," she said. This statement launched the group into a discussion of the glorification of violence in the novel and whether it merely feeds on "middle-class fears." Some argued, "Adiga knows his craft"; "It's readable"; "It has a good style." Others countered with "It is journalistic, not literary"; "There are no real characters"; "It's about marketing"; "He has the formula right"; "It's all about the hype; the timing of the book was perfect." And then, a chorus of voices: "*Sea of Poppies* should have won!"

THE POLITICS OF LITERARY GEOGRAPHY

In India, as elsewhere in the world, the social distinction of English has alienated non-English speakers to such an extent that people speak not of "knowing" English but of "having" it.[23] The social reality of linguistic haves and have-nots stands in stark contrast to the realm of elite cultural production, where Indian fiction in English has brought writers such international acclaim and prestige that many assume—much to the chagrin of writers in the other Indian languages—that Indian literature only comes in English.[24] In this realm of literary production English is often put in contrast to and is often at odds with "the languages" or "bhasha," the appellations commonly used to distinguish English from the other Indian languages. *Bhasha* literally means "speech" and is the Hindi word for "language." Yet the word has now also become part of the English language as spoken among Indians. For instance, sometimes people refer to the "bhashas," pluralizing the word as if it were an English one, or they use the word as an adjective, meaning Indian language other than English, as opposed to "regional" or "vernacular."[25]

If "the bhashas" or "the languages" has a clubby ring to it, it is not because English is not seen as an Indian language in these circles but that English carries a different symbolic meaning in the Indian context. These are the issues—the competing values, ideologies, and identities associated with language—that I explore in the context of literary production today.

English is spoken fluently by close to 5 percent of Indians and is "known" by as much as 10 percent of the population (i.e., about 50 million to 100 million people of a population of just over one billion).[26] As the journalist and former *Times of India* editor Dileep Padgaonkar said to me, "The percentages of English speakers are small, but the numbers are large." Its numerical strength puts English on par with many of the regionally based languages or bhashas. Its place in the global order of things and the fact that it is entwined with modern, urban culture give

MAP 1. Some of the languages of the subcontinent.

English great prestige in the Indian context, while its lack of regional specificity within India often marks it as being culturally inauthentic. Just as there is a global geography that privileges English and its Anglo-American sponsors, there is a linguistic geography within India that recognizes twenty-two official, or "scheduled," languages, as listed in the Eighth Schedule of the Indian Constitution. It is this geography that at once confirms and marginalizes the place of each language in its regional context. Sisir Kumar Das links the competition among languages in each region to "the rise of the middle class within each language community" and to its members having "legitimate aspirations to share political and social power." The result is what he calls "language tension," which becomes "more acute" in such situations. He gives the examples of the sociocultural power of standardized Hindi over the Hindi "dialects," of Urdu over Kashmiri, Bengali over Oriya and Assamese, Tamil over Telugu, and Marathi over Konkani.[27]

English might be irrelevant to some of these interregional linguistic tensions, but it often factors in, either by assuming a more neutral position or by exacerbating class or caste tensions. And it is this linguistic geography that has inadvertently impinged on many regional and national literary and cultural debates. It may be true, as Pascale Casanova has written, that language is the major component of literary capital, but it is perhaps most vital to understand how the nature of that capital changes in different geographic contexts.[28]

In 1949 the Constitution of India included a proviso whereby Hindi was to be "phased in" as the language of national integration, in order to mark a national "resurgence" in the service of the "ordinary citizen." English, after all, had been the language of the erstwhile British colonizers. Meanwhile, Hindi was the most widely spoken language in India, even if its speakers were concentrated in the North. During the proposed fifteen-year transition period, English would retain its bureaucratic and political functions, while there would be "the progressive use of the Hindi language for the official purposes of the Union." The *Report of the Official Language Commission, 1956*, documents the copious debate and analysis regarding the uses of English in India and imagines its role in the future. It is not that the members of the commission did not see the value of English, especially in the realms of science and technology, and the way in which India had benefited and would continue to do so by using the language. In fact, there were as many proponents of keeping English as the official language of the union as there were those who wanted to switch to Hindi.[29] The report itself was in English not only because it was an official government document, but because it was the only language that could link the committee members who came from all corners of the country, north, east, west, and south.

Hindi became a cause and a symbol of national unity, but the language debates pointed to a larger malaise: the Indian languages in general had languished under colonial rule. As one committee member put it, the Indian languages "failed to develop a sufficiently rich and precise vocabulary for the requirements of modern social life, during this period when the progress of scientific knowledge wrought a great revolution in the physical conditions of living in the country."[30] It was perhaps this conflation, of English being not fully Indian and seeing the Indian languages as having suffered under British colonialism, that opened committee members to the idea that Hindi could stand for all things linguistically Indian at the national level, that there could be some postcolonial linguistic redemption after all.

The broader aim after independence, in large part, was in developing not only Hindi but also the thirteen other major languages "so as to make them adequate vehicles of thought and expression" (a somewhat paternalistic attitude to the bhashas that goes back to Macaulay) leading to "the eventual displacement of the English language." At the same time, for reasons of administrative practicality, the official bureaucracy at the national level could only occur in one language. Where English had previously forged a pan-Indian consciousness, credited with enabling a countrywide nationalist leadership to orchestrate the ousting of the British, Hindi would now take over and spread. There would be a "changeover" to Hindi, especially in the fields of "education, administration, and law courts, so as to bring them in a live and continuous communion with the common people of the country."[31] In deference to the other Indian languages, Hindi would not be referred to as the "national language" but the "official language of the Union."

The long-term goal was for Hindi to enable a pan-Indian dialogue and consciousness among all classes of Indians. To this end, the Ministry of Education was charged with creating a new scientific vocabulary in Hindi, organizing the massive translation of administrative documents, teacher training, correspondence courses for Indians in non-Hindi regions, subsidies to Hindi publishers and prizes to their authors, and the elaborate distribution of Hindi books to non-Hindi states, schools, colleges, and libraries. Beyond the rhetoric and debates, what was being called for was nothing less than a linguistic revolution.

But in the decades after independence, the English language was not "phased out," as had been planned by the first postcolonial government. Instead, the language became even more entrenched in public life and the change-over to Hindi never happened. At the same time, governmental programs to promote Hindi have had long-lasting effects on institutions such as publishing houses and cultural bodies such as the Sahitya Akademi. This lopsided cultural "development" kept the reins of Hindi in the firm grasp of its cultural elites, who effectively became the custodians of Hindi culture.

The place of English is defined vis-à-vis Hindi, and also in relation to the other bhashas. In 1956 India's Official Languages Act organized states along linguistic lines, despite the fact that nearly every state has sizable linguistic minorities. So, for instance, although Marathi is the mother tongue of nearly three quarters of those living in the western state of Maharashtra, about 8 percent of Maharashtrians count Hindi as their mother tongue and a little less than 8 percent Urdu. Literature is nevertheless largely mapped along those same state borders to the extent that bhasha literatures are often referred to in English as "regional literatures." In addition, most of these "regional" literatures serve reading populations larger than those of most European nations. For example, there are close to 80 million Hindi speakers in the state of Bihar alone, 74 million Telugu speakers (largely in the state of Andhra Pradesh), and 83 million Bengali speakers, mostly in West Bengal.[32] Hence both the size and the dimensions of a vernacular literary culture become obscured by the idea of the regional. This obfuscation becomes a veritable distortion when regional literature itself is continually juxtaposed with the "global" literature written by Indians in English. In the face of globalized English literary production and the prominence of Indian English writing, the regional has to some extent become a diminutive. Being confined to a limited geographic space has in many respects come to restrict the stature of bhasha literary texts when placed side by side with Indian English ones, as they increasingly and inevitably are.

It had not always been this way. When there were fewer Indians writing in English, in the 1930s, 1940s, and 1950s, for instance, these writers (e.g., Mulk Raj Anand, Attia Hossain, Kamala Markandaya, R.K. Narayan, and Raja Rao) were thought to be writing against the grain. They were thusly perceived in part because they were not taken as seriously by the English literary establishment based, naturally, in London. Yet they were also not taken as seriously in India, since at this time English was not an Indian language in the way it is today.

The change in the relationship between English and bhasha literatures is partly due to the shift in how Indian English writing has been received and published abroad, a dynamic that, I argue (in chapter 8), generates a new politics of place. Yet Indian literature in English also has more validity and social resonance because of a thriving Indian English culture in India itself. English is not tied to any region but is the "second mother tongue," as it is sometimes called, of the urban elite.

Despite all this, the politics of language in India cannot only be understood simply in terms of the position of English vis-à-vis "the languages." The languages have their own rivalries and similarities among them and have varying levels of power nationally. This power derives not only from the numerical strength of each language but also from its perceived cultural worth. This "cultural worth," not surprisingly, is often defined by a language community's elite members in their chosen fields of cultural production.[33] If we consider the language debates and commission report of 1956, we may see, for instance, how English and Hindi were in some ways pitted against each other from the start. They, and their elites, vied for the role of official language *(rajbhasha)* of the union as well as for the unofficial role as link language. As a result, English and Hindi are in some respects competing national languages.[34] This competition exists not only in Delhi, where there is a concentration of elite discourse in both languages, but also in north India more broadly where Hindi is most often recorded as the mother tongue. What we see in the relationship between English and Hindi is a dovetailing of the cultural and the political.

Forty percent of Indians, over 400 million people, are Hindi speakers, though within the appellation "Hindi" are some forty-eight "dialects," such as Bhojpuri, Haryanvi, Marwari, and Awadhi. Hindi is not only a regional language but also, by virtue of being the most widely spoken Indian language, a national language.[35] Like English, its hegemonic power is contested but for quite different reasons; for many south Indians, for instance, Hindi is a symbol and arbiter of north Indian cultural hegemony. The major south Indian languages—Telugu, Tamil, Kannada, and Malayalam—are Dravidian based and use different scripts from each other and from the Indo-European languages of the North. This north-south linguistic divide is as relevant to contemporary Indian language politics as the global promises and pretensions of English. Yet English is also implicated in this divide.

The South, especially the state of Tamilnadu, famously opposed Hindi becoming India's national language in a fierce and occasionally violent cultural war. In 1835, during colonial rule, the British made English the language of government (replacing Persian), and knowing English became necessary to obtain coveted government jobs, including those in the railways and the police force. Over a century later, if Hindi were to replace English at the national level in post-independence India, access to government jobs would require knowing Hindi instead.[36] In this context, English was curiously a more neutral language and, paradoxically for an elite language, one that promised more equality between north and south Indians. If Hindi was to become the national language, as leaders such as Mohandas K. Gandhi had fervently hoped and planned, the practical consequence would be that south Indians would all of a sudden be at a disadvantage.[37] It would be incumbent on them, and not their compatriots from the Hindi belt, to learn an entirely new language (and script) to be in a position to vie for a lucrative government job. For educated, largely Brahmin or other upper-caste south Indians, English was already the language of social advancement and cultural comfort. It did not threaten their regional linguistic identities precisely because it was not the language of another Indian region; yet it allowed them a place to assert themselves on an equal footing with English-educated north Indians and to excel at the national level.[38] The anti-Hindi agitations in the South had the distinction of having the support of nearly all factions of the political spectrum. For non-Brahmins (the overwhelming majority) in Tamilnadu, for instance, Hindi was threatening on at least two accounts: first, it drew away from education in Tamil and represented Sanskrit-based north Indian cultural hegemony; and second, if they had to learn a second language, they wanted it to be English, which they saw as a world language and one that Brahmins had already had the opportunity to master.[39]

Like Hindi, English is able to divide and unite depending on what is at stake; for all its documentation of Hindi and English and its comparisons to other linguistic situations the world over, what the *Report of the Official Language Commission* fails to stress enough is the relationship and rivalries among the Indian languages themselves. The afterglow of independence and desire for unity did not mean that upper-class Indians were going to change their linguistic priorities if they didn't have to. English thus became more deeply entrenched in the postcolonial government bureaucracy and also became the official language of higher education. The Official Languages Act of 1963 allowed for the continued use alongside Hindi, even after the fifteen-year phasing out period that was to come to an end in 1965. In 1964, when there were more attempts to institute Hindi alone, more protests in the South and elsewhere ensued. By 1967 English was officially sanctioned, albeit in reluctant official prose: it would be a "subsidiary official language." What English became instead, to use Aijaz Ahmad's phrase, was "*the* language of national integration and bourgeois civility."[40]

Unlike Hindi, English could never be viewed as representing "the people"; hence its authenticity was always questioned, even after being accepted as an Indian language in a variety of realms. As Alok Rai makes clear in his analysis of the competition between Hindi and English elites in contemporary north India, it is only political discourse and cultural production in Hindi that may "liberate those democratic energies of the Hindi belt."[41] What Rai is pointing to here is a language's social and political potential in society. Despite its pan-Indian pose, English comes with ready-made restraints. Hindi is not only the language of the home, the street, and popular culture (film, radio, television, pulp fiction, comics, music, theater) in north India but also the language of conversation and asides in the very spaces where English is supposedly the most entrenched: government halls and university campuses.

The very fact that political constituencies may be defined in terms of language of course means that these constituencies themselves may be in flux. For instance, English education of dubious quality is increasingly being "sold" to the masses. The widespread opening of "global language institutes" in villages and small towns is just one indication that aspiring to know English is no longer the reserve of the urban middle classes; from construction workers to security guards to domestic servants—everyone wants their children to have English.[42] What distinguishes these institutes (which may be located in office blocks or, more often, in ramshackle buildings in local bazaars) is that unlike the traditional English-medium education available to upper-class and upper-caste Indians by way of convent schools run by nuns, or today, by mostly private Indian trusts and religious societies, these new centers are open to lower-caste and lower-class groups who could not afford private English-medium schools. Contemporary language politics in fact hinges on the politics of both caste and class. English, in the meantime, is signified less and less as a colonial remnant and more as a contemporary global attribute.

THE CASTE OF LANGUAGE

The globalization of English has been especially relevant for the most socially disadvantaged, those who are from the lowest castes. In the realm of Dalit (what used to be called "untouchable" or *harijan*) and Dalit-*bahujan* (which includes a wider group of lower castes) politics, access to the English language has come to symbolize a new political consciousness. In fact, some see the language as the most feasible and direct method of social empowerment. They are less concerned with the so-called linguistic authenticity of the bhashas since the "culture" (and specifically, religion) associated with that authenticity is one from which they are already excluded. As detailed in the scholar and activist Kancha Ilaiah's contemporary political tract, *Why I Am Not a Hindu*, since Dalits were excluded from Hindu society in terms of day-to-day life on the scriptural principle of being "polluted," why should they embrace a Hindu identity now?[43] Ilaiah's tract hit a nerve precisely because he connected the issue of caste to religious identity and practice, challenging the idea of a large, all-encompassing Hindu cultural umbrella. In one fell swoop arguments such as his threaten the Hindu vote bank, one that is dependent on lower-caste and Dalit voters.[44]

In many respects, Dalit and Dalit-*bahujan* intellectuals who advocate English are responding to an already apparent desire by urban and rural lower classes to have English education for their children. However, for the English education of "the masses," there will have to be more than an array of private and unregulated language institutes. The real question has become whether or not government schools, which are administered by each state, will offer English-medium education and not just English as one among many subjects. What may seem linguistically expedient to some is a fierce cultural debate for others. Proponents of vernacular, or "mother tongue," education are opposed to such a measure because they fear the end of the mother tongues in terms of their social and cultural relevance. These proponents tend to be from the ranks of the cultural and political elite, who see language as a key associative symbol in consolidating vote banks; the mother tongues are to be defended from everything from urban elites to the forces of globalization. Most centrally, perhaps, is the notion of what the mother tongues are in the first place. With the standardization of grammar, a more Sanskritized vocabulary, and the choice of script, the bhashas as modern, written languages are also expressions of upper-caste culture.[45] In this sense, English, even with its colonial past and globalizing power, is in the context of Dalit activism a more neutral language. Its neutrality is premised on more direct access to power, one that bypasses more traditional or engrained social boundaries. Ilaiah and other activists also point out that those same mother tongue proponents, not to mention many mother-tongue-loving politicians who see Dalits as being essential for their own Hindu vote banks, make sure to send their own children to private English-medium schools.[46]

Chandrabhan Prasad has been most associated with the promotion of English for Dalits in his column, "Dalit Diary," which appears in the *Pioneer,* a national English-language newspaper. His method of instilling this desire and what he frames as a right to the language has come in the curious form of proposing English as a "Dalit Goddess." Prasad's immediate aim is not historical revisionism but instead to instill the desire for English, a desire that he hopes will turn into a serious demand for the language among Dalits themselves. He wonders why in the past six decades of Indian independence the demand for government-sponsored education in the language has not flourished. In line with this cause is what many see as his audacious valorization of Thomas B. Macaulay as a kind of saint for the oppressed Dalits.[47] Since 2006 Prasad has made headlines for hosting parties each year in Delhi to celebrate the anniversary of Macaulay's birth.[48] What is unclear at this point is how much of an effect this kind of valorization—to what extent it is a real movement or a gimmick—will have in the actual education of Dalits or even the creation of Dalit literature in English. It is clear, however, that the idea of English education as being the sole provenance of the elite is changing.

For these reasons and others, thinking about English solely as a postcolonial language fails to capture the complexity of the distinctions associated with language in India today. The term *postcolonial* has come to flatten our sense of a variety of social and cultural changes in over sixty years of post-independence cultural politics, mostly because it relies on the colonizer/colonized model of power and cultural interaction, and it sidelines competing nationalisms and regionalisms and their ideologies. Even in Delhi, where the architectural and governmental remnants of the British Raj are most obvious, English is no longer a postcolonial language. Instead, as I argue throughout, it is a mediator in a variety of cultural and political realms.

THE CITY AS A LITERARY FIELD

This mediation is, perhaps, most apparent in Delhi, a city that is not only the political and bureaucratic capital of India but also the center of English and Hindi publishing as well as home to the country's preeminent universities and a wide array of cultural institutions representing local, regional, national, and international concerns. Recognizing Delhi as the site of the major publishing houses in English and Hindi first enabled me to see the city as a literary field. There would certainly be other places in which to study Indian literary fields, in Mumbai, Kolkata, or Chennai, to name just three important sites of cultural production; however, to understand the nature of Hindi and English as competing national languages in the cultural and political arenas, there is no more significant site than Delhi. In addition, Delhi's role as the cultural capital of north India and as the bureaucratic center of the nation makes it a clearinghouse for a range of cultural production; hence I also contend that seeing literary production through Delhi allows one to understand the relationship not only between English and Hindi but also between those two languages and the bhashas as a whole, thereby allowing an understanding of the most important cultural debates of the past few decades. While my research took me to other places and people in those places, it always brought me back to Delhi. At the same time, this book is not a case study of literary production in Delhi; rather it views questions *through* Delhi and its institutions.

My inquiry began by focusing on the city as the publishing center for Hindi and English, the two most published languages in India. On the roadside the connection between publishers, distributors, and consumers seemed very direct. I would see the small publishing houses on Ansari Road just within the walls of Old Delhi and often buy books directly from them. This exploration led me to the Hindi publishers Rajkamal Prakashan and Vani Prakashan, with informal chats leading to longer interviews. It was the artisanal bent of these publishers, and also of the English publisher Ravi Dayal, that I found most interesting. They were small operations, yet pioneering ones that had become major cultural institutions. The life histories of the publishers themselves—how they came to publishing, how they related to the various languages they spoke, how the publishing endeavor itself was a way of imagining postcolonial India—said much about Hindi and English from the decades just after Indian independence to the cultural changes that economic liberalization brought from the 1990s onward. I saw that there was a larger significance to Delhi being the center of publishing of these two languages in particular since they are competing national languages. Furthermore, as I soon discovered, other languages—Bengali, Tamil, Marathi, for instance—figure prominently in the story of both Hindi and English. These interests in literary publishing dovetailed with the historic and contemporary site of the city as the bureaucratic center of the nation's cultural institutions and policy making, where discourses around nation and region but also around gender, caste, class, and religion are continually being made and remade. It was in this sense that I started to see certain literary discourses and the multilingual literary field itself as moving through Delhi and its institutions. In this latter case the relationship between Hindi and the other Indian languages and English and the other Indian languages comes into sharp relief. In part, my argument is that what is produced (not only books but also ideas, policies, attitudes, experiences, and discourses) in Delhi, by virtue of its position as the former colonial capital and current, increasingly globalizing cultural capital of India, frames and influences debates regarding *other* Indian languages in their respective regions. However, rather than merely finding a hegemonic Delhi-centric discourse, what I came to see were its obstinacies, fissures, and inconsistencies, spurring me on to unravel what I saw as the decentering politics of identity, language, nationhood, regionalism, and globalization.

Delhi is the place where many writers from regional centers come to work and live, so the interaction between region and nation also plays out in the everyday life of the city and its institutions. Several of the figures I engage with throughout this book come from language backgrounds other than Hindi (e.g., Malayalam, Bengali, and Marathi); yet they are individuals who here in some way contribute to the construction of the regional, national, or global via the prism of Delhi's bureaucratic and cultural worlds. Delhi has, not surprisingly, played a dominant role in defining the parameters of national culture, yet these definitions are more often than not contested in regional milieus. This book explores what is at stake in some of these contestations by positing Delhi not only as a site of literary production but also as a producer of cultural meaning.

People like to say that Delhi has no literary culture of its own. This perception is due in part to the migration of Punjabis (and their language) to the city at the time of partition, in 1947. The language on the street changed forever, as, to the chagrin of many, you now hear a mix of Hindi and Punjabi. Yet the city has the largest concentration of Hindi writers and publishers. Though Delhi is the geographic center of the Hindi belt, where many Hindi writers, publishers, academics, and other elites live, it is not the only cultural center of Hindi. Centers of Hindi culture are also to be found in other places in the Hindi belt, places where Hindi is spoken without as much English (or Punjabi), where fewer people speak English fluently, and where the daily culture is saturated with Hindi rather than a mix of Hindi and English. Most of these Hindi centers—such as Allahabad and Varanasi—are in the state of Uttar Pradesh, which borders Delhi and is the most populous state in India. In the state of Bihar, it is the city of Patna where Hindi books are sold en masse. And in Madhya Pradesh, it is the city of Bhopal that is a cultural center for many Hindi novelists and poets. These other places, not Delhi, are commonly referred to as the "Hindi heartland." However, the "Hindi heartland" does not only refer to geography; it is also an idea about the place and role of Hindi. In this sense, the Hindi poet and literary administrator Ashok Vajpeyi told me, "Most small towns can't contain Hindi writers." It is precisely the institutional and cultural offerings of Delhi that have made it a center for Hindi writers and a place where their own ideas have come into contact with those of writers in many other Indian languages, including English.

AN ETHNOGRAPHY OF LITERATURE

The process of English becoming an Indian language, alongside Hindi and vis-à-vis other Indian languages, is the story that I tell from the perspective of various individuals and institutions in Delhi. My reading of Delhi, my conversations with publishers, writers, and others, and my analysis of texts is meant to suggest how the meanings of a language, from the everyday to the ideological, emerge from the places in which it is located and lived through. In this sense, the individual's feeling for language is a prism through which I analyze contemporary society.

In the chapters that follow I document subjective relationships people have to language and their own linguistic histories. I locate them in particular places and in different paradigms, including the local, national, regional, and global. This book is not a survey of all I saw and everyone I met but instead is organized around key figures and places in the literary landscape that I believe encapsulate the most important features, moments, and problems that have defined Indian literary life since the early 1970s. In this respect the chapters offer three interlinked narratives: the cultural history of English vis-à-vis Hindi and the bhashas, debates about cultural and linguistic authenticity, and the city of Delhi as a postcolonial and now increasingly globalized literary space. Each chapter moves *across* the literary field, from text to institution to publisher to author or translator, highlighting and expanding on key ethnographic moments and milieus. My approach is not only a method but also a vision of how to understand English in India and the relationship between literature and politics in the world more generally.

In terms of my day-to-day methodology, I began by visiting publishing houses and bookshops and going to events at the Sahitya Akademi, the Habitat Centre, the India International Centre, and other cultural venues in the city. At first I relied on newspaper listings for cultural events, crunched in extra small type at the bottom of pages in newspapers such as the *Times of India*, *Hindustan Times* (in Hindi and English), and *The Hindu*. Then, as I got to know people, I was invited to events or often just had a sense of where to show up or whom to call. As the writer Pankaj Mishra told me in one of my first interviews in 2001, there was no real literary "scene" to speak of in Delhi. He was right in terms of—and this is what Mishra emphasized—the quality and standards of writing, editing, reviewing, and publishing that one found elsewhere and were essential to creating an informed reading public leading to that somewhat elusive scene. Yet my sense was that there *was* something to be found and discerned, even if it might not look the same, or feel the same, as it did elsewhere. I started to see English in relation to the bhashas, especially when listening to writers who inhabited multiple worlds, such as Gagan Gill, Nirmal Verma, K. Satchidanandan, Kiran Nagarkar, and Geetanjali Shree. And when I had conversations with publishers such as Ashok Maheshwari and Ravi Dayal, who offered their own linguistic ethnographies of the city, a map of the literary field began to emerge. As I connected my knowledge of texts to places and people, I began not only to read differently but also to see how a variety of literary practitioners were connected to each other and to recurring notions, realities, and moralities of place. Most of all, I started to see how different languages stood for different things to different people and what was being created emotionally, intellectually, and politically—on the page, in their lives, and in society—because of it.

The more research I did, the more my methods adapted to what I was seeing and listening to and the more I saw how language ideologies exist not only in political realms but in everyday life as well. For this reason, I propose the "ethnographic study of literature" as a way to link the practices of literary production to the politics of language in discrete and overlapping literary fields of actors and institutions. Literature reflects and represents, but it is also produced and consumed under particular social and political conditions. An ethnographic approach emphasizes the connection between literary analysis and the meaning of everyday life, even as it interrogates and unravels it. However, the point is not merely to juxtapose the methods of ethnography and literary analysis for some kind of layering effect, interpretation upon interpretation. Instead my method is to intercut between ethnography and the study of literary texts. I use the insights gleaned from one practice or realm to question and inform the analysis of another. It is this intercutting, a practice that emerged from my own experience of research, that is central to the critical perspective I introduce in the pages that follow.

CHAPTER 2

Two Tales of a City

On family visits to Delhi in the 1970s, South Extension was a sleepy place. It was always summer, and we spent the afternoons under the fan. My cousins and I would quiz each other over world geography, they with their British-inflected accents and spellings, me with my wide American syllables. By early evening one of my uncles would show up with a bag of warm samosas and a few bottles of sweet, sizzling Thums Up. Later, another uncle would whiz me around on his scooter to the market. He would get a *paan,* and I would stand next to him and invariably be approached by street children for a rupee coin.

Once on the outskirts of the city where partition-era refugees bought government-subsidized plots of land, today South Extension is a congested, central, and upscale residential area and shopping hub. Over the years I have watched as the area has become emblematic of the new New Delhi, surrounded by flyovers, jammed with cars, and home to an array of Indian and multinational shops. Land prices have skyrocketed, and today the horseshoe-shaped market looks like a car dealership, its mass of metal gleaming under the sun. My grandmother's small pink bungalow on B-block, with its open courtyard, has long since been sold and its flowering tree replaced by an imposing multistory house built to the edge of the road. I still visit the market to eat *gol gappas* standing outside Bengali Sweets, admire the costly fabrics at Heritage, and visit Tekson's Bookshop, but I lament the passing of time and people more than the place itself.

This chapter unearths a cultural history of English, one whose origins I locate in the realm of colonial-era political discourse and in Delhi's Urdu, sublimely poetic past. In the post-independence era, it has become a truism to say, "English is an Indian language." And yet its path to becoming one, especially in the literary realm, has been contested at every step along the way. I reflect on the "authenticity" of English by providing a genealogy of it from the political to the literary realm. I argue that it is precisely *how* English becomes indigenized and compromised in specific instances and discrete contexts that will come to characterize the language and its eventual role as mediator. On the one hand, the back story of any understanding of English as an Indian literary language necessarily involves its role as a language in the nationalist movement and, more specifically, as being integral to India's political modernity. English was accepted, by necessity, in the political realm because it allowed a pan-Indian movement, one that was at first merely critical of British rule and then eventually anti-British, to take shape. On the other hand, it is not that English came to represent a national consciousness in any holistic sense but rather that the language created a new set of compromises, both emotional and ideological.

A VERY SHORT STORY ABOUT ENGLISH BECOMING INDIAN

As Indians became increasingly critical of colonial rule in the last half of the nineteenth century, the British started to monitor Indian-language publications; in the aftermath of the 1857 Revolt in particular, they were naturally worried about seditious ideas that could reach the masses in their own languages.[1] *Amrita Bazar Patrika,* a Bengali newspaper launched in 1868, was one such publication; the periodical was known for its support and promotion of Indian nationalist causes. In 1878 the British colonial government in India passed the Vernacular Press Act, which allowed legal censorship of the Indian press. *Amrita Bazar Patrika* responded by switching to publishing in English overnight, effectively evading a law meant for "vernacular" languages.

English, of course, was not a vernacular language, and, in this case, publishing in English turned out to be a safe zone for Indians. The British were not willing to censor the English-language press, among which *Amrita Bazar Patrika* could now be counted, since doing so would go against their own notions of free speech. In line with their liberal values, freedom of the English-language press was paramount. Freedom of speech for Indians in their own languages—the bhashas—was not. That the editors of *Amrita Bazar Patrika* switched from publishing in Bengali to publishing in English suggested an attempt to alter the language-knowledge-power equation to their advantage.

For Partha Chatterjee, the story of the Vernacular Press Act reveals the true nature of British liberalism and what he calls "the rule of colonial difference."[2] He argues that the universal claims of British liberalism were in fact undermined and curtailed by its own racism, since there was one rule for the British and another for Indians.[3] In another way, we may also read this event as symbolic of the myriad ways in which the English language, by necessity, ingenuity, and compromise, has become Indian. There was a social and political cost to the Indian editors, who in a move to retain their right to publish, had to turn their Bengali newspaper into an English-language one. There was also a cost to the newspaper's Bengali readers, many of whom were not able to read English. Their "rights"—access to information and ideas in their own language—were surely diminished in the process. It is this kind of process that created a wedge between Indian English-speaking elites and Indians who did not have English, a wedge that would create its own set of problems for the subsequent nationalist movement. And yet if English was seen as the language of whites alone, this was beginning to change.

GANDHI'S PLEA

A year before Indian independence nationalist leaders were necessarily reckoning with what would stay and what would go. In a column that appeared in English on August 25, 1946, in the consciousness-raising journal *Harijan,* Mohandas K. Gandhi wrote, "I love the English tongue in its own place, but I am its inveterate opponent, if it usurps a place which does not belong to it."[4]

In Gandhi's view, the English language had come with the English, had become rooted in elite Indian society, and had gone on to become a contributing factor to what divided elite Indian interests from the masses. Gandhi's diatribe against English was part of his larger critique of modernity, most cogently presented in *Hind Swaraj* (Indian Home Rule) in 1909. In that book, written as a polemic, Gandhi emphasized that self-government (the rule of one's self by the self) was a precursor to home rule and that for Indians to rule themselves they would have to draw on Indian, not Western, civilization. This line of reasoning, of course, required a definition of what constituted Indian civilization. It did not matter to Gandhi that he himself had been educated in London, an experience that enabled his work as a civil rights lawyer in South Africa and his ultimate return to lead the anticolonial movement in India. Gandhi saw his critique of English in India as a critique of the class of people (in India and those abroad, such as the Indian expats in London whom he had met) who spoke English and claimed to represent the nation.

Despite the fact that English may have been one of the factors leading to the very creation of the first pan-Indian national organization, in the form of the Indian National Congress, established in 1885, Gandhi saw English as another example of what divided Indians and argued that it obstructed real freedom, or *swaraj* (self-rule). The seeming contradiction of what English allowed and prevented fit perfectly with Gandhi's larger critique of the nationalist movement—that it was elitist and out of touch with the masses. In *Hind Swaraj,* written originally in Gujarati as a dialogue between a newspaper editor and a reader (and then translated into English by Gandhi himself), he writes:

> *Reader*: Do I then understand that you do not consider English education necessary for obtaining Home Rule?
>
> *Editor*: My answer is yes and no. To give millions a knowledge of English is to enslave them. The foundation that Macaulay laid of education has enslaved us. I do not suggest that he had any such intention, but that has been the result. Is it not a sad commentary that we should have to speak of Home Rule in a foreign tongue?
>
> . . .
>
> Is it not a most painful thing that, if I want to go to a court of justice, I must employ the English language as a medium; that, when I become a barrister, I may not speak my mother-tongue, and that someone else should have to translate to me from my own language? Is not this absolutely absurd? Is it not a sign of slavery? Am I to blame the English for it or myself? It is we, the English-knowing men, that have enslaved India. The curse of the nation will rest not upon the English but upon us.[5]

English was, however, not only a symbol of class division; rather it actively jeopardized the nationalist movement. Gandhi saw it as an impediment to the winning of independence and self-government. How could Indians come to know themselves in English? For him, it was not a question of English being a window on the world for some Indians but of there being an unbridgeable divide between poor and rich and between rural and urban, a divide along the lines of one's experience and way of life. To be sure, Gandhi did not want to imagine an independent India where English was still entrenched.

What did not fit in with Gandhi's polemic on things foreign and things Indian was that English in India did not exist in a vacuum; it was not something that had been casually set down and was now to be brushed aside. It had not merely usurped a "place," but had created a place for itself. Gandhi, as much as the more comfortably Anglicized Jawaharlal Nehru, saw the great utility of English as a "link language" among Indian nationalists from across the incipient nation. But even if English had its place during colonial rule, that place would have to change after independence had been won. Gandhi's diatribes against English emphasized the symbolic, class-oriented meaning of English in India rather than its existence alongside other Indian languages. At the same time, his own strategic uses of English, Gujarati, and Hindi, depending on whom he was addressing or in which form and genre he was writing, were in some respects a precursor to how issues of language in post-independence India would unfold. And in this regard, it is also important to note that Gandhi's advocacy of Hindi as the national language was not for the Sanskritized Hindi associated with Hindus but for Hindustani, the common spoken language of north India that was a mix of Hindi and Urdu.

In this chapter, I consider how the meaning and "place" of English changes from being a strategic language to an Indian one and how this shift alters not only the language and its meanings and uses in India, but the urban landscape itself. This shift is not wholesale; instead, as I will show, English comes to take on a mediating role. In considering Delhi's linguistic history as showcased in two novels—Ahmed Ali's *Twilight in Delhi* and Anita Desai's *In Custody*—I detail how the process of English becoming Indian is closely linked to its relationship to the other Indian languages. This relationship has to do with the social locations of language—of Urdu, Hindi, and English—and the conflicts that arise therein. Both novels happen to be classics, although that is not why I write about them. Rather, I was struck by the resonances—relating to language, genre, and narrative—between them as I thought about the corpus of writing in English by Indians as a whole. This resonance tells a story about the temporal and political disjuncture between the colonial and the postcolonial and relays a social and cultural narrative of acclimatization.

WHERE THE NOVEL TRUMPS POETRY

In the case of north India, the place of English is moderated by the shifting relationship between Hindi and Urdu. English becomes a way for Indians to reflect on their own society and to speak to different publics but also, most crucially perhaps, to assess the other Indian languages in its midst. The question of genre, of the novel versus poetry, and how the former trumps the latter, is also integral to these two tales; it is a mirror of the place of English vis-à-vis Urdu, whereby English plays the part of the novel, or prose, and Urdu of poetry, or verse. This mapping of genre onto language has, as Dipesh Chakrabarty has detailed, much to do with how prose, rather than poetry, has become associated with political modernity, with its attendant notions of the "real" and an "objectivist engagement with the world." Poetry, meanwhile, comes to be seen as existing "outside of historical time."[6] This distinction plays out in my reading of *Twilight in Delhi* and *In Custody* both at the level of genre and of language, as we see the English-language prose novel take center stage.

The work of Ahmed Ali offers a literary understanding of what it meant for English to "usurp" another place, language, and cultural sensibility. His 1940 novel, *Twilight in Delhi,* brought us Mir Nihal, a Muslim patriarch steeped in the traditions and language of Urdu, living in Old Delhi at the peak of Britain's colonial enterprise in India, from 1911 to 1919. Forty-four years later, Anita Desai wrote another novel about the demise of Urdu; *In Custody* recounts the tale of a Hindi (and Hindu) lecturer from the provinces who comes to Old Delhi to find and interview one of the last great Urdu poets.

By reading the texts as a pair, one may see how Delhi is transformed by its own linguistic history from the colonial period to a postcolonial one and how the English language becomes central in the reformulation of people's identities as Indians and as Dilliwallahs (residents of Delhi). Read one after the other, the two novels create a surprising narrative of their own. This narrative is not a straightforward sociology or history of the city of Delhi but instead has to do with the kinds of artifice being created by each author. It is also a narrative whose resonance is felt precisely because of the gap in time between the writing of the two texts. English, it turns out, was not about the relationship between Indians and Britons but more about Indians' relationships with one another. Where Ali directs his English prose to English speakers outside India, Desai is speaking to a homegrown audience of Indian English readers, people essentially like herself. Further, both novels recount prose stories about Urdu poetry; in Ali's tale it is the poetic imagining of Old Delhi; in Desai, the tale of a degenerating Urdu poet living in Old Delhi. Both tales highlight a disjuncture in terms of language and of genre, whereby the form of the novel is summoned to explain, as it were, the poetic.

Franco Moretti intriguingly writes of the relation between verse and prose to suggest why prose prevailed "so thoroughly" in the historical formation of the novel. He writes that "a line of verse can to a certain extent stand alone, and so it encourages independent clauses; prose is continuous, it's more of a construction. I don't think it's an accident that the myth of 'inspiration' is so seldom evoked for prose: inspiration is too instantaneous to make sense there, too much like a gift; and prose is not a gift; it's work."[7] The distinction between "work" and "gift" plays out especially, and to great comic effect, in *In Custody,* where the poet Nur sees his poetic utterances as gifts that can never be returned from a prosaic, Hindi world. Both novels tell tales of how poetry is romanticized, comically and tragically, and how it is ultimately squashed by a less forgiving, prose-dominant world. The lament for language is also a lament for genre.

Ali (1910–94) was part of an earlier generation of Indian English writers, those whose literary consciousness was formed during the colonial period. By writing a history of Delhi in literary form, Ali assumed the role of historian in the colonizer's language, and he achieved this within the temporal space and climate of the British Raj. His novel employs the English language to tell Britons of the emotional toll on their colonial subjects in a language they will not only understand, but uncannily recognize, as it describes a foreign city they themselves have come to dominate. Desai (b. 1937) is closer to the Salman Rushdie (b. 1947) generation of Indian writers. She came of age just after Indian independence but is usually not included in the post-Rushdie Indian fiction boom. In many ways the style and themes of Desai's fiction form a bridge from one generation of Indian English writers to the next, whereas Rushdie's marks a more decisive break.

Desai's *In Custody* is especially interesting for the way it almost seems to take up temporally where Ali's left off. The protagonist changes from an Urduwallah to a Hindiwallah; Delhi is still the capital but is no longer ruled by the British; most important, the population and character of Delhi have changed considerably after the partition of 1947. Yet, reading Ali's novel and then Desai's, it is also as if the same tale is being passed down and retold. Both novels recount the demise of

Urdu literary culture in the city of Delhi, even if the manner in which they do so points to two different moments in what could be called the "localization" of English in India. Ali's is a mournful tale, heavy with despair and dilapidation; Desai fills her pages with sly humor and linguistic caricatures, balancing the personal failures and unfulfilled longings of her characters. In an attempt to locate Ali and Desai on the same map but then chart the distance between them, I will illustrate the shift from one kind of English to another, a movement that illuminates both the fact of Indian independence from the British and the complicated legacy of the social and linguistic upheavals of the partition of the Indian subcontinent. As a result, *In Custody* may be read as a satirical coda to *Twilight in Delhi* and an index of how English has gone from dominator to the mediator of other Indian languages in the postcolonial era.

TWILIGHT IN DELHI

Twilight in Delhi was originally written in English by a writer who usually wrote in Urdu, and critics have rightly pointed to the Urdu rhythm of Ali's English.[8] Ali made an explicit decision to write the novel in English in order to reach a wider audience outside of India. He writes that he saw the broadcasting of the loss of Urdu culture as a "cause" that "deserved a world-wide audience" and feared that "if presented in Urdu, it would die down within a narrow belt rimmed by Northwest India."[9] In the historical frame of 1930s India, writing in English is quite literally strategic. Ali admits that he must disavow Urdu in order to highlight Urdu, a move that may appear to us today as a classic postcolonial maneuver. His novel writing begins with self-consciousness about the very language in which he chooses to write. And yet, while there is a certain utility in his decision to write in English, his use of the language also leaves a deep literary impression: it marks the very death of Urdu in Delhi that it laments. Ali writes in English in order to "write back to Empire," but it is a lonely, isolated voice, far from Rushdie's triumphant literary arrival in 1980s Britain.

Twilight in Delhi chronicles the decline of Urdu culture in the face of colonial infringements on city space and lifestyles. The novel is an elegy to a Muslim cultural sensibility that by the early twentieth century is inextricably linked to the Urdu language but must now adapt to the new spaces of British-inspired rationality. In this adaptation, as Ali poignantly renders it, Dilliwallahs become subject to the built environment of colonial India.[10]

The novel is set in 1911, two years after the British shifted the colonial capital from Calcutta to Delhi. It should be emphasized that until the early twentieth century the core and political heart of Delhi had always been Old Delhi, the Old City, or Shahjahanabad, as it is still sometimes called. The British reorganization of Delhi, then, is seen as both an assault and containment of this core of the city and the culture within it, both of which over time will become increasingly peripheral.

At the start of the novel British authorities are implementing a number of changes to the urban landscape and infrastructure: the removal of native trees, the widening of streets into boulevards, new sewage systems. Changes in urban form are accompanied by the pomp and circumstance of the public coronation of George V and the grand architectural constructions of what will come to be called New Delhi. In the opening paragraphs of the novel, the narrator chronicles the broad sweeps of history that have come to roost in the city, in grandiose phrases such as, "It was the city of kings and monarchs, of poets and story tellers, courtiers and nobles. But no king lives there today, and the poets are feeling the lack of patronage; and the old inhabitants, though still alive, have lost their pride and grandeur under a foreign yoke."[11] The narrator emphasizes that these alterations to the city's landscape have changed not only the way people live but also the way they feel. The narrator dwells on what was, but even more powerfully, the tone of the novel is such that the reader continually feels as if something is still being taken away. Lament is not a leftover sentiment but something that seeps from the cracks in the soon to be demolished city walls.

These descriptions of early-twentieth-century Delhi are paralleled with flashbacks to the humiliations that Muslims experienced at the hands of the British in the 1857 Mutiny and the First War of Indian Independence. The narrator creates a continuum between these two historical moments to fashion his contemporary despair. But most significantly, Ali creates a narrative of Indian history in English to be "broadcast" beyond the borders of his Urdu-speaking world. The lament begins in 1857 and is literally cemented when the British create a new colonial capital that will be New Delhi. Old Delhi, meanwhile, is home to the historic Muslim quarters of the city, especially in the adjoining by-lanes of the Jama Masjid. This religious containment is mirrored in the Urdu language. Urdu represents a lifestyle through which a cultivated Muslim sensibility is lived. The loss of language as lived in the city is the loss of an entire world.

Ali contrasts the public events and changes to the city with the private world of his protagonist, Mir Nihal, an aging, pigeon-flying, china-collecting Muslim patriarch, "an aristocrat in his habits."[12] As the colonial power intrudes in the city's alleyways and by-lanes, Mir Nihal's life and spirit are in a state of decline and degeneration. In one passage the narrator describes the alleyways of the old city as "tortuous and winding, growing narrower like the road of life" and terminating "at the house of Mir Nihal."[13] Mir Nihal's beloved city is literally closing in on him. He must accept that it is not only a new world that he is no longer part of, but as the narrator describes it, it is a "unity of experience and form" that no longer exists for him.[14] This breakage in the unity of experience and form is paralleled in the form of the novel itself, as Ali renders an Urdu idiom of life in English. While others around him—even members of his own family—adapt and even embrace these changes, Mir Nihal suffers a cultural paralysis that is mirrored by a real paralytic stroke by the novel's end.

Priya Joshi has argued that what prompted Ahmed Ali to write *Twilight in Delhi* was that he had become (and his protagonist Mir Nihal by proxy) an "exile at home," a foreigner in his own land.[15] But it might be more accurate to characterize Mir Nihal as dislocated since his tragedy is precisely that there is no possibility of return and no new place to go to. His dislocation goes beyond the colonizing presence of the British; it is indicative of a sea of cultural changes that are occurring within his own family and in his own neighborhood. Further, this dislocation is a mirroring of the linguistic dislocation in the city itself. It comes at a time when the political distinctions and agendas of Hindus and Muslims under colonial rule have grown, and the shared north Indian language of Hindustani has split into a Sanskritized Hindi and Persianized Urdu.[16] Even if Urdu becomes the language of Pakistan (as it does), the strongest Urdu-language communities in Delhi, Lucknow, and Hyderabad, will unravel but not be able to be reconstituted elsewhere.[17] It is both the city and its language that make the cultural distinctiveness of Urdu life.

In narrative terms, the loss of Urdu culture and its replacement by a crass modernity introduced by the English and their language is most powerfully relayed as a classic generational struggle between father and son. Mir Nihal is increasingly alienated from his son, Asghar, and is resentful of his habits and ways, everything from the English boots his son wears—"You are again wearing those dirty English boots! I don't like them. I will have no aping of the Farangis in my house. Throw them away!"[18]—to his son's fervent desire for a love marriage. When, three quarters of the way into the novel, Asghar finally succeeds in marrying Bilqeece, with whom he has been obsessed from the start, the sad disconnect between the newly wed couple epitomizes the kind of emotional disjuncture with which Ali is preoccupied. The narrator explains:

> Sometimes when they were alone, Ashgar would put his hand round her waist, but this annoyed Bilqeece. She did not say anything to Asghar, but she felt constrained, and would become silent.
>
> 'Why are you so quiet?' Asghar would ask her.
>
> She would sit gazing in front of her and say:
>
> 'I do not know what to say.'
>
> He would have liked to hear her talk of love and happiness, her voice flowing like a sweet murmuring stream, talking of sad and beautiful things. He wanted her to kiss him and caress him, put her arms around his neck and whisper: 'I love you, I love you . . . '
>
> . . .
>
> Now and then Bilqeece looked at him with beautiful, furtive eyes. At such moments Asghar loved her more than anything in the world, and smothered her with kisses. But she was not romantic at all. This damped Asghar's feelings. He thought of his Mushtari Bai and other sweethearts. He remembered the warmth of their passion and their loving ways. By contrast Bilqeece looked so dull and insipid. But she was young and beautiful; and Asghar had built most beautiful castles around her lovely frame.[19]

As English sensibilities trump Urdu ones, and in the novel's triumph over poetry, Ali seems to be saying, love will be domesticated. It is not a simple question of love becoming an exclusive part of so-called private space but rather that the male gaze turns inward to a love unconnected to the city itself. The imposition of new ways of thinking and being (or, importantly, in the case of Asghar, the yearning for and grasping of those new ways) begins a process of shifting social norms. Ashgar puts his modern desires and expectations onto his new, unsuspecting bride. For Ali, English is the language of his text, but it is also a sign of the intrusions of a Westernized, English sensibility. The mounting tragedy of the novel is that Mir Nihal continually refuses the possibility that he can find a place in this changed world. For him, there is no possibility of a dual cultural consciousness, a world of Urdu and English. But even the younger Asghar, in his grasping of English ways, is stymied in his modernistic impulses. He does not become at home in a new world but instead is completely lost (though not destroyed, like his father) by the end of the novel.

IN CUSTODY

At least three historical developments separate the writing of *Twilight in Delhi* and *In Custody.* After the partition of India and Pakistan, Urdu became the national language of Pakistan and hence acquired a nationalistic association for the first time in its own history. This association not only symbolically "consolidated" the newly formed Pakistani nation, with its own host of competing regional languages (Bengali, Punjabi, Sindhi, Balochi, Pashto), but also made official the perception of Urdu as being the language of Muslims. Meanwhile Indian cities like Delhi, Lucknow, and Hyderabad, once centers of Muslim culture and Urdu poetry, lost large sections of their Muslim populations who migrated to Pakistan or were killed in the violence of the partition itself. At the same time, Hindi, though the most widely spoken Indian language, was rejected as the Indian national language (mostly by southern India) despite its majority status. In what could be seen as a sad linguistic farce, Hindi and Urdu, once spoken as a lingua franca of north India in the form of Hindustani, were delinked to represent two nations with two national languages (Hindi and Urdu) that did not adequately represent the people in whose name they were created.[20]

By this time, English had become a sign of bourgeois India and middle-class aspiration, symbolized not only by the urban conglomerate of government, higher education, and commerce but also by such popular publications as the *Illustrated Weekly of India,* scholarly publications by Indian intellectuals in the 1960s and 1970s, and the burgeoning canon of Indian English literary texts themselves. That there is and will be cultural production in English became a given, and its contestation became part and parcel of local and regional struggles, with little or no reference to empire. These major sociological shifts created a new linguistic and political culture in the city of Delhi, and *In Custody* reflects some of those changes.

In Desai's novel, and as distinct from Ali's, English is no longer a sign of Westernization but instead mediates an internal Indian discourse. If Ali's lament of Urdu is focused on the imposition of English modernity, in Desai's satirical portrait, Urdu culture has already become a relic. We may detect farce even in the setup of Desai's novel, which tells the story of Deven, a glum, small-town Hindi lecturer whose real and perhaps sole passion is Urdu poetry. Part of the satiric power of *In Custody* is that it is a hapless Hindi lecturer who goes to interview and record the poetic utterances of one of the last great living Urdu poets, called Nur. Deven is slight and unsure of himself; the narrator tells us that Deven's early life experience had taught him how to get by: "to lie low and remain invisible."[21] The title of the novel refers to Deven's quest to have Nur's poems in his custody, for safekeeping and for the possible revival of the Urdu poetic tradition. As in *Twilight in Delhi,* the demise of one literary form (poetry) is being told through another (the novel). However, Desai's novel relies on a different spatial order to do so. Where Ali brings to life the public and private spaces of Old Delhi, Desai highlights the space between Old Delhi (seeped in culture) and the new hinterlands of Delhi (devoid of culture). Where Urdu culture was symbolized as being on the decline in Ali's Delhi, in Desai's Delhi it is a nearly dead literary presence. In this regard, her novel is also a post-partition view of the state of literary language in Old Delhi; but, unlike Ali's novel, it illuminates the space of Hindi as much as Urdu. So for instance, Murad, a buffoon-like character in the novel who has started up an Urdu literary journal says, "Someone has to keep alive the glorious tradition of Urdu literature. If we do not do it, at whatever cost, how will it survive in this era of—that vegetarian monster, Hindi? . . . That language of peasants . . . raised on radishes and potatoes."[22]

The notion of cultural refinement is central to both novels, but Desai's novel views Delhi from the provinces and structures the relationship between Hindi and Urdu accordingly. The spatial ordering of Hindi, Urdu, and English is not dependent on a distinction between public and private space, as it is in *Twilight in Delhi.* Instead, it is reflective of an urban–provincial divide. It is a moment in which English takes the place of Urdu as the language of urban sophistication. Mir Nihal views Delhi as the center of his world, and as the city changes, he becomes emotionally dislocated. For Deven, Delhi is the locus of his desires, which from beginning to end is always just beyond his reach. The space of the "countryside" is never the site of action but a space that Deven must traverse in order to travel to and from Delhi, as the narrator describes:

> Of course the stretch of land between Mirpore and the capital was so short that there was no really rural scenery—most of the fields looked withered and desolate, and tin smokestacks exhaling enormous quantities of very black and foul-smelling smoke, sugar-cane crushing works, cement

> factories, brick kilns, motor repair workshops and the attendant teashops and bus-stops were strung along the highway on both sides, overtaking what might once have been a pleasant agricultural aspect and obliterating it with all the litter and paraphernalia and effluent of industry: concrete, zinc, smoke, pollutants, decay and destruction from which emerged, reportedly, progress and prosperity.[23]

In this passage, the bucolic ideal is unmasked for the industrial wasteland it has become. And yet country and city are tied by this space, or perhaps tied up by it.

What is the "really rural scenery" that Deven expects and hopes for? Would that landscape redeem his position as a small-town Hindi lecturer? Would it perhaps make his spatial positioning more palatable if he were surrounded by something "really rural"? The narrator continues to probe Deven's spatial past:

> As a student he had known the countryside only as a background for an occasional picnic with his friends: they had gone out into it on their bicycles, bought sugar cane from some surly farmer and sat in the shade of a ruined monument to chew it and sing songs from the latest cinema show and talk lewdly of cinema actresses. That countryside had had no more connection with the landscape celebrated in the poetry he read than the present one. Then, after he graduated and married and came to Mirpore to teach, it became for him the impassable desert that lay between him and the capital with its lost treasures of friendship, entertainment, attractions and opportunities. It turned into that strip of no-man's land that lies around a prison, threatening in its desolation.[24]

In this passage, Deven has discovered the despoilment of the space that Hindi was meant to occupy in his ordering of the landscape. But this spatial setup is further betrayed, since Delhi itself only disappoints. It continually offers Deven the possibilities of poetic exaltation, of cultural renewal amid decay, but takes them away before he can grasp them. Do they exist at all, he wonders?

Where Ali's Mir Nihal was a cultured and romantic gentlemen quoting Urdu verse as part of his daily life, Desai's Nur has let his love for food and drink, the sycophantic antics of his admirers, and the bitter rivalries between his two wives overtake his poetic life. The satiric setup is played out as Deven, longing for Delhi, for its urbanity, and for an Urdu way of life, enters the world of Nur. Deven is longing for a different life, whereas Nur is biding his time until he is released from the one he is in. Deven, like Ashgar in *Twilight in Delhi*, is of a younger generation and yearns for modernity, even if, unlike Ashgar, he is looking for it in an older, now-lost tradition of Urdu poetry. In Desai's tale, tradition itself is longed for and refabricated with tape-recorded recitations in order to make sense of modern selfhood. But the recording itself shows up the futility of the longing. In one scene, Nur vehemently resists the management of his art by Deven:

> Frantic to make him resume his monologue now that the tape was expensively whirling, Deven once forgot himself so far as to lean forward and murmur with the earnestness of an interviewer, 'And, sir, were you writing any poetry at the time? Do you have any verse belonging to that period?'
>
> The effect was disastrous. Nur, in the act of reaching out for a drink, froze. 'Poetry?' he shot at Deven, harshly. 'Poetry of the period? Do you think a poet can be ground between stones, and bled, in order to produce poetry—for you? You think you can switch on that mincing machine, and I will instantly produce for you a length of raw, red minced meat that you can carry off to your professors to eat?'[25]

In other scenes, Deven and Nur are able to strike up moments of understanding, but it is a story that will ultimately offer little redemption.

LAMENTING URDU IN ENGLISH

Reading *Twilight in Delhi* and *In Custody* in tandem, one is struck by their surface similarities: they are both set in Old Delhi and reflect the waning of Urdu literary culture within a male world of cultural pleasure. A sense of bleakness and loss pervades both narratives, as does a palpable forlornness in the principal characters. For both Ali and Desai, Old Delhi symbolizes the Urdu language as well as a declining Muslim sensibility and culture that came to life through Urdu. Urdu itself is a translated idea in Ali's text; we might sense the meaning of the language to his protagonists, but we never experience it for ourselves. Desai has explained that she wrote the verses that were to stand for Nur's Urdu poetry by "concocting poetry" that she then attributed to him. In the process, a new kind of literary question, and perhaps conundrum, arises: How does one write Urdu poetry in English? Desai's method was to "write verses in English that echoed their Persian origin," verses that employed "traditional images and metaphors" and followed "Persian verse forms." She goes on to say that despite their authentic ring to some ears, she saw them as "pastiche, not poetry." And yet, when Nur's verses (her concoctions) had been translated into Urdu for the film *In Custody,* directed by Ismail Merchant, she writes: "Hearing the translated lines spoken, I felt myself translated into an

Urdu poet—a surreal experience."[26] A concocted language is returned to Urdu to complete the fabrication begun by Desai. Yet her research and writing also come from her own experiences of speaking and living in Hindustani in 1950s Daryaganj, part of Old Delhi. There is both remembrance and resonance in her text, even if it is sociologically—happily so—unsound. It is in this way that Desai's text, and perhaps all literature, "refracts" rather than reflects.[27] It is her imagination and vision that achieve "accuracy," not merely the representation of a single social reality.

In other moments, Desai's narration is more removed from the language. For instance, she writes of "flowery Urdu," "ornate Urdu," and "chaste Urdu." Here, Urdu is object and nothing more. But the meaning of Urdu in both texts—Desai's and Ali's—was perhaps never meant to be the language itself; how could it be in an English-language novel? Instead the idea of Urdu is the locus for drama, regret, discussion, and the delving into dense emotional webs of disappointment. In both novels, language and place are symmetrical, as both narratives continually inscribe the loss of language onto the physical structures and landscapes of the city and its environs. What is revealed is how the politics of language is an intimate affair in modern Indian life. So it is not surprising that the question of language—who speaks what, when, and where and how they feel about doing so—becomes the engine of both novels' narratives. For the principal characters of each tale, it is the very right to create and exist in different languages that is at stake.

In the temporal move from Ali's novel to Desai's, Urdu's decline is mirrored by the greater influence of a Sanskritized and so upper-caste Hindi, a Hindi that is slowly but surely purged of its Arabic and Persian vocabulary. And it is the shifting places of Hindi and Urdu that influence the changing place of English. These "political dismemberments of language"—to use Gayatri Spivak's phrase—have both social and literary consequences.[28] The political dismemberment of Hindi and Urdu—whereby vocabulary changes and becomes less representative of average people's everyday speech while also becoming symbols of national and religious difference—allows for English to emerge as a more neutral and secular language. And it is the very process by which English becomes an "Indian" language. The "Indianness" of English, then, is not merely attributable to its being able to represent a national consciousness but instead to its ability to mediate the sensibilities of other Indian languages. It offers something new, yet it is as partial and compromised as they are.

In Ali's text, the demise of Muslim Delhi is a direct consequence of British colonial rule and the way his community reacts to that rule, whereas in Desai's post-partition tale, cultural ruptures have been made more strident by the realities of shifting borders and population exchanges. It is not the case that Indian modernity is captured solely or most ably in English but instead that English takes on a mediating role. It is this principle that may be abstracted from the novel. It is precisely the interlingual dialogue in each text that sheds light on the ways in which language politics has been central to the articulation of Indian modernity. In contrast to Hindi-Urdu's dismemberment, Desai's English prose becomes further solidified, as it offers a seemingly neutral and yet also authoritative rendering of the cultural aftermath of the split of Hindi and Urdu and the trauma of the politicization of religious identity inherent in that split.

A CINEMATIC INTERLUDE

The demise of Urdu as a story line arises not only in literature but also in popular Hindi film. In Manmohan Desai's classic film, *Amar Akbar Anthony* (1977), the audience witnesses how Urdu can also play a mediating role in the Indian landscape. And yet in this case the language is reduced to being the vehicle of expression for a single religious community. The film's conceit is that the three brothers named in the title are separated in their childhoods and go on to be raised in families of different religious backgrounds only to meet again as adults. Amar is Hindu, Akbar is Muslim, and Anthony is Christian; they are played by three titans of Hindi cinema: Vinod Khanna, Rishi Kapoor, and Amitabh Bachchan, respectively. A pivotal moment occurs near the film's climax when Akbar is being held hostage by the villainous Robert and tries to send out a call for help to his brothers, Amar and Anthony. Robert allows Akbar to send a note to his tailor shop for more materials, which are required to alter the wedding dress of one of the heroines (who is also being held hostage and is about to be forced to marry her former bodyguard turned thug). Instead of writing down a list of supplies, Akbar pens a plea for help to his brothers. In a voice-over, Akbar explains that he writes the note in Urdu so no one will be able to read it except for the Muslim tailor at his shop. A close-up of the note is then shown on camera as having been written in the Perso-Arabic script. In the next scene, the tailor reads the note and then verbally relays the message for help to Akbar's brothers; a rescue ensues, eventually leading to a happy ending uniting all the brothers of differing faiths with their common mother. The message: religious diversity may exist side by side in a single, unified mother India.

What is not reunited is the language of Hindi and Urdu, a matter that brings us to the question of script. Before Hindi and Urdu were distinct languages with Sanskritized and Persianized vocabularies, respectively, they were commonly written in the same script, the Perso-Arabic or Urdu script as it is called. Part of the "collapsing bridge" between Hindi and Urdu occurs when Hindi began to be written in the Devanagari script.[29] Harish Trivedi has called this switch to the "Nagari" script a "triumph" that "gave a tremendous boost to the morale of the users of Nagari and Hindi" and thereby "led rapidly to a reversal in the balance of power between Urdu and Hindi, resulting in a virtual rout of Urdu in the public domain of authorship and publishing."[30]

It is precisely this loss of literate comprehension of the Urdu script that we see in the film. The change in script signifies a larger linguistic and, in this case, religious divide, cementing the idea that only Muslims read and write in the Perso-Arabic script and Hindus in Devanagari. And yet, in the film at least, Urdu literally mediates in an improbable yet telling way. It supports the premise of the film, that religious cultures are "separate but equal," the hallmark of the Indian secular ideal. Urdu as a sign of difference enters mainstream Hindi cinema—an industry that is ironically made up mostly of Hindustani speakers. Even more telling perhaps is that in today's Mumbai cinema, the often ridiculed "filmy Hindi" screenplays and television scripts are written in Roman script, since many actors do not read Hindi anymore, whether in the Perso-Arabic or Nagari script.

A SHIFTING LINGUISTIC LANDSCAPE

To return to the realm of the Indian English novel, what does it mean for Ali and then Desai to recount the demise of another language? And to do so, not as triumphalist accounts, but as mournful tales? By writing about Urdu in English in this satirical mode, Desai emphasizes her own complicity in Urdu's demise. Her satire is far from the world of Hindi comedy, yet creates its own measure of ironic distance. For lament has turned to satire on the very question of language itself, as Hindi is ridiculed and the desire for Urdu is doomed from the start. English meanwhile has become a normative narrative presence. It embodies a self-consciousness that becomes part of its very definition as an Indian language. In this sense, the novel tells the story of the relationship between English and the bhashas. English enables Indians to look out onto the world (the most common refrain of Indian cosmopolitanism), but in Desai's reckoning, it perhaps even more significantly allows them to reappraise their own linguistic backgrounds and struggles.

Thus, English in India is shaped by internal struggles over language as much as it has been by the colonizer-colonized relationship. This shaping of English goes beyond the interpretation of each text on its own. By reading the texts as a pair, it is possible to see the ways in which English has sparked the social and literary consciousness of modern Indians, of the work that English does on that consciousness, and the effect that English has on lives and livelihoods. Indians who write in English do so not merely because they have been educated in that language. The language has become part of the social fabric, and that fabric includes intersections with and relationships to other Indian languages. Both novels show that to live in a particular language is to inhabit a different cultural world, and what it means for English to "usurp" a place (to return to Gandhi) is really a story of how individual subjectivities change with the adoption of new linguistic sensibilities. In Delhi, and many other parts of north India, English changed the way Urdu and Hindi exist socially and politically. People sometimes speak of "Englishwallahs" and "Hindiwallahs" not to denote which language someone speaks—most people are at least bilingual—but instead to denote the relationship they have to that language, their worldview, the family they come from, the type of education they have had, the beliefs they hold and promote.

In the novels of Ali and Desai, the shifting linguistic landscape changes what people think, believe, and desire. It is this larger social and historical texture of English in Indian society and the meanings of the uses of English for Indians in everyday life that then becomes paramount.

CHAPTER 3

In Sujan Singh Park

In 1967 Nirad Chaudhuri issued a characteristically dire pronouncement on the place of Indian writers in the world. "It is essential," he wrote, "from every point of view to secure the imprint of a London or New York publisher, and the higher the status of even these publishers the better for the writer."[1] For Indian writers of English, Chaudhuri seems to be saying, the only path to literary recognition is through the publishing apparatus of the Western world. Further along he continues in a slightly more ominous vein: "But one warning I must give. To be acceptable to Western publishers, an Indian must write English not only with competence, but with distinction. The competition with the natural writers of English is so severe that British and American publishers will not submit to the impact of any English from an Indian writer which is not quite out of the ordinary."[2]

In Chaudhuri's mind, and in the minds of many of his generation and class, the intellectual center of the English-speaking world could only ever be located in the West. And, by implication, the traffic in ideas could only ever be directed by the demands of London-based publishers, the "natural" speakers of the English language. It was they who would judge literary merit and disperse literary capital accordingly. And in the evaluation of the literary, there would be a measurement of linguistic competence. In Chaudhuri's passive, double-negative construction regarding publishers not willing to submit to "the impact of English that is not quite out of the ordinary," it is almost as if the Indians have the upper hand, wielding their wanton prose through the streets of London. Chaudhuri's advice to other writers details a classic center-periphery dynamic: how to turn the colonizer's gaze to one's own advantage, to "write back" and get published. And yet if postcolonial writing was meant to be about the reappropriation of the colonizer's language, would not the place of publication also have to be refigured?

The last chapter detailed how English mediated the linguistic realms of Hindi and Urdu, emphasizing key shifts from the colonial to postcolonial periods. This chapter argues for English as mediator in the realm of elite intellectual life, specifically in the decades after independence. It is a story of a particular upper-caste background and upper-middle-class sensibility, one in which secular and liberal values become defined and associated with cultural production in English. It is a set of values that I identify as emerging from a dual sense and experience of one's own place in society. From the 1970s onward Delhi was the major hub of this intellectual life, largely because the academic and then literary publishing outfits in English moved there and, along with other institutions, became the center for the exchange of ideas in English, ideas that would ultimately inform the larger multilingual intellectual and literary spheres in the city and beyond.

POSTCOLONIAL PUBLISHING

A writer's location may at first appear to be a more interesting story than a publisher's, but an inquiry into the latter reveals more about the relationship between knowledge and power. The production and consumption of books, especially "serious literature," has been yet another way in which societies are measured and compared to one another. In the decolonizing era of the 1950s, 1960s, and 1970s, publishing in the "third world" was a way to assess the intellectual health of society, often measured by the degree to which nations both produced and consumed ideas. Statistics on book production and consumption were supposed to indicate levels of development and the overall health of the nation and its cultural life. UNESCO keeps track, for instance, of the number of books published in every language, as well as the number of books consumed per capita. It also defines a book as anything bound and having at least forty-eight pages. Its 1972 Charter of the Book states, in part, "Everyone has the right to read," and "A sound publishing industry is essential to national development."[3] Behind these definitions and proclamations are questions about literacy, the ability of average people to buy books, the lack of government funding for libraries, the nature of educational systems, and the accessibility of alternative media. However, the real issue at hand is not merely about quantities published, but about the flow and directionality of ideas.

The higher education scholar Philip Altbach has called the situation of most postcolonial nations a kind of "literary colonialism." Despite having achieved independence, he writes, formerly colonized nations were subject to an international environment of publishing that was dependent on laws—regarding copyright, the import and export of books, the cost of equipment, and the international price of paper—already set up by industrialized nations. What is important to note about Altbach's formulation is that "literary colonialism" comes *after* independence, at the precise moment when the limits of independence become apparent. It comes at a time when new infrastructures and programs must be molded to already existing business models. A running theme in Altbach's work on India in the 1960s and 1970s is how political independence does not always lead to intellectual independence, and how for that, just like for the former, a society needs to have its own institutions.[4]

Although Chaudhuri's assessment of the intellectual health of India was not promising (in his view, it was derivative and not Western enough), the book in which he made his pronouncements, *The Intellectual in India* (1967), was actually the first of his to be published in India.[5] The book inaugurated the publisher Orient Longman's Tracts for the Times series and nearly coincided with the 1968 Indian takeover of the formerly British publisher. The case of Orient Longman is one example of how British publishing in India became Indian.

Before independence, Orient Longman was known as Longman and in 1906 was one of the major British publishers in India, along with Macmillan's, established in 1903, and Oxford University Press, established in 1912. In the years after independence, Longman's became Longman Greene and then, in 1968, Orient Longman, when it became an Indian company and had an Indian board of directors. Becoming Indian entailed shifting the majority of shareholders to Indian ownership and the major decision making to Indians. By 1968 the educationist Raja Rameshwar Rao was named chairman of the board of Orient Longman, a post he retained until 1984. Rao's family had long been interested in education, and his wife, Shanta Rameshwar Rao, was a schoolteacher deeply involved in issues of pedagogical reform. The idea of working for the nation was a persistent theme among all the publishers I spoke to—English and Hindi—who were publishing in the decades immediately after independence. Rao's daughter, Vidya Rao, told me that her family members were "Gandhians and idealistic," and she said that her father saw the chairmanship of Orient Longman as a good opportunity to produce "good books" and "to do something."[6]

The idea of producing "good books" came up in the rhetoric of both English and Hindi publishers I spoke with in Delhi. I found it curious at first—such a general, almost bland statement for the entire process of book production and the more nebulous notion of literature. I came to realize, however, that a "good book" was not just a good book, or *koi acchi kitab,* as the Hindi publishers referred to it. The idea had more to do with the publisher's relationship and responsibility to society, to readers and buyers of books. In Rao's telling, it often had something to do with the past. In the colonial era English-language textbook publishing in India essentially meant doing reprints of English textbooks and grammar books to be sold to a ready-made Indian market whose education was based on British curricula. In line with the grandest ideals of nation building, the postcolonial incarnation of Orient Longman saw itself as a way to create Indian texts for Indians.[7] And yet postcolonial publishing was not a simple switch from being British to being Indian. Instead, the networks of authors slowly changed as some publishers and editors began to mine and promote Indian ideas. By the 1970s English-language publishing in particular became a mediator and clearinghouse of ideas in Indian intellectual life.[8]

Ravi Dayal (1937–2006) was someone who was emblematic of the changes in the Indian-English ethos of Delhi in the 1970s, in part because he helped instigate some of those changes and in part because of his background and linguistic sensibility. Dayal was the first Indian to head the Indian office of Oxford University Press (OUP), and during his tenure there he changed the face of OUP India. Dayal's legacy at OUP and his network of associations put him at the center of the Indian English literary world. After retiring from OUP, Dayal went on to establish his own publishing imprint specializing in literary fiction, Ravi Dayal Publisher. It is a small, independent publishing house and, in some respects, a regional player in the international trade in Indian English novels by virtue of the fact that its distribution is only within India. And yet because of who and how he published, it was a central node, I would argue, in what has since become a boom in Indian literature in India and abroad. Dayal's role as a publisher and his background speak of the generation of English-educated Indians who gave rise to the intellectual and literary flourishing of English-language culture in Delhi.

When I met Dayal in 2001, he was, as always, involved in all aspects of the publishing process, from reading new manuscripts to editing and designing book covers. He also took care of all the correspondence relating to matters as diverse as distribution, dispensing royalties, and ordering paper. Dayal was known for downplaying the role of the publisher; he did not even like to be thanked in his authors' acknowledgments. He was considered by most to be a fine manuscript editor, and in the middle of one of our conversations he went to a back room and emerged to show me the manuscript he was currently working on, covered with editorial marks in red ink. Still, he saw a publisher as someone whose main purpose was to reflect the intellectual currents around him. He told me, "It is writers who write books. The publisher works as a kind of junior partner. He shouldn't flatter himself to think he's the generator of ideas."[9]

Over the course of our conversations, I saw that he seemed to take a quiet satisfaction in every aspect of his trade. I also began to see how the way he narrated his life's work said much about the ground on which he came to stand as a publisher. For Dayal, publishing was a craft, but it was also an expression of his responsibility to "the nation." This responsibility was defined by an ethics that stressed egalitarianism, even as its aim was to foster a cultural milieu that was unquestionably elite. Dayal did not seem to feel conflicted by this apparent contradiction. He was, in this sense, a prototypical Englishwallah, someone who is not just an English-speaking Indian, but in whose vision of Indian society English is central. An Englishwallah might also be described as someone who imbibes the ideology of English in India, that of a cosmopolitan, liberal, and secular elite. For Dayal's generation it is a set of values that are part and parcel of the English language. It is not that these values were British or "foreign" in any simple way, but they were values that elite Indians came into contact with and molded to their own needs, which were often anticolonial and nationalistic. In the 1960s and 1970s the nationalism of Indian English intellectuals was tied up with doing good for the nation.

Dayal's linguistic orientation did not mean that he was indifferent to the other Indian languages in his daily life or even outlook, even if he was skeptical of their potential to harness intellectual creativity. English was simply the language to think with. He believed it to be an Indian asset and a social necessity. He said he thought that Hindiwallahs—the Hindi cultural elite—minimized the importance of English. It was not that Hindiwallahs did not know English, but they were oriented both culturally and politically to Hindi and to some of the ideologies associated with Hindi promotion. Hindiwallahs not only had the numbers on their side; they could also more easily win debates over cultural authenticity, even if the formal, Sanskritized "Hindi" they espoused was not spoken on the streets. For Dayal, the significance of English in post-independence India was not its numerical strength or weakness but its cultural influence. In 1991 he wrote that the burgeoning of English in India was evidence of "the growing independence of the Indian mind."[10]

This statement, which set the stage for a range of debates in Indian society, encapsulates a line of thought that sees English as liberating to Indians and as the language that enables a fully modern life. In a larger sense, this independence was also a way for Indians, over time, to reverse the intellectual traffic that formerly began in colonial metropoles and moved out to the peripheries. Having imbibed English ideas in India, Indians through English could have their ideas known in the world. In this sense, Dayal's statement could be coupled with one written by his protégé Rukun Advani, who in his obituary of Dayal wrote that his mentor had "put India on the world's intellectual map."[11]

The flip side of Advani's comment is that it is very much the English-thinking India that is on that map. Would Indian thought only have international resonance in English? By the 1970s the answer already seems to have been a resounding yes, and the question was only how.

SECULAR, MODERN, AND MIDDLE CLASS

Dayal lived in Sujan Singh Park, the epicenter of Delhi's English-speaking elite. The area happens to be a tiny colony by Delhi standards—more of a large square than a colony—but it is where the city's linguistic, social, and architectural capital meet. One writer describes Sujan Singh Park as forming "a golden triangle" with the India International Centre and the India Habitat Centre and, in a more satiric vein, calls it "the land of the concerned liberal, pale pink in hue, likely to be clad in handspun and rarely in synthetic, with some ancient books and jewels and old frames with ancestors to add a touch of vintage and class." Of its residents, she writes, "Most would also be card-holding secularists."[12]

The most well known literary resident of Sujan Singh Park was not Dayal but his ninety-something father-in-law, Khushwant Singh (b. 1915). It was Singh's father, Sobha Singh, who was the building contractor for much of New Delhi, including Sujan Singh Park, the South Block, the court of Rashtrapati Bhavan, Vijay Chowk, the War Memorial Arch, Baroda Palace, All India Radio, the National Museum, and, as Singh has written, assorted "bungalows, chummeries, and clerks' quarters." He further tells us that his father "shared with Lutyens and Baker a vision of the shape of things to come. . . . Like his other colleagues, Sobha Singh taught himself English, became president of the New Delhi Municipal committee and member of the Council of States" and was eventually "knighted by the British government."[13] It should come as no surprise that in the colonial period learning English was key to gaining a government building contract. In fact, the story of Delhi's history and modernity is most often told through its architecture: the striking tombs, landscaped parks, and assorted Mughal and British colonial monuments. "New" Delhi was an English-knowing Delhi laid out in stone or, as in the case of Sujan Singh Park, brick by brick.

By marrying Singh's daughter, Mala, Dayal inadvertently became a resident of the colony. The Dayals met through the small world of publishing in Delhi in the early 1970s. Mala Singh had been editing children's books at the National Book Trust (NBT) when a friend asked her, "Why are you working with the government? Why not OUP?" She was open to the idea and had an informal meeting with Dayal. Nothing came of the job, so she stayed on at the NBT but ran into Dayal at book fairs. Her father was at the time living in Bombay and editing the *Illustrated Weekly of India,* the most widely circulated English-language magazine in India. Singh knew Dayal independently of his daughter, and when he came back to Sujan Singh Park to see his family and saw Dayal outside the house, he invited him in, assuming Dayal had come to see him.

When Mala Dayal told me this story, she emphasized that there was no way she could have told her father that she and Dayal were seeing each other since he was such a gossip that the news would have been all over town by the next day. Anyone who has read Khushwant Singh can understand this; part-scribe, part-gossip, he writes about everything and everyone, in multiple eras. And this talent is precisely what made his editorship of the *Illustrated Weekly* so notable. It also explains why the magazine was part of the burgeoning of the English-language cultural sphere, especially from 1969 to 1979, when Singh was its editor.[14]

Unlike the sober, exacting Dayal, Singh is known for his bawdy irreverence. Yet Singh is also perhaps the most popular Indian English writer ever. One of the major Delhi booksellers told me that he was simply "a perennial bestseller." His appeal to the English-educated masses was also apparent when it came to his editorship of the *Weekly.* Not only did everyone I speak to about the *Weekly* say that it was at its best under Singh's editorship, but it was also the decade in which it hit its peak circulation of 400,000. Why were people buying it?

In my subsequent reading of archival issues of the magazine, I was not always sure. I saw certain aspects that made the publication distinctive during that period; it was light reading with a lot of pictures and had something for everyone. It was popular, and yet it was also in English. That used to be a contradiction in the Indian context, but under Singh it started to become less of one. It was not aimed at the intellectual elite but at a pan-Indian urban English readership that all of a sudden seemed to have come into existence.

The *Weekly* was part variety, part lifestyle magazine. It was the frivolity of the *Weekly* that first caught my attention, even as I sat reading it in an austere library, trying to imagine it in drawing rooms across urban India. I talked to my English-speaking Indian contemporaries who had come of age in the 1970s and 1980s, and nearly all of them told me it was something that was always "lying around." Yet it was something that was "not taken seriously." It was also, for many, a source of great titillation, with its risqué back-page photos. Its notion of "variety" in a family magazine seemed to extend quite far.

The British established the *Illustrated Weekly of India* in 1880, and after 1947 it became an Indian magazine edited by Indians. The magazine folded in 1993. Dileep Padgaonkar, then editor of the *Times of India,* whose larger group owned the *Weekly,* told me that the Times Group lost interest in the publication and that circulation had steadily gone down after Singh's landmark decade. Singh's editorship of the *Weekly* reflected his own writing persona: crass and risqué, with flashes of seriousness. It had mass appeal but was also described to me on more than one occasion as being "vulgar, barbershop reading." One of these indictments came from the veteran journalist and former *Times of India* editor Sham Lal as we sat amid his skyscraper bookshelves in Gulmohar Park.

Despite its mixed reviews, the *Weekly* was *the* place to be published if you wanted to be read across India, and writers and scholars but also jokesters and others were eager to have their work appear in it. It is for this reason that in its pages you might see the words of a great playwright, like the late Vijay Tendulkar, next to a Dennis the Menace cartoon or an essay on Muslim identity by the scholar A. G. Noorani next to a photoessay on basket weaving. "Everyone bought it," says Rukun Advani, and despite (and, I suppose, because of) its bawdy photographs (usually of Indian and European women), it was ubiquitous on coffee tables across urban, English-reading India.

In the pages of the *Weekly* I also saw how a middle-class consumer identity—what is now so commonly associated with what English represents in India—was being forged. This identification came through most obviously in the advertisements, where everything from blenders, upholstery, and men's suits to shampoo, health tonics, and batteries were being showcased, the accouterments of a modern life. It told readers the story of what their lives could be. Take (at random) the issue of October 3, 1971. The front cover story was "Harijans," featuring a photo of an exuberant young woman clutching a handwoven basket with a sweeping implement inside it. Turn the page, and on the inside front cover are four 4-inch by six-inch advertisements: "No ghee no oil!" promises an ad for saucepans, followed by "Making Living a Pleasure" featuring a smiling couple who have presumably just taken some Okasa, "modern tonic-restorative tablets." Further down, "There's a job waiting for you. Get ready with ICS training!" reads an ad for International Correspondence Schools offering courses in commerce, hobbies, technology and industry, and professional examination coaching. And finally, "Are you qualified and yet not suitably employed?" asks the Overseas Booking Centre, which explains, "Among the persons registered with us, in 1970 alone, 257 Indians are already holding lucrative jobs overseas."

The essays and exposés were equally telling. They were, in fact, about "India." Defining India for Indians came to be central to forging middle-class values and identity. If language, religion, caste, and ethnicity could not be shared, there was still class and urbanity. At times the magazine read like *National Geographic* (another best-seller among the Indian middle classes, though produced abroad), with stories and photoessays about different caste, ethnic, religious, and regional groups in India. In addition to the feature on Harijans, topics in other issues that same year included "Kashmiri Muslims," "Eminent

Banias," "The Rajputs," and the "Niramkara Sikhs." Exposés included "Black Money"—"millions of Babus, miles of red tape"—and the situation of Indians who were living in England. Was there racism? Were they assimilating?

Although it was light reading, there was also something serious going on, especially if one looked at years of the *Weekly* in back-to-back issues rather than at a more leisurely week-by-week pace. The *Weekly* promoted a kind of class awareness and what I would venture to call a kind of cosmopolitan secularism. Secularism in the Indian context has never been about eschewing religion or separating it from other domains; instead it has, in theory and often in practice, been about accommodating diverse religious beliefs and practices in public life. The secular is not a space void of religion but a space filled to the brim with it. For this reason, the discourse on secularism in India has also, essentially and most important, been about the rights of minorities and the definition of minority groups. Seen in this light, it is interesting that in the pages of the *Weekly* there was an "enumeration" of caste and religious types, but unlike the infamous anthropological excess on these topics, the *Weekly* showcased "all of India" as a form of social edification. It went hand in hand with the promotion of India's "unity in diversity," where all trades, religions, and castes had something to offer and a rightful place in the national mosaic.[15]

RAVI DAYAL, PUBLISHER

Two years after Dayal's death, I went back to Sujan Singh Park to talk with Mala Dayal and their daughter, Naina. I wanted to talk to them about the chapter I was writing, not so much for their approval (though I'm sure I was looking for that too), but more because I wanted to share with them what he had said, on several hours of tape, about himself and his life.

During my visit Naina came in and out of the room a couple of times as Mrs. Dayal and I were conversing. Naina, who at the time was a college lecturer and finishing her Ph.D. on ancient Indian history, lived across the road and was involved in a verbal dispute with the Delhi metro workers. An entrance to the Khan Market metro stop was being built next to her flat, and her garden was in jeopardy. But when she was present she chimed in a few times to echo a point or add another angle. On one occasion she took issue when I used the word *elite* in relation to her father. I had used this word in the larger context of the world of English and the fact that her father had been at the helm of Indian English publishing. I tried to rack my brain for some scholarly definitions of elite and elite groups, but instead I said something cheerful like, "*Elite* also refers to the best in a group, in terms of the quality of work or other activity, such as 'elite athletes.' These two qualities of *elite* may go hand in hand; someone who is able to become the best at something may have had the grooming that only an already elite background could afford." Of course, I also meant that he was a cultural elite, and for Naina, the word used in relation to her father was nearly a slur. This reaction was not surprising, since in Delhi and among liberal, urban elites the question of the haves and have-nots in Indian society is a moral one. How one lived, what one did. Yet I believed that the fact that Dayal was both fair-minded and an egalitarian did not preclude him from being elite, though he was certainly not an elitist.[16]

As had been noted in obituaries of Dayal (by friends and colleagues such as Girish Karnad, Amitav Ghosh, and Rukun Advani), he practiced egalitarianism in his management of OUP, and this was unusual for the time and the place. First of all, it meant everyone ate together in the canteen, from the drivers and office assistants to the editors and prized authors. But it also meant that Dayal chose not to avail himself of a car and driver or an air-conditioned office, two taken-for-granted perks for anyone at the helm of a major Indian enterprise. Mrs. Dayal explained that her husband had not wanted to be dependent on such perks. It was a way for him not to feel beholden to his position; he wanted to feel, she said, that he could pack up and leave whenever he wanted to. For Naina, her father's quirks were part of his ethical universe and evidence that he practiced what he preached. She recalled with amusement that this practice extended to their family trips, when they always stayed in "uncomfortable, mosquito-ridden places."[17]

A CASTE OF MIND

Ravi Dayal's background speaks to a dual heritage that was not uncommon for many of his generation, class, and caste. He grew up in Uttaranchal (now known as Uttarakhand), part of the western Himalayan range, though he made it clear that his family were not *pahadis* (mountain people) strictly speaking. They were Mathurs, a subcaste of Kayasthas, who were traditionally in the fields of "reading and writing" and usually assumed government posts. The hill station of Nainital was the site of their old family home, where he said his family had been "for over a century." This location, away from Delhi and in the mountains, was to be a central part of Dayal's identification throughout his life.[18]

Considering his family background, Dayal remarked, entering publishing was entirely accidental. His father died when he was only four, and so he spoke of his uncles, most of whom were officers in the Indian Civil Service; one taught English at Allahabad, a city in Uttar Pradesh known for its universities and intellectual life. His civil service uncles spoke English, but "out in the districts" they spoke Urdu and at home a mix of dialects. Of his uncles, he said, "They all went off to England at some point, were all ambassadors and diplomats." And with his usual wry sense of humor, he added that "going into publishing was almost a caste blemish."

Of his cultural upbringing more generally, Dayal noted, "We were Islamic in everything but our faith; we spoke Urdu, and used the greetings of *khudah hafiz* (may God protect you)." It was a shared pre-partition, Hindustani sensibility and northern Indian cultural milieu, a mix of Persianate and Sanskrit vocabulary, of Muslim and Hindu. This mixing was not meant to conjure up an idyllic past of Hindu and Muslim brotherhood (though that existed in some places) but rather a shared cultural ethos that was commonplace and natural enough to be reflected in everyday language. At the same time, Dayal was sent to an English-medium school and described the mood of his household as having been "a good civilized Victorian Indian home." He explained that the family came from a community that was at once committed to the revolutionary, pro-independence Gadar Party and in the civil service, that is, serving the empire by working in the colonial British administration and acting, he added, "as if they were serving a national purpose." As elsewhere in the world, the question of what constitutes national purpose and what it means to serve that purpose is a matter of much societal debate and historical reflection. It is this dual consciousness that Dayal cites as having formed his family's moral sensibility. He said, "You were caught in the usual debates over whether you were collaborating with imperialism or actually subverting it by joining its ranks."

Dayal compared the dexterity of living in two or more languages with the ability to straddle two civilizations: "To be familiar with Indian classical music and Bach and Beethoven at the same time—some would say what happens is that you don't know either culture very well, that it's always surface, a mannerism, but that's not really true." I took this to mean that Dayal did not think of himself as English in taste and

Indian in blood. And I also took it to mean that what was "Indian" and what was "English" were not static cultural traits or practices to begin with. Throughout, I was struck by the cultural "duality" that Dayal emphasized in his own background, and how this duality differed from accounts of hybridity in postcolonial theory. Hybridity, as theorized by Homi Bhabha, for instance, is certainly more political, and in the colonial context, it is a concept that emphasizes cultural conflict and compromise with a strongly subversive edge.[19] Duality, at least as expressed by Dayal, seems to have emerged from a less fractured place. English became an Indian language for a significant number of Indians, and so for a certain class of people it stands side by side with other Indian languages in the making of their own identities. The idea of duality could also be seen as an acceptance of a kind of cultural surfeit, where one cultural tradition does not threaten the other but in fact props it up. In the essays of Sheila Dhar, another Mathur Kayastha who moved in Delhi circles and wrote memoirs about the culture of the city, the Kayasthas are portrayed as being refined by their use of Persianized Urdu and holding their own in English. In her telling, they have a very particular idea of what it means to be "cultured," a world of English education, classical Hindustani music, and Urdu literature, one that is echoed in Dayal's narrative.[20] What is significant about this positioning of English is that it does not stand in opposition to the other Indian languages. It in fact engages with them and is produced alongside them, even if it also supports a linguistic hierarchy that in many domains puts English on top. Dayal connected this form of bilingualism, which he saw as a kind of bicultural fluency that was pervasive in urban milieus, to what he called "such interesting writing." It is a positioning of language that a certain kind of caste privilege allows and encourages. It was from this milieu—of a dual heritage—that Indian English thought percolated, and Dayal's role as a publisher was to notice it and bring it to everyone's attention.

A FIELD OF CULTURAL PRODUCTION

Dayal came to Delhi for college. His entire family had gone to university in Allahabad, so, as he phrased it to me, he and his brother decided *not* to go there and went to St. Stephen's College instead.[21] Dayal was at St. Stephen's from 1954 to 1959, a time, he said, when the college "wasn't as English medium as it is now; you still heard Hindustani and Urdu." He went on to say that university life in general "still wasn't quite so Anglicized; you had students from Daryaganj, Chandni Chowk, etc." These other parts of Delhi, the ones that now constitute "Old Delhi," are often contrasted to central (bureaucratic or Lutyens') Delhi and south (middle-class) Delhi. But in the real geography of the city, these distinctions are never so clear-cut, especially when one considers the poor, *basti* neighborhoods that dot the entire Delhi landscape.

When I was reading this passage from my conversation with Dayal to Naina, she stopped me and said that she and her father often used to argue about how university life and its composition had changed from his time to hers. Where I had thought his emphasis was on language (who had English and who didn't), on being "Anglicized," and coming from parts of Delhi that were less so, Naina began to speak of caste. It was caste and caste consciousness over which she and her father had disagreements, she said. She explained that her father thought her generation was more "caste conscious" and felt that in his generation caste was "less of an issue," since, after all, they had the nation to think about. Naina vehemently disagreed with him. She explained that she went to college "post-Mandal commission," meaning that there was such a focus on the issue of caste, in order to make university education open to lower-caste and Dalit groups, that it was impossible not to be caste conscious.[22] Was it perhaps that in the elder Dayal's generation, class and caste were less of an issue because they were less visible to those in their ranks?

When Dayal recounted his experiences after college, it was as if he were telling the story of his generation and class:

> Nineteen fifty-four at St. Stephen's, did an M.A., still wondered what to do: Civil Service or try learning a little more. Can you get a grant to go off for a year or two to actually hear the people you have been reading? So you apply for scholarships. My brother got the Rhodes. I got a grant. You sailed to Britain on the cheapest wretched ticket possible. Your cabin is under the sea almost, and you can't open your porthole. It takes twenty-two days getting to Tilbury. You land up at Oxford, which is interesting. You work quite hard; you relish it at one level. You go on learning and developing. Like everyone who has been too long in university you're fit only to go on staying in university, so then you wonder. In those days I don't think people wanted to be expatriates in quite the way they do now. I certainly could have stayed on and done a D.Phil. and taught and done a Ph.D. working, oddly enough, on India. That seemed a bit absurd.

Instead of studying India in England, Dayal returned to India to publish English books at Oxford University Press. He was first based in

Bombay, working under the British head of OUP, Roy Hawkins. Next he went to Madras, where he worked with and befriended the Kannada playwright Girish Karnad. In 1971 he came to Delhi to set up the new OUP head office; five years later, in 1976, he became the first Indian general manager of OUP. Dayal said that it was during this period that there was the realization that one could look at and use the resources within India for bookmaking. He described the intellectual scene of the late 1960s and early 1970s when he returned from Oxford to Delhi.

> Immediately you know when you come back to India the place is bubbling a bit, new frameworks are being worked out. In history, Irfan Habib's changing the face of modern India, Amartya Sen is working on something. Because you belong roughly to that period, you can follow the importance. The earlier lot of people at OUP were out of touch—they didn't know the nature of the debate. They had fine editors, even when I joined, but they really weren't following what was happening in post-independence India, even though they were quite sympathetic to independence. This happens in publishing; a publisher can lose touch with ideas.

This was a turning point in Dayal's narration—that it took Indians educated in English to keep up with the intellectual currents (which were leftist and Marxist at the time) and to know they were indeed the currents and seize them. One could identify this kind of shift as yet another moment when English became Indian. The language was now attuned to the experiences and ideas of a certain class of Indians and allowed the expression of common goals, as well as a wider discourse. It was the medium of elites but in the service of the nation. On the other side, because of the indigenizing of intellectual life in the English language, OUP, still a British-owned company, was able to make a name for itself in India. It became known for being on the cutting edge intellectually and was the place to be published on topics relating to the subcontinent.

Dayal emphasized that what was important about this burgeoning space of English-language intellectual production was not the numbers of English speakers but *who* was using the language and *how*. Delhi's cultural milieu, including its political and bureaucratic aspects, was also implicated in the shift in the leadership of nearly all the major houses from Bombay to Delhi. Delhi had a higher concentration of universities, scholars, and readers, and it also possessed the infrastructure that government agencies provided for the production of books. Dayal described the culture and convenience of working as an editor in Delhi during this time. Around him were institutions that were being set up or expanding. There were institutions of higher learning, such as the Delhi School of Economics (D-School) and Jawaharlal Nehru University (JNU). There were also the social imperatives being set forth by the Green Revolution. As for book production, libraries were being set up, and they became a big market for publishers, sometimes keeping them afloat.

The new OUP office that Dayal was to head was located in the hub of the book trade on Ansari Road. It was ideally situated, with its reasonably low rents, in more ways than one. Being on Ansari Road meant being near Chawri Bazaar where the paper merchants were, as well as near the Delhi Railway Station where you could dispatch goods and drop mail off at the post office across the road. The area had a host of *dhabas* (roadside food stalls) and restaurants where you could take authors for lunch. And it was not far from Delhi University. Overall, it seemed to Dayal "a sensible place." It was also not too far from the Feroz Shah Kotla cricket ground. Dayal chuckled as he described how he would sometimes stand on the roof of OUP, watching "the odd cricket match while editing a manuscript."

Delhi fast became the center of this web of creative and intellectual influences and personalities. Or, as Dayal put it: "The economist reads the historian reads the sociologist reads the novelist." In his view, the flourishing not merely of English publishing in India, but of the intellectual and creative climate, was no mistake. He saw the literary flourishing as part of a larger cultural movement. He likened Indian-English intellectual production to such culturally and creatively significant movements as the German Bauhaus movement, whose members created a new aesthetic in art and design and whose ideas influenced at least a generation of intellectuals, writers, and artists. Dayal's central point was that the kind of high-caliber creative writing being produced by Indians in English was not occurring in isolation; instead there was a rich web of ideas that produced each author and work. He said that creative writing does not come out of an "intellectual vacuum" but is in fact connected to an "intellectual hinterland." For Dayal, the examples were plentiful, from Vikram Seth, who trained as an economist, and Amitav Ghosh, who was a social anthropologist, to Shashi Tharoor, who studied political science, and Mukul Kesavan, who teaches history. "They're all part of, have been to some extent nourished, by ideas in their back garden," Dayal noted, a garden that included the preferred institutions of Delhi and Calcutta.

Implicit in Dayal's discourse is that the social infrastructure that supports the exploration and development of thought in a particular language is necessary for this kind of intellectual and creative flourishing. Part of what Dayal emphasized was the way in which English was used to gain knowledge about the world and, crucially, the world of ideas outside of India. It was at this juncture that he offered what has now become a shared view among many Englishwallahs regarding the limitations of the scope and range of ideas in academic publishing in the other Indian languages:

> Well, from the sixties, there was an enormous expansion in the university system. There were maybe ten or fifteen universities at independence. By the sixties there were about one hundred—the good, bad, and the indifferent. But each university had one or two faculties or one or two teachers who were influential teachers or supervising interesting research, so even if you went to what seemed like the backwaters, there were one or two very good departments there, working on something interesting. I traveled a fair amount for OUP just to find out what was happening everywhere, and this is what struck me: what little work was being done in the Indian languages. There was a fair amount of plagiarism, a lot of subcontracting. They get research grants and don't do the research themselves. There was all this talk that the truth lay in the Indian languages, but that was not the case.

For Dayal, "new" and progressive thinking was happening in English; the cultural influence of the language—including its difference—was its virtue. In some sense, his estimation of the role of English during this period gives Dayal the license to dismiss what is happening in the bhashas. In his intellectual map of India, the bhashas were regional languages, outposts to be traveled to. Yet Dayal did not dismiss bhasha writers, especially the ones who had a cosmopolitan aspect to their work, a cosmopolitanism that he, not surprisingly, identified in relation to their exposure to English. Dayal emphasized the effect that English had on Indian writers and intellectuals, regardless of which language they wrote in. Even the best bhasha writers, he said, were deeply affected by what was happening "in the world." In his view, English-language culture was the way in which many of them not only earned a living but also became cosmopolitan; and he firmly believed that this wider outlook benefited their writing: "Even the Indian-language writers are teachers of English, from Ananthamurthy, to the Bengalis, to Vilas Sarang in Maharashtra; Krishna Vaid, his major critical writing was on Henry James. Vatsyayan, great Hindi poet, knew his German and his Eliot. Firaq Gorakhpuri, the great Urdu writer, taught English in Allahabad. People who have been to university at some point."

And then he continued: "In a way it's a bit of a fantasy or romanticization that every person off the street can be a writer or poet; you have to be lettered at some level. All right, you can be a *bhakti* (devotional) poet, suddenly so spiritually attained, that you are able to give vent to all your wonders of the world. But it should take a form; there's no harm if the person is aware of other *bhakti* poets, too."

Dayal saw English learning as part of the more general process of education and awareness of a class of people, regardless of the language in which they ended up writing, but essentially he was also describing an urban middle-class and upper-caste identity. Some would argue that a "wider" cosmopolitan outlook could actually dilute the "authentic" regional outlook; others would say this regional outlook or grounding makes writers parochial. This may seem to bring us back to the question of a writer and his or her location, but in some sense this shift in perspective between what is cosmopolitan and what is parochial might be more a question of class and sensibility and less about language. Dayal would have been the first to agree that there is a Marathi, Malayalam, Hindi, or Bengali cosmopolitanism, but he might also have insisted that English had a role to play in it.

Dayal left OUP in 1987. He was forty-nine years old at the time, and after twenty-five years at OUP, he had become tired of the work there. And yet he could not help but work obsessively. Under his editorship of the academic section, OUP was doing well financially, and Dayal said he felt he had "built up a fine team," a situation that perhaps made it easier, or at least possible, for him to consider leaving. He had also been grooming Advani to take his place.[23] Dayal described his life after OUP, saying he "did nothing for a year." He in fact traveled around the country and was an occasional adviser to OUP. "Then stray manuscripts starting coming to me," he said. "[People were] asking me, can you do something? But I didn't want to do academic manuscripts; I didn't want to poach on OUP territory. So I passed those on to them."

At the same time, Dayal said that it seemed like a good idea to try publishing nonacademic books. After all, he was familiar with many types of writing, and he happened to know all the leading novelists, playwrights, and poets. It was the very circle of people he associated with. Even more important, Dayal had always been a great reader of novels and poetry and had kept up with what his poet and writer friends were working on. "I'd edited so many manuscripts," he said, "that people probably thought, this man has an eye for detail."

By September 1988 Dayal had set up his own one-man publishing operation out of his home in Sujan Singh Park and had published his first set of titles. He not only edited all his books but also designed their covers and did all of the related illustrations, including the owl that became the publisher's logo. He was lucky, as he described it, to have started with the highly successful *The Shadow Lines* (1988) by Amitav Ghosh, a book that is now in its fourteenth impression. In many respects, Ravi Dayal, Publisher, as the official publishing house is known, is a product of the genealogy that Dayal outlined earlier. Having been at the academic helm of Indian English writing, along with his literary education and bicultural upbringing, he was the perfect candidate to catch the new wave of Indian English novels that were written in the 1980s and 1990s. By 2001 he had published sixty-five titles in all. At that time Dayal told me that he received at least one manuscript a day, packages that arrived unceremoniously on his doorstep.

> I would liked to have published some [authors] I haven't, but they don't all come to me of course. But I'm very glad I've published Amitav [Ghosh], Firdaus Kanga, Mukul [Kesavan], Rukun [Advani]. It's nice to publish people when they are unknown as well, not just the celebrities, so I hope unknowns keep coming to me; that's what makes publishing exciting. And it's nice if you can hold onto the celebrated writers, because often for a small publisher, they become too big. They might be able to get bigger advances, or their sights may become bigger; they might go to a publisher who has a bigger marketing reach. I'm fortunate. I've got Orient Longman distributing here, but they can't reach the market outside of India.

Dayal was aware of the limits of his own publishing apparatus, as well as the particular cultural cache he had within the literary publishing world and within Delhi itself. The English-language literary publishing scene was nurtured by idiosyncratic relations of production and networking. Dayal had a great sense of obligation to each of the manuscripts that landed on his doorstep, yet he was also aware that his kind of boutique publishing was not what the future of Indian literary publishing would look like. He said, "I'm glad what I've done has seemed to have a small impact. HarperCollins, Kali, Seagull are others doing good fiction. I can't go on forever. At some point I may just want to put my shutters down. I don't even know how to do that. I can't abandon my obligations. Still, I will probably do four or five titles a year. But I want to do other things now, just being a nonpublishing person, loitering once more."

Dayal was in all respects a gentleman publisher, and with him went an era. In Dayal's narrative, we see that even in its elite positioning within Indian society in the 1970s, English comes to have a role that it had not had previously. Dayal's view was that the publication of English-language social science texts written by Indian academics established a base for the larger intellectual and creative scene in English. These issues, about development, poverty alleviation, and neocolonialism led to monographs on a variety of social and economic theories. This flourishing in the social sciences was sparked and then nurtured by the expansion of universities in the 1960s, with English as the medium of instruction at the level of higher education. The forum of debate, then, often on the most salient issues of culture and politics of the day, tended to be in English, especially in the urban centers that housed the best universities—Delhi, Bombay, Calcutta, Allahabad, Hyderabad, and Madras.

LOCATING *CIVIL LINES*

Rukun Advani, who followed in Dayal's footsteps and then charted his own path at OUP before leaving to start his own publishing venture, emerges from a different generational ethos than Dayal. When I spoke to Advani in 2001, I was struck by his view of the increasingly marginalized position of Englishwallahs, despite some of the obvious cultural capital they hold. This attitude was apparent in the way he talked about his coeditorship of the literary magazine, *Civil Lines,* named after what was once the British cantonment area of Delhi, just over the ridge from Delhi University and north of the Old City. *Civil Lines* marks a different cultural moment in the position of Indian English literary culture, even if it represents similar networks of people. As a magazine title, it is both a place and an attitude; *Civil Lines* may stand for civility, but if so, only in a mocking, satirical way. These Englishwallahs had already made English their own and were now looking for "fresh" and "new" ideas, unfettered by colonial or postcolonial angst. The subtitle of the magazine is also telling: "New Writing from India." Not in India or by Indians or about Indians or India but *from* India. The writing would be solicited and edited from here, from Delhi, maybe even from Civil Lines and then published and sent out elsewhere. It was in the end about editorial location.

The idea for *Civil Lines* came about in 1993 when the economist Dharma Kumar, who, Advani remarked, "was a great literature enthusiast and had strong literary interests," approached Advani when he was still at OUP, telling him that she wanted to fund a literary journal. Advani then "asked a few friends" to help him, including the historian and novelist Mukul Kesavan and the journalist Ivan Hutnik, a British Ukrainian based in Delhi. Advani said, "Ram Guha would also sometimes show up. He was a cousin of Dharma's."[24]

Advani described how the magazine got under way: "We would meet in her house [Kumar's] next to the zoo. We naturally spoke English, only using Hindi if a certain idiomatic expression was needed. The talks by the zoo would revolve around who we could get—we wanted writers who were iconoclastic, irreverent, serious but not stodgy, and who would write pieces that were not footnoted."

The "talk" among the editors, in Advani's words, "was of our alienation, angst, how deracinated we were, but the point was getting people who were not bogged down by those issues." At the same time, many of the leading Indian writers were academics, and perhaps this was why they stayed clear of the dreaded footnote. They wanted to create a literary and not an academic platform. Literature "from India" was not going to be an exercise in theory, especially not postcolonial theory. When I asked him who the journal was for, if he had an idea of the audience, he said, "It was for everybody we knew, our own circle of friends."

His dispassionate, matter-of-fact tone would describe the editorial introductions to the first issues of *Civil Lines*. There was an unabashed desire to emphasize that the selections only had to be liked by the editors, that they only looked for what they thought were "good reads." There was an attempt to eschew ideological platforms, as in this typical introductory salvo: "Manifestoes are strident, bullying things and it's nice to do without one; but it does mean that we feel and grope our way around each issue till it's good enough (and thick enough) to print."[25]

The magazine was already wrapped in both the ideology (liberal, secular) and identity (upper middle class, connected) of the English language. They could afford their attitude precisely because of the elite (in terms of status and access) and marginalized (in terms of their position in the larger sphere of cultural production of the other Indian languages) position of English. This position—English literary expression as being hemmed in by issues of authenticity—was perhaps best expressed in a slightly tongue-and-cheek poem written by Mukul Kesavan as part of the editor's introduction to *Civil Lines 4:*

Sternest are the guardians of Hindi:
can alien okra ever taste
of bhindi?
The words of life and fiction must be one:
in everyday vernacular
their-will-be-done.

Like many Indian English novels in the Indian market, each issue of *Civil Lines* (which is bound as a paperback book) sells only about two thousand copies. The magazine has been heralded as a place where Indians writing in English may send their prose rather than, let's say, to *Granta* in London, and *Granta* was in fact one of the models for *Civil Lines*. But the existence of the magazine did not necessarily herald the burgeoning of the Indian market for writing in English. Advani remarked, "Sales are pathetic." At the same time, he added that the bigger publishers like HarperCollins and Orient Longman take notice of who is being published in each new issue.

Ravi Dayal eventually put money into *Civil Lines* as well and became its publisher, with the first issue appearing in 1994 and subsequent issues in 1995, 1997, and two in 2001. The content of the magazine, with its mix of literary reflections by academics and journalists along with those of novelists and others, unwittingly mirrored Dayal's own movement from academic publishing to literary publishing. Dayal's economists, historians, and sociologists of the 1970s spawned and in many cases became the feminists, subalternists, and novelists of the 1980s. The world of English in Delhi had flourished in those two decades, and the writers and editors came from overlapping worlds, neighborhoods, and ideological stances. And perhaps more interestingly, the magazine's contributions bypassed the central paradox of English writing from India: the question of representing others. This was achieved mostly by the autobiographical quality of many of the contributions, from André Béteille's "My Two Grandmothers" to Sheila Dhar's musical remembrances. The magazine gives a sense not of "this is India in English," but instead, "these are the perspectives and attitudes of English-thinking Indians." While the magazine is meant to be literary and not sociological, most of the contributions fall somewhere in the realm of documentary, well written and considered, though not breaking new literary ground.

After her husband's death, Mala Dayal knew that she did not want to become a publisher, but she was very much concerned with the list that her husband had created. Over 90 percent of the list of Ravi Dayal, Publisher, is now being produced and distributed by Penguin India. Its future seems secure with a large publisher and is indicative of the trends in Indian publishing that Dayal himself had envisioned.[26] There are continued and sometimes vigorous debates within the publishing industry on the impact of multinational publishers on small, independent ones. For most, these debates have gone beyond issues of what is "Indian" publishing and what is not. Instead, they have to do with the persistent challenges of production—from the price of paper to the efficiency of distribution—as well as the need to cultivate audiences and the book-buying habit. This discourse, for the most part, is one of business interests and economic globalization rather than of identity and authenticity. That there is an Indian field of cultural production in English is a given. Dayal's role in publishing was one of a kind, yet his trajectory both mapped out and aligned with larger publishing trends.

CHAPTER 4

The Two Brothers of Ansari Road

I first went to Ansari Road for the same reason many writers and scholars do, to buy discounted books from the rows of distributors and publishers located there. I was living next to the Golcha Cinema then and felt, for the first time, a faster pulse of the city. Daryaganj and the net of gullies leading through Old Delhi—Chawri Bazaar, the Jama Masjid, and Chandni Chowk—are famous for showcasing just what it is people get up to during the day: buying and selling paper, cloth, wedding cards, plastic toys, and sweets; flying kites, washing dishes, sweeping garbage; praying, walking, watching.

Once there, I remembered that this was not the first time I had come to Daryaganj; my mother had taken me there as a child to show me where she was born. She had lived there for fifteen years in a two-room flat with her parents and three brothers, one of the many Punjabi partition families that had settled in the area after 1947. I decided that while I was in the neighborhood I would look for the building. The problem was, I had no idea what the building looked like, and I did not have the address. All I remembered was her pointing to a window, and the image I had of it now was of a window against a pale green wall. So, after buying my discounted books, I went looking for my mother's window in the wall.

I never found the window, but on my walk around the neighborhood I did keep noticing how, while reading the signboards for various publishers in Hindi and English, the two languages seemed to exist side-by-side, the Roman and Nagari scripts almost interlaced at times. On closer inspection, I came to see that they in fact inhabited different worlds.

This chapter concerns the world of Hindi publishing, one that has undeniably been shaped by the presence and politics of English. On the one hand, as we will see, Hindi *does* stand alone as a national presence and in terms of its numerical significance; on the other, its claim to nationality has been vexing for its own literary practitioners. Like all languages it is riddled with contradictions, reflecting the very complexity of the everyday vis-à-vis the ideological; in many respects what has shaped Hindi the most since independence is the tension between its regional and national significance.

AN INTIMATE AUDIENCE

Early on in my research I had a conversation with the Hindi poet Gagan Gill about who she understood her audience to be. It was the late 1990s, and the question of linguistic authenticity was linked to who one thought one was writing for. It was perhaps an unnecessary question for a writer who wrote in the most widely spoken language in India, yet I was curious to know how she conceived of her audience. She started by recounting several stories of "common people stopping and recognizing" her husband, Nirmal Verma (1929–2005), who was one of the most important living writers in Hindi at the time (and was recognized in 2000 with the Jnanpith Award, which is India's highest literary honor). She recalled one instance (of which there were many, she said) when she and Verma were walking on a bridge in the Himalayan foothill town of Rishikesh and a young man approached Verma and asked him to sign a book. It was the fact that he was recognized on the street and far from urban literary worlds that had meant something to her. She then shared a story of the time when a young man wrote to her and explained how one of her books of poetry had been serving as a go-between between him and his beloved. He was writing to Gill to ask her to sign a copy of the book and send it to the beloved on his behalf. Perhaps he saw this as sending his beloved not only the poetry but also the poet, as a way of further consecrating their impending union. In this individual plea for authorial consecration, I had the sense from Gill that it was her own consecration that she was refusing. In the end, she did not send the book to the beloved but signed a copy and returned it to the reader. To do otherwise would have broken the integrity between the author and the reader, she explained. Gill throughout seemed to have a keen sense of the relationship she wished to have with her audience. She refused to be co-opted by too much publicity, she said, a situation that might lead to having an inflated sense of her own importance. Like many authors I spoke to, Gill had some disdain for the kind of celebrity bestowed on Indian English authors and took pride in cultivating what I understood to be a relationship to one's readers that was at once more intimate and more measured, though this was surely also because she was a poet. At the same time, she continually stressed to me how she felt Hindi (and hence Hindi writers and Hindi literature) had a kind of visibility in India that other languages, including English, did not have. Her point in these stories was to relay the pervasiveness of the Hindi audience, the idea that readers could spring up anywhere, and as such create an organic, continuous audience, unlike the fragmented English one. The audience was not in a fixed location, such as an elite institutional or cultural space in Delhi, but out in the country at large. Hindi was also the only real literary link language in India in Gill's view and the only language in which she could identify a public that meant something to her. As Gill spoke I could sense that part of the distinction of being aware of one's audience in geographic terms was also a claim to a kind of literary nationality, predicated on having a regional identity first. For her, Indian authors who write in English forfeited this claim, as did nationalist Hindiwallahs. At some level, it seemed that Gill was questioning if someone who had a pan-Indian identity alone—whether in English or Hindi—could speak to Indians at all. The regional, then, for her was a badge of specificity, authenticity perhaps, that unlocked the door to national recognition and belonging. Hindi is pan-Indian, but it may also be located in specific regional settings in the Hindi belt. Gill, meanwhile, comes from a Punjabi background but writes in Hindi, a choice that in her literary world is less problematic than if she had chosen to write in English, which cannot claim to have an authentic audience in the way Hindi can.

HINDI LITERARY PUBLISHING

Usually it is writers who think of audiences (or decide not to, as the case may be), while publishers think of markets. However, one set of Hindi publishers in particular has powerfully shaped the business and meaning of the Hindi language in the literary realm. There has been a burgeoning of English since independence, and alongside the gains of English in the education, commerce, and media worlds, there has been a proliferation and growth of Hindi too. The perceptions of the languages and the ideologies sometimes associated with them differ, yet they both have central roles in contemporary Indian society. What does it mean to publish—as literature, in newspapers or online—in the most widely spoken language in India, albeit one that has repeatedly been rejected as the national language and whose own currency vis-à-vis English is continually debated?

The story of Rajkamal Prakashan and Vani Prakashan, in particular, showcases the way Hindi literary publishing had a mission to carve a distinct space for itself in line with its unique position as a regional and national language. Theirs is also the story of the national aspirations of Hindi in post-independence India. Publishing was one of the areas highlighted by the Official Language Commission in its report on how Hindi would grow and take the place of English as the language of public discourse. There were government subsidies for Hindi publishers in the 1950s and 1960s, but even more significantly, there was a desire among publishers to contribute to the nation through their work in the Hindi language. Their story enables an understanding of how and why language becomes a crucible for modern Indian identity.

Although Hindi books are sold most heavily in Bihar (the city of Patna being the focal point of sales in the region) and across the Hindi heartland, the relationship between Hindi and other linguistic regions in India has always been extremely important in giving legitimacy to Hindi as a national language. While Hindi has generally succeeded as a link language in popular culture—in the form of newspapers, movies, songs, and national and cable television—it has not become the link language for intellectual and literary exchange to the extent that the Hindi intelligentsia had expected. How, then, has the position of Hindi as a contested national language affected the perspective of Hindi literary publishers, who would arguably be in a different cultural and economic position if Hindi had achieved a broader appeal across India and if Hindi had been the language—even if via English translation—by which India had been represented globally?

According to statistics from the National Library of Calcutta, the compiler of the national bibliography, of a total of 24,856 books published in India in 1959, 3,751 were in Hindi and 12,585 were in English.

Of the other major Indian languages—Bengali, Gujarati, Marathi, Tamil—1,000 to 2,000 were published in each. A decade after independence, the colonial hangover in publishing was still apparent. English was the language of government and education, and its publishing enterprises had been greatly privileged by the colonial apparatus.

In 2004, of a total of 77,537 books published in India, 21,370 were in Hindi and 18,752 were in English. Tamil came next, with 7,525; then Bengali, with 5,538, and Marathi, with 5,475. In a mostly steady increase over the past four decades, Hindi has caught up to and surpassed English in terms of the number of books published, but considering the number of Hindi readers versus the number of English ones overall, there are many more books per capita for English readers. English is still dominant in the literate public sphere. This discrepancy has mostly to do with the trade in English-language textbooks and technical manuals, but 25 percent of English-language publications are also in the "general" category, which includes literature. It is hard to say whether the growth of English is at the expense of Hindi, since the possibilities of a multilingual public domain would seem limitless. Yet, considering the richness and diversity of Hindi in north India, it would appear that the potential of Hindi has not been fulfilled. Below I consider various kinds of literary nationality, or attempts at forging one, and argue that it has to do with how Hindi is deployed in literary and related realms rather than on any inherent strength the language has based on its numerical majority.

The first time I visited Rajkamal Prakhashan, I entered the cramped but neat office space and scanned the bookshelves lined with the distinctive thin black spines of the publisher.[1] The shelves told their own story of Hindi, as books by most, if not all, of the luminaries of Hindi and Urdu literature were there: Premchand, Ismat Chughtai, Nirmal Verma, Krishna Sobti, Mohan Rakesh, Shrilal Shukla, Bhisham Sahni, Vinod Kumar Shukla, Omprakash Valmiki, and dozens of others. There are a few things to notice about this list; the first is that Premchand and Chughtai wrote in the Urdu script, and like many of his generation and hers, they may be read in either the Urdu or Devanagari scripts, since the Hindustani language is a mix of Persian and Sanskrit vocabulary. While today Premchand is categorized as a Hindi-Hindu-Indian writer and Chughtai as an Urdu-Muslim-Pakistani one, both hailed from a shared, subcontinental, Hindustani milieu. Krishna Sobti, meanwhile, writes in a Hindi that is so colloquial it has little to do with the standard Hindi one finds on national television.[2] This may be said about most good Hindi literature—that it reflects the everyday speech of diverse milieus in the Hindi belt—but Sobti has been perhaps the more inventive in this regard and has pushed the idea of "writing on the margin" to the point where her oeuvre is considered central to the literary significance of post-independence Hindi. Finally, Omprakash Valmiki represents the vanguard of Dalit writing in Hindi, the first wave of writers who entered the literary mainstream with powerful autobiographical narratives imbibing histories of degradation, caste exploitation, and a new political consciousness.[3]

I met Rajkamal's owner, Ashok Maheshwari, who promptly invited me to his home for lunch. Republic Day was two days away, and there would be a family lunch at his home in Patparganj, an area just across the Yamuna River from central Delhi. I bought some books and said I would see him in two days.

At first Patparganj seemed a bit desolate. It was true that I had come on a Sunday when the market was closed, but there didn't seem to be anyone on the streets; all I saw were some tumbleweeds rolling in the wind, a far cry from the lively, signboard-filled alleyways of Ansari Road. In the coming months, as it turned out, I would make many visits there, since it is where many of the city's Hindi and English writers and publishers lived. It was one of the few areas of the ever-expanding Delhi that was affordable, yet it was fast becoming middle class and soon would be less affordable for those who had already been living there. Somewhat predictably, services and amenities were becoming too expensive for the lower class and poor in the area, including the service class on whom the middle-class households depended. And yet simple gentrification does not capture the dynamics of the variety of changes across the Yamuna.

Maheshwari had an uneasy position in this new urban configuration; for one, once he and his family moved to Patparganj, he could no longer send his children to Hindi-medium schools, as he had in north Delhi. In Patparganj, the only option for a "good," middle-class education was at an English-medium school. Maheshwari was irked by this and perhaps even slightly embarrassed. At the root of Hindi literary publishing is a continual reckoning with the social value of the Hindi language. Again and again, publishers are faced with the onslaught of English culture and prestige, fortified by better infrastructure, resources, and organization. In this case, the language of the sphere of cultural production of which Maheshwari was at the center was not even available as a medium of instruction to his own children. It is not that Maheshwari did not want his children to know and benefit from knowing English, but it is that with English education comes a different value system, one that frames bhasha education as second-rate. It is one thing to learn English as a second language, another for it to be the medium of education. For Maheshwari, this was part of the larger cultural problem of Delhi, where a "good" education was more and more inevitably a privatized English-medium one.

That Sunday, I met Maheshwari and his family at their flat in a large medium-rise apartment complex, surrounded by many more such complexes. Although one Hindi writer had joked with me that Patparganj was like the Left Bank of Paris, unlike its Parisian equivalent, from Patparganj central Delhi was nowhere in sight.

At the Maheshwaris, before we ate lunch, I asked him questions about publishing and Hindi and the history of Rajkamal Prakashan. He was disappointed that I had not brought a tape recorder. I was embarrassed that I had not. I had convinced myself that it was better to have informal conversations without one, that people would thus be more comfortable. The line between interviewing and having conversations was also often blurred. In Delhi, I soon learned some people expected you to bring a tape recorder, especially publishers and newspaper editors; it spoke of your own professional seriousness. Writers, on the other hand, did not like them at all. It soon became easy to know when to pull one out and when not to.

After lunch we sat upstairs on the roof, the nicest place to be on a cold, sunny afternoon. There Maheshwari began to ask, somewhat to my surprise, about my own experiences in publishing in the United States and the United Kingdom, how publishers worked, and what the major problems were in English-language publishing. We talked about literary agents and the lack of them until quite recently on the Indian scene; about advances, which again have only recently been available to writers in India, and then only in the English-language world;[4] about editing and the use of computers. His publishing outfit, I began to realize, was in many respects a one-man show. He had copy editors and an office manager, but in terms of real responsibility, it all fell to him. The other people at Rajkamal were "peons," more like office boys than editors. Talking to him, I also realized then that there was very little if any communication between English- and Hindi-language publishers in Delhi. In fact, there is little direct competition between publishers of different language presses. Maheshwari's main competitor, it turned out, was his brother.

Ashok's brother, Arun Maheshwari, owns Vani Prakashan, the other leading Hindi literary publisher, also located on Ansari Road. The Maheshwari brothers had not always been each other's biggest competitor. They had started out by working together and only later split into two separate publishing houses. Vani Prakashan was established by the Maheshwaris' father, Shri Premchand Mahesh, in 1955. Rajkamal was developed by Om Prakash, who came from Amritsar, Punjab, in the late 1940s and had an instinct for Hindi literature; in the 1940s and 1950s the house published a range of social science titles, began a number of series, and mostly survived off government bulk purchases. When the brothers went their separate ways in 1991, Arun took over Vani, and in 1994 Ashok took over Rajkamal from Sheila Sandhu, who had been running it for thirty years and had already maintained it as the leading Hindi literary publisher.[5] The two brothers were both inspired by the work and life of their father, and their own publishing work began in the context of this family business.

Ashok and Arun Maheshwari have spent their lives carrying on the work of their father. As with Vidya Rao, in relation to her father's generation of English-language publishers, the notion of making "good books" was tied up with doing "good for the nation" after independence. "Good" was described in different ways in my time with both brothers, as well as with Ameeta Maheshwari, Arun's wife. My first few visits to Vani Prakashan were spent waiting for Arun and having tea and samosas with Ameeta. She was from a Hindi-speaking family in Hyderabad, where she told me she had been more "in touch" with English, since that was "how it was in the South." When she married and moved to Delhi, she started "to read Hindi newspapers and get back into the language"; after all, she had married into a Hindi publishing family. As she described it to me then, she had left her "household works" to come "sit in the office" and "have a look on people, just to see what they're doing." What was clear to me over several conversations with her was that she not only looked after the office when Arun was away, but that she also had her finger on the pulse of Vani Prakashan. She, too, spoke of making "good books."

In the language of a publisher one might expect a "good book" to mean the entire production value of the book, from its content and quality of editing to its cover design and binding. It is true that the quality of paper and its expense in India is troublesome for Ashok, but when he says "a good book" *(koi acchi kitab),* he told me, "I am asking myself if the book is worth reading."

The Maheshwaris' connection to the production of books was not only a matter of business and competition, but sprang from the legacy of their father, whose aim it was to promote the Hindi language. Part of the success of that promotion depended on the commercial aspects of the trade. The infrastructure for many English-language publishers had been established by the British during the colonial period, while the vernacular presses had been commercially marginalized and often denigrated through censorship. This favored status made both the distribution and the dissemination of English-language books and ideas, partly through an already established network of distribution by big companies like OUP and Orient Longman, travel and flourish. So, for someone like Ravi Dayal, by contrast, the promotion of English as a language was never an issue. Instead, the language became "Indian" as Indian economists, historians, and sociologists expressed their ideas in it and those ideas traveled. But, in the case of Hindi publishing, what was at stake was no less than the assertion of a language for the nation.

BUILDING BOOKS FOR THE NATION

The Maheshwaris are Banias, that is, members of a merchant caste, and they started their own book publishing business from their residence in Kamla Nagar in north Delhi, before moving their office to Ansari Road in 1983. Though Ravi Dayal came from a Kayastha subcaste, where reading and writing are prized, and the Maheshwaris come from a Bania background, both of the narratives show the ways in which family history, rather than a simple association of caste affiliation, influenced their commitments to the publishing business and fortifying the respective languages they work in. There is no clear-cut narrative in this. Ravi Dayal pointed out that for him going into publishing was a "caste blemish"; and yet, even in his seemingly new profession, Dayal was very much continuing in a kind of Kayastha preoccupation with words and ideas even if he did not enter the higher-status world of civil servants like his uncles had. The Maheshwaris meanwhile began a business sparked by the literary aspirations of their father. Arun and Ashok, as well as Ameeta, Arun's wife, explained that Premchand Mahesh had been a good writer who wrote several children's books and was working on a doctoral thesis but died before completing it. Arun began to explain the beginnings of the family's connection to publishing by recounting how his father had been part of an informal collective of writers who wanted to have their works published. In the tradition of many writers' collectives, this group appears to have been trying to change the norms of the market by asserting their own ideas about society. Along with their larger mission of publishing good Hindi books, the Maheshwaris seemed, even this many years later, propelled by the specter of their father's unfinished work.

The brothers narrated a common story about their father that begins with his aspirations but then moves to the business of publishing, especially in the years after independence, and ultimately to the idea of the promotion of Hindi itself. I have included Arun's version below, only because it happened to be the more expansive of the two. Arun narrated this to me in Hindi, and I have translated it somewhat literally.

> Thirty years ago Vani Prakashan began. Our father was a writer himself; he had written some history books and children's stories and some poetry. We used to live in Thapar [Uttar Pradesh], which is about seventy kilometers from Delhi. It was there that my father and some of his friends decided to start their own publishing house. You know, publishing houses are limited by their own interests. What you as a writer may like, they might not have an interest in, and so won't print it for you. Every writer has his own views about his writing, but the work may not be marketable. It's the publishing house that decides. Because they didn't get the publishing house to publish what they thought was good, some friends got together and formed their own publishing house. Sometimes a good writer does not have the idea of what the market wants. Every writer has his own view of his writing. It may be good writing, but the market does not want that. But it is what the writer wants to give to society, even if the publisher doesn't value that. So these writer-friends formed their own association. Then they published some poetry and some writings. And they were published and distributed their works locally.

In the world of English publishing in the years after independence the goal was to renegotiate the management and sometimes ownership of British-run companies, as a precursor to shifting the focus to "home-grown" ideas. In the case of Hindi, it is a different kind of story, more of a negotiation between the regional and the national. First, there is a move from the Hindi heartland of Uttar Pradesh to the capital city, a place that affords greater resources, infrastructure, and possibilities for a small business. Arun continued:

> After that we moved to Delhi. Delhi is the capital, and it's obvious that it's very big and it's spread out. We had an interest in books, so we thought we will do good by working towards books. The problem was my father was a teacher, employed by the government, and there were certain boundaries he couldn't cross. At the same time, he was a writer, and he was anxious. He was really dying to write. A writer's heart is anxious, is really dying to publish what he has written, to share with people. So with my mother's collaboration, he started this publishing house, and she was the proprietor. Because he was a government teacher, he couldn't put the business in his name. Their bank accounts, income tax, and everything was in her name. It wasn't just that it was in her name. It's not that she didn't do anything; she used to take the books and go to various institutions and meet with a lot of important people to market them. We were very small, but even we children used to take the books and go [to market them]. My parents used to go to booksellers and to some institutions, and if nothing else, we [he and his brother] would go to get orders. Sometimes we would just go to the post office. We were publishers and distributors in Delhi in a small way.
>
> As our father's thoughts started to develop, he saw that in the South, at that time, Hindi was starting to become popular, and in our trade at that time, even now, we don't have educated agents and marketers to spread Hindi, to make it more popular. My father and mother both used to go to the South and meet with Hindi scholars who were settled there. In that time, these scholars were there spreading the use of Hindi, but it was also their livelihood *(roz ki roti)* since most of them were teachers of Hindi. They were not only teachers; they wanted to do more for Hindi. They wanted Hindi to progress *(agay budne)*. This is how my parents had this connection with them. Since then we have a rule; we always try to give some space, a percentage, to south Indian writers. Because our father had thought of this, we have continued this notion. We publish their writings or thoughts. After that, slowly, Vani Prakashan books came to spread all over. Then after our father died, we started to take over. And the result of that is for all to see.

Despite their work with south Indian writers, Arun never spoke of liaisons with Tamil or other south Indian–language publishers. The point was not to publish Hindi translations of Tamil, Telugu, or other writers but instead to publish and promote Hindi writing beyond the Hindi belt. In Arun's narrative publishing is linked to the betterment of society and, in the case of post-independence publishing, to the spread of Hindi. A larger goal seems to have been: How to create not only a pan-Indian language but also a set of discourses within that language? In many ways, the focus was necessarily on creating a kind of literate nationality, even though this might have paradoxically limited Hindi's scope and range.

Today the issues in Hindi publishing have to do with the technical advances in the promotion and development of Hindi, seen as part and parcel of raising professional standards. The English words most noticeably incorporated into the Hindi newsletter of Vani Prakashan, *Vani Samachar* (Vani News), for instance, are "hand composing" versus "computer composing," "internet," and "font." More recently this goal of extending the reach of Hindi has been through translations, hence a focus on bringing in new ideas rather than trying to gain more Hindi readers. Vani has a Hindi-English bilingual series, and it is translating books from English and the bhashas into Hindi. Topics such as the various aspects of globalization as well as religious identity and women's rights are featured on the book list. Ameeta Maheshwari stressed to me that their mission was to let people know what was going on in different parts of the world. She cited the Hindi translation of the Bangladeshi writer Taslima Nasrin's *Lajja* (Shame) as one of their most popular Hindi books sold.[6] Arun said more explicitly, "It's a sign of development—taking from other languages—we're satisfying what our readers want." In his use of the idea of development, he not only refers to increased growth and sales, but a notion of cultivation, allowing readers to read about different societies through translation.

There are at least two strands in contemporary Hindi publishing, one favoring its promotion as a language and the other directed toward the cultivation of Hindi readers. Rajkamal and Vani are at the center of Hindi literary publishing, and many others I spoke with in Delhi who were involved in Hindi promotion were connected to one or both publishing houses in some way. They bought and sold their books or formed publishing partnerships with them for particular series, forging new topics in Hindi literature or translations from a range of other languages. Yet in these other satellites in the Hindi world, the people I met were grappling with the failure of the nationalist vision of Hindi as promoted in the 1950s, 1960s, and 1970s. What was the way forward as English was globalizing and Hindi seemed to be stagnating? I discovered different responses to this question and kinds of projects that were forging new intellectual and creative avenues for Hindi. I saw that these avenues inevitably had to do with the creation of a kind of cosmopolitanism within the language itself, of finding a "window to the world" in Hindi, one that had previously only been possible in English.

HINDI COSMOPOLITANISM

Not far from Ansari Road is Asaf Ali Road, a busy crescent-shaped thoroughfare dividing Old and New Delhi. Here, the Punjabi bookseller Amar Varma addresses some of the more practical concerns about language dissemination. For Varma, who is in the business of selling and occasionally publishing Hindi books, the "culture" of book consumption is not amenable to the promotion of Indian languages. Varma explained to me one day in his office that there was "no habit of buying books in our country" since there was "no reading habit to the extent there should be." This perceived lack extended to the notion of what a book was more generally: "When I was getting married and my in-laws were inquiring about me, they came to know I am in books and said, 'What kind of books do you have?' And they asked, 'Are there any books besides textbooks?'" Varma saw this as proof that "people will spend money on cinema but wouldn't like to buy a book."[7]

Varma went on to tell me that his family had been in the book business for the past fifty-five years. They had been booksellers in Multan, a Punjabi town that became part of Pakistan at the time of partition. In 1947 his family migrated to Delhi and opened a small, "low-scale" bookshop, selling Urdu-language books on Chandni Chowk in Old Delhi. Varma himself joined the family business in 1956, after he had completed his studies. A turning point in the family's book business occurred in 1958 when they started publishing books in addition to selling them, first Hindi and then Urdu paperbacks. They became known for these paperbacks, and in 1969 they moved to Asaf Ali Road, a location that afforded them more space than Chandni Chowk had. Varma's shop, the Hindi Book Center, is one of the largest bookstores in Delhi in terms of its stock and floor space. Unlike many of the English-language bookshops in Connaught Place, Khan Market, Greater Kailash, and South Extension, which tend to be cramped and have limited stock, the Hindi Book Centre feels like a small library, with patrons milling around between the roomy aisles and with men and women taking care of accounts and patron queries at large desks in the back of the shop.

A pivotal event occurred for Varma in 1969, when he was invited by the British Council to go to England to meet other booksellers and publishers; this was "good exposure," he said. He came back to India inspired to focus exclusively on being a bookseller, not a publisher as well. To be a bookseller exclusively was to flout the business practice of most Indian booksellers at the time, he explained. They tended to be publishers and distributors, since the specialized practice of bookselling did not give enough of a profit margin. The Hindi Book Centre had received a major distribution contract from the Library of Congress, which had appointed it to supply books in Hindi, Urdu, and Punjabi to twenty-four American universities. Now, Varma said, "I'm sure I can claim to be the largest Hindi book distributor in all of India. Bombay filmmakers come to us to find Hindi stories." His main competitors were not other booksellers but Hindi publishers. They "undersold" him when customers came to buy books directly from the publisher. He told me, "In our country, bookselling has not developed," citing the fact that there was only one major Hindi bookshop in the national capital. For him, this pointed to a "big handicap" in the promotion of books. Since there was "no coordination between publishers and booksellers," he explained, "Indian publishers will undersell the booksellers." What ended up happening was that "the publisher becomes the competitor of the bookseller." He linked this situation to the feasibility of owning one's own bookshop, of paying rent for a shop floor, and the reasons for the dearth of such shops in Delhi and elsewhere. "Bookshops are so expensive here," he added, referring to the high cost of rent for shop space, "unless someone has some old property at his disposal."

I had begun talking to Varma after browsing in the Hindi Book Centre and finding him sitting behind his desk in a large, glass-windowed office in one corner of the shop floor. I noticed he was speaking to another man who was seated across from him. A thick manuscript was sitting on the desk between them. Seeing him through the glass gave me the idea to set up an interview with him. When I asked one of the staff if I could make an appointment to see Varma, I was instead ushered straight into his office and found myself sitting next to the man he had been in conversation with. I explained to Varma that I needed to talk to him for perhaps an hour or more and that I would be happy to come back when he was not in a meeting, but he insisted that now was a good time and proceeded to call for tea. I found that this kind of experience was more typical in the Hindi publishing world—less so in the English one—where I was unexpectedly invited into other people's conversations. The man to my left, one Professor Subramani of the University of the South Pacific, smiled and agreed that he was happy to remain while Varma and I conversed. Subramani, it turned out, was a Hindi writer from Fiji.

Although Varma had told me that he had abandoned publishing to concentrate on bookselling and distribution (after his revelatory trip to England in 1969), he said that from time to time, he published a book that would otherwise "fall between the cracks." Subramani's novel, he believed, was once such book. Varma explained that because of the worldwide distribution networks of the Hindi Book Centre, he had more international contacts than most Hindi publishers; those contacts included writers and publishers in Fiji.[8] Varma told me that he thought of himself as a kind of roving ambassador for Hindi, and in his travels to distribute Hindi books around the world he had developed a vast network. Subramani, meanwhile, based in Fiji and writing in "Fiji Hindi," was not linked to the Hindi literary sphere in India but came to know about Varma and eventually approached him with his novel. The meeting I had inadvertently joined was Subramani's delivery of the completed manuscript. Since by this time we were all part of the same conversation, Subramani explained that in Fiji people speak "a mixture of Puri and other Indian languages" but that many are "still maintaining Hindi and have learned the Devanagari script." Varma added, "We feel quite proud and happy to go to that part of the world which is so far away; even if there is a mixture with other languages, we see the signboards in Hindi." What seemed clear was that the discourse of Hindi had widened: a bookseller's network brings a diasporic Hindi author—and a new form of and perspective on the Hindi language culled from the migrations of indentured labor—into mainstream Hindi literature. The connection between other Hindis and the language politics of overseas Hindi populations is another layer through which Hindi may be viewed.[9]

Subramani's novel, *Dauka Puraan,* went on to be published by Varma's publishing wing, Star Publications, in 2001 and has since been lauded by critics for having captured the argot of Fijian Hindi. Subramani has been praised for his ability to reflect the "actual speech" of Fijian Hindi, especially as spoken among the poor and working class of rural Labasa. It is not the "high" or "Sanskritized" Hindi of north Indian elites, but it is written in the Devanagari script. The novel plays on the "high/low" concept in its title, *Dauka Puraan; "dauka"* means "lying con man," literally, someone who pulls a fast one on you, as in *dauka dalna;* the *puraanas* meanwhile are sacred religious texts, originally written in Sanskrit. Most critics, both in Hindi and in English, saw Subramani's novel as irreverent and hilarious, though a few said that it denigrated the Hindi language. In his book *The Literature of the*

Indian Diaspora, Vijay Mishra lauds the novel as representing "the discourse of the silenced subaltern diaspora" as it creates "an alternative reality" imbibing social resistance and protest. It is a unique discourse, explains Mishra (who himself is a Fijian Indian and links the novel to his own biography), since it is made of "the original vernacular of the indentured laborers." Most interestingly, he points out that Fijian Hindi is "no one's mother tongue, but belonged to anyone with an indentured background."[10]

Farther into central Delhi, where cultural bureaucracies reign in the area known as Mandi House, the conversation about the cultivation of Hindi and the process of its becoming more cosmopolitan took on different proportions. It was in my discussions with Ashok Vajpeyi in 2008 that I began to see the possibilities and limitations of a "top-down" approach to Hindi promotion. Of all the people I came across in Delhi, Vajpeyi most aptly fits the title "literary practitioner." Many writers carry out aspects of literary promotion or administrative work, but Vajpeyi has held one arts-related post after the other. In the press he is sometimes referred to as a "culture activist." As for Vajpeyi himself, he seems to relish his position as a "power center" in Indian cultural life, even if, when speaking about the Sahitya Akademi, he told me that it was "a contradictory organization" since it was "the nature" of literature and the role of writers to "suspect power." This contradiction, it would seem, also held for Vajpeyi himself. One afternoon, while chatting in his new office at the Lalit Kala Akademi (India's National Academy of Art), of which he had been appointed chairman in 2008, he said that at times he is "undercut" by the Hindi literary world but that even so, "It is difficult to bypass me. I am a power center. I can't wish it away."

Vajpeyi is a lauded Hindi poet with thirteen poetry collections; he won the Sahitya Akademi award for one of them, *Kahin Nahin Wahin,* in 1994. However, regarding his own place in Hindi letters, he said that he was often "looked down upon" because he is a civil servant. "I was seen as an officer-poet," he told me. He is, in his words, an "overnoticed" institution maker and an "undernoticed" poet. He has also written eight books of art criticism, hence his appointment at the Lalit Kala Akademi. He joked that another writer once told him he was the only person who could fill the presidency of all three of the national art academies (art, music, literature).

Vajpeyi grew up in Sagar, a town 120 miles from Bhopal in Madhya Pradesh. His father came from Uttar Pradesh and was a university administrator. Vajpeyi studied in a Hindi-medium school and was exposed to literature from around the world through English translation. He told me he would always be "indebted to the English language" for opening up the world of poetry to him. He went to St. Stephens College in Delhi for his master of arts degree and then taught English for a few years. He said he was not fluent in English the way other students at St. Stephen's were, yet he had read Rilke and many other poets in translation. Even then, it seems, he had a strong sense of his own cultural worth. He explained that his "small town boy's revenge" at the urbane St. Stephen's was "to acquire an accent." Vajpeyi's accent could be described as having a Cambridge hue, though he never studied abroad. He was thirty-two years old when he took his first trip abroad, and that was to the former Soviet Union.

It was Vajpeyi's twenty-six years as an IAS officer (1966–92) in Madhya Pradesh that shaped his interests but also gave him the tools to pursue his passion for cultural life and its development. He worked on a variety of projects during those years, including founding a department of culture within the state's Ministry of Education, known as the Kalidas Academy. In 1980 he began to shape Bharat Bhavan (India House), a more personal endeavor that was completed in 1982. Bharat Bhavan was a "multiarts" center, bringing together visual arts, fiction, theater, music, and poetry. The Hindi poet Gagan Gill told me that it was "a place where you could get feedback from other writers, which is what all writers want." She and other Hindi writers told me of their productive stints at Bharat Bhavan in the 1980s and 1990s and of Vajpeyi's generosity and vision. Some others alleged that he looked out for his family and "his own interests" more than he should have. The sense I got from Vajpeyi was of his awareness that he was as much of a "political animal" as a literary one.

We talked about the "location" of Hindi literary culture and how places like Bhopal, Allahabad, and Lucknow compared to Delhi. I had met several Hindi writers who felt their sense of place and language came from elsewhere, often from Uttar Pradesh. In Delhi they were transplants, much as writers in many societies might be who flock from villages or small towns to big cities. Vajpeyi simply said, "Delhi has no literary culture of its own, but the largest concentration of Hindi writers and publishers is in Delhi." At what point, one might ask, does a "concentration" create a culture of its own?

Vajpeyi's biggest venture yet, meant to bring together his passion for the Hindi language and for the development of Hindi culture more broadly, turned out to be his biggest disappointment. From 1997 to 2002 he served as the first vice-chancellor of the Mahatma Gandhi Antarrashtriya Hindi Vishwavidyalaya (MGAHV), or Mahatma Gandhi International Hindi University, in Wardha, Maharashtra. Wardha was chosen because it was the site of Gandhi's Sevagram ashram from where he largely directed the freedom movement. The university aims to connect Gandhian ideals and history to the contemporary study and promotion of Hindi, though Wardha is geographically remote from any other universities that have strong Hindi or other departments. The university is funded by the government of India and was meant to be, according to Vajpeyi, a "British Council of Hindi," meaning that it would promote Hindi internationally. It was also meant to be "just a university," focusing on literature, language, culture, and translation. Most of all, it was intended to promote Hindi to its legitimate place as an international language.

As vice-chancellor Vajpeyi had a mission to confront what he saw as a number of "obstacles" within Hindi. Hindi scholarship, to take one example, had declined in the previous decades. He wanted to address this issue by creating a dialogue with foreign universities at which Hindi language and literature was being taught. To this end he started a Hindi journal, called *Hindi,* which appeared in English, so that it could serve as "an international forum for Hindi scholars." Vajpeyi also started two Hindi-language journals, *Bahu Vachan,* which he described as "a series of conversations among scholars and creative persons"; and *Pustak Varta,* a wide-ranging review of books. He began to publish anthologies of major Hindi writers and of poetry for use in university courses. He wanted to have a partnership with publishers such as Rajkamal Prakashan as a way to enlarge the lists of publishers while also serving the needs of students. "The Hindi domain is not adequately addressed by Hindi publishers. They are very conventional," he said. "A 'daring' is required." By this he meant that publishers should be involved in commissioning books and starting series. He criticized Hindi publishers in general for being "too comfortable with library purchases."

Vajpeyi's plans for the university extended to the classroom and the cultivation of students. He was at once trying to subvert areas of Hindi scholarship that had been mired in controversy—the Sanskritization of Hindi, for instance—and had led, in his view, to "mediocrity" in all things Hindi. He advocated an "alternative syllabus" that placed Hindi within the realm of world literature by including Hindi texts alongside those from the world's major languages. Students would gain from English and Hindi reading materials, while classroom and written assignments would value Hindi expression. Master's degrees would be offered on Ahimsa (nonviolence), Women's Studies, and Hindi-Urdu. "If Hindi and Urdu are so closely related," he said, "why not study them together?" But the course drew only three students initially, he went on to say, and there was a problem with the availability of texts. "According to the Urdu scholars," he explained, "while much Urdu literature had been translated or transliterated into the Devanagari script, Hindi had not been put into the Urdu script."

Within the classroom itself, Vajpeyi wanted to revive the *tika* tradition from Sanskrit, consisting of close line-by-line readings of texts. He also wanted there to be a focus on Hindi grammar and lexicography, and he started a special unit to create a new grammar for Hindi by young linguists. The idea was to bring in the many ways of speaking Hindi across the Hindi belt, "to take into account all the Hindis"; they would carry out a proper linguistic survey of the country, beginning with the states of Jharkhand and Chattisgarh, areas far from mainstream Hindi cultural centers. "After Grierson," he said, referring to the early-twentieth-century *Linguistic Survey of India* (1898–1928) that had been conducted by the colonial-era civil servant George Abraham Grierson, "there has been no linguistic survey."

Vajpeyi spoke proudly of his ideas and initiatives, but then his voice dropped as he explained how his efforts were stalled by the university administration. The university came about during BJP (Bharatiya Janata Party) rule, and Vajpeyi said that he did not want to be influenced by their politics. Perhaps because he was all too aware of how institutions worked, he set a few rules for himself: the university had to be a pluralistic space, one that reflected the pluralism within Hindi itself; he would be bound by the Constitution of India; and politics would not interfere in the running of the university, to which end he said he never invited politicians to come to campus.

Instead, Vajpeyi drew on his contacts in the Hindi world—professors, novelists, essayists, and poets. These occasional visitors added something to the atmosphere of the university and to students' morale, but longer-term academic life was stalled. It became impossible to hire anyone. "You can read the report by the UPA [United Progressive Alliance] government," he told me. I consulted the report, brought out by the coalition government that had been voted into power at the national level in 2004, defeating the incumbent BJP. The report had been "convened" by the respected historian Bipan Chandra, and its pages contained a detailed recounting of academic politics gone wrong. It is a tedious story of blocked appointments, including key positions such as the registrar, the financial officer, and members of the Academic Council. In a never-ending interim, the university was run by the Executive Council, "without the aid of any academic person from the university." The report unequivocally states at the outset, "The University failed to develop fully or adequately primarily because the Ministry of Human Resources Development acted as a road-block virtually from the very beginning." Further on, the report specifies, "From certain oral evidence, it seems that the University has been implicated in local institutional Hindi politics."[11]

Part of the problem, Vajpeyi admitted, was one of location. "I was here in Delhi," he said, as were his resources and contacts; Wardha was an outpost. It was hard to oversee what was going on. Students were unhappy. The university administration had plans to build better hostels, for instance. Those plans were discussed and drawn up by an architect, but then construction never began. He explained that ultimately the government was against his vision of the university, but so, he found, was the academic world. "They were comfortable with the way things were."

Vajpeyi reflected that he should have started a research institute instead, "something like a World Hindi Institute" rather than a university. Something smaller and more manageable but also something, it seemed, he would have been able to manage without the interference of forces greater than himself. And then he returned to the realm of big ideas, of how "there should be a movement to protect and preserve languages and mother tongues, just as there is an environmental movement." India should take the initiative, he said. "India is plural and things 'Indian' should be taught in plural terms." With this, Vajpeyi seemed to return to firmer footing. He was smiling again; his cheerful demeanor had returned. He seemed happy in his new post; he liked to be asked to head big ventures and to be given the leeway to implement his ideas.

Vajpeyi's story seemed to me a quest for not only the promotion of Hindi, but of another kind of Hindi cosmopolitanism, one that meant to expand the parochial study of Hindi literature. The desire for Hindi to enter the international discourse on literature ultimately needed a new pedagogical framework and a new style of university administration. There was also the question of the language itself—the history of its grammar and the ways in which it is spoken and written in contemporary India—and there was the influence of its ideas. Many of those ideas, about the relationship between language and religious identity inherent in the Hindi-Urdu debates, for instance, were sites of contestation that Vajpeyi sought to bring into the university curriculum itself. There were also the ideas associated with "Hindi culture" that were admired all over the world: Gandhi's nonviolence movement, which rested on such Hindi and Gujarati concepts as *ahimsa* and *satyagraha*. It seemed like a viable way to make Hindi part of a world discourse not only through its literature but also through its contribution to society. What were the capacities inherent in Hindi, and how could they be "unblocked"?

A CRITICAL DISCOURSE IN HINDI

The question of Hindi cosmopolitanism took on yet another meaning in my discussions with the historian and translator Ravikant, who works at the experimental research program, Sarai, which is part of the Centre for the Study of Developing Societies (CSDS) in the Civil Lines area of north Delhi. Ravikant, who is in his early forties and equally comfortable in the intellectual worlds of Hindi and English, taught history at Delhi University for many years before moving to the Hindi lab at Sarai. He became interested in the way popular and new media are bringing a new liveliness into the Hindi discourse, especially in the implications and possibilities of new media forms in Hindi popular culture. In this regard, he edits the Hindi media reader *Deewan-e-Sarai,* which is published out of Sarai, and keeps track of new developments in Hindi free software, satellite channels, and "tactical media." He himself is involved in creating viable fonts and interfaces for Hindi to allow for greater online cultural production. We can see how the interests of traditional print media like the publishers of Ansari Road might dovetail with the interests of new media technologies, and in fact there are more and more collaborations happening with "traditional" and "new" media entrepreneurs. Sarai's few Hindi publications are all published by Rajkamal Prakashan, the most recent of which, *Bahurupiya Shehr* (2007), is a celebrated collection of reflections on Delhi in various narrative forms, including blogs, by "ordinary" Hindi speakers and writers who have grown up in the city's *bastis* (informal settlements).

One afternoon at Sarai, Ravikant explained to me that "scholars of Hindi-speaking culture" have been "obsessed with print culture from the nineteenth century." It was this realm of cultural production that came to inform both the value of and the trends within the Hindi language. "They have a love for literature, " he added, "but today there are more ways of looking at the world. Film and TV now constitute language."[12]

What this means for Ravikant and others who work in the Hindi lab of Sarai is that the "authority" over the Hindi language no longer comes exclusively from the literary elite. It is becoming both more anonymous and more collaborative, as befits the technologies associated with the digital world. Yet the nature of this collaboration was also new, since when one works online one may not know with whom one is collaborating. In the constant adding and remaking of knowledge and language, many more people from different backgrounds and regions are involved in what are essentially collective practices. Ravikant sees great liveliness in Hindi, from newspapers like *Dainik Bhaskar* and *Dainik Jagran,* which are now the highest-circulation dailies in the country in any language, to the high Hindi content of television channels, to the variety of accents and lexicons audible on FM Hindi radio stations. Yet he also sees the need for a "higher level of intellectual discourse" in the language.

The problem for Hindi, according to him, is that the critical discourse on various forms of Hindi culture is happening in English. For instance, the best books analyzing the Hindi public domain have been written in English. Similarly, experts on Hindi film publish only in English. His point is that the intellectual discourse on Hindi should also be happening and be available in Hindi. There came a point, he seemed to be saying, where English as mediator became an intellectual problem. But it is not enough for people just to write in Hindi. Ravikant believes that the discourse on Hindi must be infused with ideas from "elsewhere," which in some respects echoed some of the failed initiatives of Ashok Vajpeyi when he was vice-chancellor of MGAHV. Ravikant has been involved in translating key texts of social science from English and other languages into Hindi, for the long-term goal of enriching the discussion on social and political topics in Hindi.

New media essentially offers new forms and methods of cultural production that are in turn changing traditional print media forms. In the process, the question of language promotion takes on new meaning. For Hindi, the emphasis is not on merely promoting Hindi, but on exposing and including many different styles and accents and ways of communicating within Hindi. The idea for Ravikant and others is that the burgeoning of styles and ideas might eventually break the ideological constraints of Hindi. Whereas Vajpeyi's version of Hindi cosmopolitanism is to improve the intellectual activity within the Hindi language and its discourses, Ravikant aims to bring new ideas into those Hindi discourses.

It is perhaps not surprising that new institutions may be required in order to implement new ideas. In Hindi there is a generational shift occurring alongside the new cultural utilities and requirements of the language. By outlining the contours of this incipient Hindi cosmopolitanism, we may see how the Hindi language may be promoted through new forms of institution building and new technologies that intersect with traditional publishing forms. In the process, this "promotion" becomes something more, as it grows beyond the confines of "the national."

Indeed, the notion of publishing itself has been under scrutiny the world over as Google and other digital ventures are changing the possibilities of what readers and consumers might expect to have access to. "Cosmopolitanism" itself is a changing concept. It has surely been shorn of some of its elite pretensions with the growing influence of the digital world, as what it means to know the world and be part of the making of knowledge continues to change.

CHAPTER 5

At the Sahitya Akademi

The majority status of Hindi and its reflection in a unified, national literary culture becomes more complicated as one leaves Ansari Road and heads to central Delhi, where government bureaucracy and Nehruvian idealism meet at "the house of Rabindranath Tagore." It is a place and part of Delhi where the task of creating a sense of nationality, national purpose, really, across different forms of cultural production is paramount. I identify this quest at the Sahitya Akademi as one for "literary nationality." In terms of literary production, to be literate is to know the literatures of each regional language and accord them equal status to the extent possible—a production, as we will see, in and of itself. English, once again, is a mediating language, even as its authenticity is continually in question, which is not to say that colonial oppositions are regressively at play; rather they are destabilized and reconstituted by literary practitioners themselves with a more complicated, if also resigned, understanding of the role of English vis-à-vis the bhashas and in their own lives.

The gray stone building known as Rabindra Bhavan is the home of the Sahitya Akademi (Academy of Literature), as well as the Sangeet Natak (Music and Dance) and Lalit Kala (Art) Akademis. In central Delhi, or Lutyens' Delhi, as colonial architecture enthusiasts like to call it, the roads are wide, and the *dhabas* are few and far between.

In February 2008, I attended the Sahitya Akademi annual awards function, an event held in the Kamani Auditorium next door to the Akademi headquarters. A reception for the award winners took place before the ceremony in a large, colorful tent put up for the occasion on the grounds of Rabindra Bhavan. I got there early so I had time to renew my library card in the Sahitya Akademi's library, one of the country's best multilingual libraries. Its holdings include literature in all the languages recognized by the Indian constitution and its amendments, over twenty-two in all. But first there was the matter of my library card.

MY LIBRARY CARD

I was renewing my card out of good faith; no one really checks your card as you enter the library. I didn't have checkout privileges to begin with, so I wasn't looking to use my card for that purpose. I was trying to write a book, and the last thing I needed to do was cart unread books to and from the library. My plan was to read the books in the library itself and so obtain a consultation-only membership. I had had a membership six years earlier, and as I peered over the edge of the first counter in the library, I wondered if I would be in their computer system. I was.

I was then told to proceed to the desk of one Mr. Kumar, to whom I would pay my membership fee. Mr. Kumar, however, was not satisfied when I told him I was in the computer system. He went to the tall metal cabinet across from his desk to retrieve a worn ledger and was only satisfied when he found my name and address inscribed in it. I liked seeing it there too. The cursive writing, my old address. He then became helpful, almost pliant. He asked me to pay fifty rupees to renew my reading-only privileges, and I happily obliged. He gave me a receipt, and I proceeded to the card makers stationed in the recesses of the library.

These people were younger and wore brighter clothes. I was sure I would have my card in minutes. On examination of my receipt, however, a slim girl with square spectacles told me that the fee I had paid was too small. I was sent back to Mr. Kumar. He was on my side now and didn't like being told he had charged me the wrong fee by these backbenchers. He insisted it was the right fee and sent me back to them. They took me back and said they would have to give me a different designation. I said that was okay. Then another person looked at my photo and much to my alarm told me that my face was too big. It was a passport-size photo I had gotten in New York and had used for my visa application. I had given the library staff an extra one I had. I was not now going to get another photo for a library card I didn't really have to have. They kept saying my face was too big. I started to get offended. I asked if I could crop the photo myself and looked at the supplies on the desk. Then I started cracking up a little, a kind of nervous laugh I've always been prone to; once it starts it's hard to stop. That was happening in the library. I motioned to some scissors lying on the desk. Couldn't I just crop the photo? No, I was told, my face would still be too big. I said that that was okay, all the better for me to be recognized by my library identification card. They looked at me strangely. I became emboldened and took the scissors from the desk and started to cut slivers off each side of my photo. They looked at me more strangely but with a hint of amusement. That gave me confidence to keep at it, though I noticed that as I cut slivers off the photo it was indeed becoming smaller, making my face appear even larger. When I was done, I placed the newly cropped photo on the small square on the card. See, it fits fine now, I said. They didn't look happy about it, but they had to agree that it now fit the square. They sent it for lamination, which in my mind spelled victory. On handing the finished card back to me, the laminator, who sat in an adjacent room, said, "Your face is too big." I said, "I know. It's okay."

After securing my card, it was time for the reception to begin. I got there early and found a few writers and some members of the press selecting plastic cups of bubbly brown, bright orange, and cloud-colored liquids from the servers circulating among them. I took the cloud-colored one and tasted Limca. Then a line formed for the buffet, with an array of mostly late-middle-aged men stacking their plates with fried food. It was a signature Akademi event. But there were some young people too, and then it occurred to me that I had only just seen some of them in the library. They had been the ones who told me what could and couldn't be done regarding the renewal of my library card. Strangely, a warm feeling for them came over me, a feeling of recognition. They seemed so normal, so human, waiting in line for tea and *pakoras*. It would be too much to say they helped me, though in the end my card was renewed. Now, here, under the red and green tent they were giving me sheepish smiles. I meanwhile was happy to see any face I recognized. By this time I was drinking cup after cup of the Akademi's good, strong tea with sugar not already added. I ate some sandwiches and struck up a conversation with the wife of one of the award winners, the Gujarati poet Rajendra Shukla. He had won for his collection of poems, *Ghazal Samhita,* and is known for his innovative renderings of the *ghazal* form. While Shukla was meeting the press photographers, his wife told me how meaningful this award was to her husband but also of how, sitting here at an event like this, one wouldn't know how important he was in his Gujarati community, where large crowds gathered to hear him recite his verse.

The Sahitya Akademi is a place where social and political battles are waged daily in the name of culture, the nation, region, and language. In the larger literary field, the Akademi offers structural support to literature in over twenty-two languages, something individual publishers and other institutions cannot aspire to. And most significant, in its conception of the "global" and in its promotion of Indian literatures the Akademi posits the bhashas in the main frame of literary and cultural debate. It is its mandate to do so. The Akademi may be old school in terms of its funding and institutional culture, but it has remained at the forefront of the issues and debates of the literary world. Even as the annual Jaipur Literary Festival, with its roster of best-selling international writers, is claiming the national spotlight, it is still the Sahitya Akademi, with its array of programs and awards, that has a daily investment in literary culture and the production of literature. And unlike the Jaipur and other festivals, it is the institution that takes "the languages" most seriously, both individually and as a whole.[1]

I came to see the Sahitya Akademi as an ethnographic site, as a place to watch people's habits and customs in order to understand a larger institutional ethos. I often ate lunch, for instance, in the canteen located behind the main building of Rabindra Bhavan. There is usually a *mali* (gardener) at work on the adjacent lawn and an old woman in a faded sari collecting weeds. The canteen has a corrugated metal roof, with exposed piping, though decidedly more ramshackle than postmodern. Inside, three rows of tables would usually be set with small stacks of stainless steel tumblers, metal spoons, and melamine plates. The gray plastic chairs around each table were new, with Nilkamal stickers still in place, assuring "100% *asli* quality." Fans would be whirring as I ordered an eight-rupee coffee along with rice, *dal,* and the *subzi* of the day or an omelet and a thick *chapati.* In the fancy English-language bookshop-cafés of south Delhi, or in one of the city's ubiquitous air-conditioned Barista or Coffee Day chain cafés, by contrast, coffees and cappuccinos go for upwards of sixty rupees a cup. Here in the canteen, it was clusters of men and a few women—office workers, not the literati—who ate lunch around the tables, while teenage boys carried in trays of food and cleared plates.

THE ESTABLISHMENT OF LITERATURE

The Sahitya Akademi was established by the government of India's Ministry of Education Resolution in 1952. It is an autonomous organization funded entirely by the government that answers to a body known as the General Council of the Akademi, made up of about one hundred members, most of whom are writers. In recent years this funding has amounted roughly to three crore rupees (about $600,000);[2] the government provides additional funds for special projects and initiatives. Aside from its annual audit of the Akademi, the government is not involved in the Akademi's activities. The actual work of the Akademi is overseen by its executive board, which consists of the president, vice president, financial adviser, two members nominated by the Indian government from among their nominees on the General Council, and one person to represent each of the languages enumerated in the Indian constitution, as well as other languages recognized by the Akademi.

The Sahitya Akademi has numerous functions and sponsors diverse programs: it gives awards, hosts local literary meetings and events in the places where the particular language is spoken and lived, organizes national and international seminars in Delhi, puts on book exhibitions, and publishes original works and translations from nearly all the Indian languages. It also publishes a series of monographs on writers in most of the languages and has commissioned film biographies of many of these same writers. It puts out two bimonthly journals, one in English and one in Hindi, with a subscription base of about four thousand each.[3] The English-language *Indian Literature* was launched in 1957 and publishes translations of creative and critical writings from twenty-one Indian languages, as well as original writing, book reviews, and interviews in English. In its description of the journal, the Akademi bulletin states, "The journal is the only one of the kind published in English in the country and is conceived as an authentic reflection of the current literary trends in India as well as a medium for the evaluation of Indian's rich literary past."[4] This statement is reflective, in some measure, of the role of English more broadly at the Akademi. The

Hindi journal, *Samakaleen Bharatiya Sahitya,* launched in 1980, also carries creative and critical translations from twenty-one Indian languages and original works in Hindi. As the national literary body, the Sahitya Akademi promotes discourse in the two languages—English and Hindi. However, of all the twenty-two-plus languages that it supports, it sees English as a mediator between the other languages rather than a medium of creativity.

The Sahitya Akademi sits somewhat uneasily between its bureaucratic and literary functions. It is a public sector institution officially dedicated to providing support and a forum for all the Indian literary languages; at the same time it is increasingly aware of its role in mediating between the regional, national, and international literary realms. It aims for this relevance in the type and scope of its panels, seminars, and future prospects and outlooks. The question remains, however, to what extent it may be representative of the national without being associated with the government.

This tension was highlighted when Arundhati Roy refused the Sahitya Akademi Award in 2004. The annual award, one given for each of the twenty-two recognized languages, is the most prestigious national literary prize awarded to individual works. Roy was given the award for English for *The Algebra of Infinite Justice,* which had been published in India by Penguin.

In her letter to the Akademi formally refusing the award, Roy stated that she had nothing against the Akademi but was against the policies of the government. As for the book itself, it is a collection of essays that excoriated the government's policies in Kashmir, over the Narmada Dam, and with regard to its nuclear program. The Akademi's implicit support of the method (at the very least) of her critique, by virtue of having given the award for the book, did not seem to matter, however. The secretary (and practical head) of the Sahitya Akademi at the time, K. Satchidanandan, made a plea to Roy to reconsider, saying that the Akademi members were both "culturally and intellectually autonomous" from the government, but to no avail.

While the Akademi is sometimes derided for being part of the "old school" government bureaucracy and for being underfunded and inefficient, it has rarely if ever been taken to task for representing the policies of the government. Some saw it as contradictory and self-serving that Roy would refuse a national award after accepting a number of international awards, most notably the 1997 Booker Prize for *The God of Small Things.* And yet, because the major Indian national award does have a concrete connection to the government, she might have found it impossible not to refuse the award precisely because of the critiques she advances in her book.[5]

Many of the national debates about literature in Delhi involve a careful negotiation between regional identity, literary language, and the sometimes artificial formulations of what constitutes a "national" literary culture. At the Sahitya Akademi, the construction of the "national" is premised on inclusion rather than exclusion. And in this sense the institution has perhaps been most successful in regard to its promotion of "small" languages, those that are not the primary language of a region and that, in some cases, have been overshadowed by another major language. One example would be Rajasthani, which has been overshadowed in the state of Rajasthan by Hindi as a written language. Other examples are Maithili, spoken in parts of Bihar and close to the Bengali language; and Dogri, spoken in Jammu and close to the Punjabi language. Seminars and the bestowal of awards have spurred literary activity in these languages, which have little institutional support besides the Akademi. For the major languages, the Akademi is less essential, and yet they too are part of the larger literary arena as framed by the Akademi's activities.

Through its programs and awards the Akademi gives national stature to the regional literatures. And yet the stature of any one bhasha literature might be greater than the "official" languages of Hindi and English to begin with. In its attempt to forge literary nationality on the basis of equal respect for the literary languages and linguistic communities of India, the Akademi tries to accord equal literary merit to each language. This separate but equal literary policy is evident in the programs and daily operations of the Akademi. For instance, a seminar on Konkani literature in Kerala (held in 1992) is as likely as a seminar on three generations of contemporary Punjabi literature (held in 1994), or an explicitly comparative topic such as a seminar on Kannada and Bengali bhakti literatures (held in 1995).

Akademi seminars, which tend to be large, well-publicized events, also take on thematic approaches, such as the 1990 seminar on Mirabai, the 1991 Indo-French seminar on the contemporary Indian and French novel, the 1995 national seminar on nativism in Indian literature, or the 1981 international seminar on the variations of the Ramayana in Asia. And yet for all its attempts to fulfill the Nehruvian mantra of "unity in diversity," the Akademi reflects the political struggles over language, especially in regard to the competing hegemonic influences of Hindi and English. It is a quintessentially Delhi institution in this regard.

The Akademi most obviously seeks to address the question of India's plethora of languages and its literary culture, but in its attempts to forge "literary nationality" across the regional landscape, a number of tensions arise. How are literary languages to be equated in a national framework, and if they are not to be equated, who is to adjudicate on the merits of one literature over another? Its stated mission gives little clue when it says that the Akademi is "for the development of Indian letters and to set high literary standards to foster and co-ordinate literary activities in all the Indian languages and to promote through them all the cultural unity of the country."[6] Many writers I spoke with questioned the very authenticity of the Delhi-based Sahitya Akademi, finding its mission statement equally bland and audacious.

The late translator and literary critic Sujit Mukherjee called this regional approach to studying and promoting Indian literature the "congenital debility" of the Sahitya Akademi and argued that the result was "a wholly distorted view of our total literary landscape."[7] The core of Mukherjee's critique was not the Akademi per se but the kind of literary policy that emerges from the institution and then feeds into literary criticism more broadly. The problem for Mukherjee is the actual connection between what we call "literature" and a single language. He is much more interested in the themes and values of a particular set of works and believes the critical assessment should begin there, in the realm of ideas rather than in the limiting arena of a particular language. Literature, he writes, becomes the "special possession" of a language and also, due to the influence of nineteenth-century European nationalism, the "special possession" of a nation. He writes that these linkages and associations put "at a great disadvantage those people whose linguistic history and whose history of nationhood have not coincided."[8]

Mukherjee speaks directly to the location of literature in the modern world, one that has been so strongly modulated through the political entity of the nation-state. The Akademi itself recognizes the eighteen languages listed in the Indian constitution, and it has also chosen to recognize Dogri, English, Maithili, and Rajasthani as languages in which its program goals may also be implemented. This does not mean that the Akademi believes it has covered all the nation's literary languages. To counter this perception and, more important, to give some support to the "nonscheduled" languages (those that are not listed in the Eighth Schedule of the Indian constitution), the Akademi gives out the Bhasha Samman Award each year to writers, translators, and scholars working in about twenty other languages.

Every so often there are lobbying efforts to add languages as well as to get rid of them. For instance, in 2002 the Hindi Consultative Committee advised the Akademi to discontinue its award for best work in English since English was not included in the Eighth Schedule of the Constitution. The Akademi did not heed their advice and cited other languages, such as Dogri, Maithili, and Rajasthani, that were also not listed in the Eighth Schedule.[9] In specific reference to the recognition of English, the amended constitution of the Akademi states that the organization would concern itself with "literary productions in English by Indian nationals." The institution's own ambivalence about the literary merit of English comes across in its *Encyclopedia,* where the author writes, "There is no denying the fact that English is a powerful and elastic vehicle of expression. . . . [I]t is therefore natural that a sensitive few who lived with the language and cultivated it with care, will feel prompted to choose English as the medium of their creative expression. If this literature in an international language can shake off its elitism, can talk of experience not confined to the denationalized city life of the country and eschew the gimmicks and fashions of imitation, it may one day grow into a viable kind of Indian literature at least in spirit."[10]

For each language that the Akademi officially supports, there is an unpaid advisory board of between eight and ten members (mostly scholars and translators) who meet several times a year and set guidelines for the language's activities. However, there is no defined vetting process for choosing translators, and this results in many poorly translated texts published by the Akademi. Sometimes "translators" are hacks, their qualifications amounting to little more than an M.A. in some language. In addition, they may have no feel for literature or for the text they are asked to translate. Most see this as an institutional problem rather than the fault of individuals. While the Sahitya Akademi must negotiate the intricacies of language politics, it is also occupied with the nature of "the literary" and so must patrol those boundaries and enforce standards. Most of the time language politics and literary production become overlapping concerns and problems.

Literary language, as Mikhail Bakhtin has written, poses a particular methodological problem, since each language contains many other languages or dialects. How does one patrol its borders? Furthermore, within literary texts themselves, there is an internal dialogue between different languages. He calls this the *heteroglossia* within each literary work, the many registers on which the work is written and on which it may be read. The genre of the novel, he argues, is especially equipped to encapsulate the heteroglossic; and novelistic prose with its "rich tension-filled verbal-ideological history," he writes, "is in fact an organized microcosm not only of national heteroglossia, but of European heteroglossia as well."[11]

In his European context Bakhtin assesses the relationship between individual nations vis-à-vis a broader, regional European identity. Identities, like literatures, are not fixed entities; they are also not stable or fully realized objects to begin with. They are always in the making and always being made in slightly, perhaps even ever so slightly, different ways. In Bakhtin's telling, literary language, with its constant refractions, is a linguistic kaleidoscope. How, then, may we affix a language and its politics to a single literary language? But this is precisely what occurs on the national literary stage.

In the Indian context, each "region" or "state" (Tamilnadu, Maharashtra, Bengal, Kerala, to name a few) could stand linguistically as a "nation" unto itself, complete with majority and minority languages. There would be some sort of equivalency between, let us say, Bengali literature and Italian literature; whereas Europe itself, in Bakhtin's formulation, would be equivalent to India, in that each entity encompasses a variety of literary languages. Because the Indian regional divisions were in fact made on the basis of language, there is a natural tendency to relate each language to a particular geographic space. But what I want to suggest is that in the literary sphere this is a false association. Like English, even if not to the same extent as English, the so-called regional languages are created across different cities and areas outside of the regional, or original, location of a language. What this means is that each so-called regional-language literature imbibes ways of looking at the world that transcend its geographic location. In many respects, there is a wealth of translation "theory" to be uncovered in and across diverse Indian contexts that would do much to refine the often crude assumptions made about the bhashas. The paucity of good translations has also been one, though not the only, reason that on the global literary stage Indian literature has almost exclusively been represented by texts written originally in English.

Salman Rushdie underscored this dichotomy in 1997 when he infamously derided regional-language writing in comparison to

Indian-English writing.[12] His critique was uninformed (by his own admission, he had not read many works written in regional languages) and mostly irrelevant to what was going on within the various literary language communities in India. Yet by arguing that English writing by Indians had reached the hallowed ground of universalism more often than regional-language writing, Rushdie struck a chord in the global literary marketplace that, on the surface, seemed to make perfect sense. Were not Indian-English writers more geographically diverse than regional-language writers, who perhaps never left their regions and worse still wrote for regional rather than pan-Indian or even global audiences? Did not writing in English allow an author to confront the British colonial legacy head-on? These insinuations incensed literary and intellectual communities in India, mostly because through his use of English Rushdie was flaunting his own linguistic and publishing pedigree, as he openly fashioned himself as the model for the best type of writing coming "out" of India; and yet because of his literary stature, he was also in a position to further marginalize bhasha writing on the international stage. One element of his critique pointed to the dearth of good translations from the regional languages—that much everyone could agree on. Also significant is that in his 1983 essay, "'Commonwealth Literature' Does Not Exist," Rushdie took the Commonwealth Writer's prize to task for assuming that all good Indian literature was written in English. At that time he wrote, "It is also worth saying that major work is being done in India in many languages other than English; yet outside India there is just about no interest in any of this work. The Indo-Anglians seize all the limelight. Very little is translated; very few of the best writers—Premchand, Anantha Moorthy—or the best novels are known, even by name." This seeming shift in Rushdie's own politics of language and literature and how it is framed transnationally will be explored in chapter 8.

LITERARY NATIONALITY

Literary nationality is expressed through an emphasis on English and Hindi at the Akademi. These two languages are dominant in terms of the journals published by the Akademi as well as the number of Akademi translations published in each language. While there may be debate about whether or not English is the lingua franca of India, there is no question that English is the language of formal exchange and proceedings in seminars, meetings, and most events. The Akademi hosts a variety of language-specific seminars, such as "Seminar on the Marathi Novel after 1960" or "Seminar on Modern Assamese Poetry," but the vast majority of the Akademi's gatherings involve the literatures of two or more languages or are on "national" themes. In these multilingual literary events, an individual presenter will sometimes give a speech or comments in Hindi or another language other than English, but it is the exception rather than the rule. What is striking is the way in which English mediates the discussion of other Indian languages, thereby retaining its iconic status. It is the link language of the Sahitya Akademi in Delhi and actualizes the discourse on all the other languages. English is a conduit through which to bring experiences, sentiments, and critiques to the national literary table, for a Kannada playwright to engage with an Oriya novelist, for instance.

It is precisely in this way that English is employed as a mediating tongue and through which a discourse on national language and culture is being forged; in the process the very ideas and circumstances of "the regional" are being translated into an urban and national discourse. It is also in this capacity that the use of English reveals the national/regional distinction to be somewhat misleading. At the Akademi I repeatedly observed how the English-knowing regional-language literary practitioner is able to "self-translate" on the spot. The multilingual consciousness of regionally located literary practitioners incorporates English-language discourse. English is at some level part and parcel of Indian literary modernity across languages. In moments, the expression of one's regionality relies on English. One could ask, Does this dilute one's regionality?[13]

In India's literary geography, the "regional" literary consciousness is in fact as "national" as the language of Indian-English writers. It is for this reason that "literary nationality" as a discourse may be expressed in relation to any Indian language. Different languages may emphasize different ways of being, thinking, seeing; nonetheless, the bhasha languages do not merely represent "regional" perspectives on India or the world. This assumption ignores the relationships *between* languages as well as the complex relationship between languages and their multiple locations (and hence articulations), which is so apparent in the Indian context. The regional in the Indian case becomes associated with provincialism (especially as formulated by Rushdie who, not surprisingly, is located, geographically and intellectually, firmly outside of the Indian context) because of the dearth of translated texts. English texts move more fluidly between the bhasha languages and therefore from one context to another. In the process, English in India becomes a sign of the cosmopolitan, the urban, and the elite, whereas bhasha literatures become artificially fixed to their somewhat artificially constructed "regional" locations.

PUTTING ENGLISH IN ITS PLACE

The tension between regional and national literary imaginaries was never more apparent to me than in my discussions with the poet K. Satchidanandan, who was secretary of the Sahitya Akademi for a decade (1996–2006). The secretary of the Akademi is not a member of any of its official boards but is appointed by the executive committee to run the day-to-day operations of the organization, including the implementation of its programs. I first met Satchidanandan in 2001 in his spacious, wood-paneled office on the second floor of Rabindra Bhavan.

Our discussions revealed how the binary between the regional and the national fed into his own creativity and his own politics of language. I also saw that what may have been resolved in the form of literary policy at the Akademi had not necessarily been resolved for writers themselves. Even though Satchidanandan always seemed a poet first, he could not turn his back on some of the major institutional questions and problems that the Akademi made him face, and to some degree he sought out those tangles for reasons that soon became clear. This, too, seemed to illustrate something particular about his generation of writers, of their feeling of responsibility to the idea of "nation," even as, in their own literary lives, they eschewed simple equations between nation and language.

Satchidanandan was born in the village of Pulloot in central Kerala in 1946, and he became known as a leading modernist poet in the Malayalam language. I had been curious about why Satchidanandan had left Kerala for Delhi, since I knew he greatly valued the community of poets among whom he lived and worked. Many people had recounted to me how auto drivers in Kerala could recite lines from his poetry—this, the ultimate in literary authenticity, to be loved and read by the common man, especially in Kerala, where Communist politics reign. I myself had heard him sing some of his poetic verses in Malayalam at literary events in Delhi; some of them were like folk songs, of the people and grounded in rural places.

Satchidanandan's midlife move to Delhi had more to do with moving away from his duties as an English professor than with any formal poetic considerations. He had been a professor of English in Kerala for twenty-five years before coming to Delhi, and by working with the Sahitya Akademi, he explained, he felt he would be serving Indian literature better than had he continued to teach English literature. He explained that many of his English literature students, for instance, found the literature they were reading "somewhat alien—culturally so different—landscapes, countries, cultures about which they know very little." After a short pause he said, "I began to think about colonialism and what it has done to our minds and our unconscious. I became more critical of what I was doing, and I began to ask myself whether I was an agent of the colonial legacy. So I accepted an invitation in 1992 by Sahitya Akademi." His last years of teaching were frustrating due to this inner conflict.

Many times during conversations with Satchidanandan I was reminded of Ngũgĩ wa Thion'go's classic set of essays on African literature and language politics, *Decolonising the Mind* (1987). That book discusses postcolonial literary production in Marxist terms, allying African languages with the peasant and working classes and English with the postcolonial elites. To writers who said that Africans could create their own identities through new uses of English as Americans, Canadians, and others had done, Ngũgĩ replies: "How did we arrive at this acceptance of 'the fatalistic logic of the unassailable position of English in our literature,' in our culture and in our politics? What was the route from the Berlin of 1884 via the Makerere of 1962 to what is still the prevailing and dominant logic a hundred years later? How did we, as African writers, come to be so feeble towards the claims of our languages on us and so aggressive in our claims on other languages, particularly the languages of our colonization?"[14]

Ngũgĩ appears—on the page, at least—to resolve the issue of postcolonial identity and language: Writers must return to their mother tongues to reclaim their authentic cultural and political selves. The political is central for Ngũgĩ since in his Marxist framework, language is an explicit ally of class membership. Ngũgĩ, who had previously written most of his literary works in English, describes why he abandoned that language for his native Gikuyu and advocates that other Africans do the same, as an act of self-possession. One senses his guilt as a privileged African (and Kenyan), and his only way of responding as through a kind of linguistic justice. He recalls specifically the way language was hierarchized in his childhood in the colonial education system, where Gikuyu had been the language through which he had learned about the world, through stories and myths but also riddles and proverbs. The more schooling he obtained, however, the further he moved away from Gikuyu. He writes of how "one of the most humiliating experiences was to be caught speaking Gikuyu in the vicinity of the school." He continues: "The attitude toward English was the exact opposite: any achievement in spoken or written English was highly rewarded; prizes, prestige, applause; the ticket to higher realms. English became the main determinant of a child's progress up the ladder of formal education."[15]

Satchidanandan described a similar situation, whereby individuals become alienated from their own "culture" through the loss of their mother tongues. There is certainly a class dimension to this loss, according to Satchidanandan, though he emphasizes the generational aspect of it as well: "People of my generation are reading books in their own language, but the younger generation . . . many are hardly aware of their own literatures, they don't know their own languages." He paused for some time and then continued, "Parents may have settled here, and depending on where they grew up, depending on which colony, in which milieu, some pick up Hindi, some pick up English. But most don't know how to read their own mother tongues, so they are practically without a mother tongue of their own."

He sees the situation as most acute in Delhi. He compared Delhi to Mumbai, a mega-city that is also intensely multilingual but where, he said, "Marathi culture is stronger, so that most Mumbaiwallahs must know Marathi to a large extent." The same was not true for Delhi; it did not have a dominant linguistic culture. He said, "Here if you belong to the elite you can manage in English, and if you have a smattering of Hindi you can manage the ordinary things of life also. So they don't feel the acute need of learning their mother tongues, unless they feel culturally thirsty for their mother tongue, or if they feel it as a real loss, a real mutilation, as if their tongue has been cut off."

What did it mean, I wondered, *not* to feel a "cultural thirst" for one's mother tongue? Did it mean one was satisfied with the cultural enticements of English? At some level—in Satchidanandan's phrasing of it—there seems to be a moral quality to the need or lack of need for one's mother tongue. Would not everyone be affected by such a cultural deficiency? But then Satchidanandan offered a practical assessment of what it would mean to preserve one's mother tongue. Even if "they" (those who have lost their mother tongue) feel an intense need to learn their original language, he said, there was little opportunity to do so. In university departments where bhasha literatures were taught, "there are very few students," and furthermore, "there is little prestige, and what will they do with their degree in the languages?"

With some resignation, he continued, "So English is really the dominant language of Delhi, of the upper middle class particularly. It is becoming more and more fashionable, more acceptable. There is also a kind of battle for hegemony between Hindi and English. Other languages are onlookers. It is a battle between two big languages, one that claims to be the national language, the other the world's language. The other languages just want to be left alone and allowed to survive."

As a poet, Satchidanandan is unable to imagine his own life without his mother tongue, though he has spent much of his life absorbed in English. Satchidanandan explained that he chose to study English so that he could have "access to other literatures," calling it "the obvious choice." Many bhasha writers have not only had some or most of their formal education in English, largely due to their upper-class or upper-caste backgrounds, but many have also been professors of English, and some have written books of literary criticism in English. For many, teaching college English became a tenable compromise for the writing life. It was more prestigious to teach in an English department at an Indian university than, say, a Hindi or Tamil department, and many writers had a great facility with the English language because their exposure to other literatures of the world had been through English translation. For many, English easily became the "natural" language of intellectual discourse.

Satchidanandan explained how he believed the mixing of cultures and identities was a very positive occurrence, especially when two parents from two different linguistic backgrounds raised children. In that case, he proffered that English as a mother tongue was a possibility. And this, I came to see, was where his "linguistic loyalty" lay, not in the division between English and the bhashas, or between the regional and the national, but between knowing one's mother tongue and not knowing it. His concern was one's relationship to language. It was the perceived lack of the mother tongue—its diminishing importance, growth, and usage in the face of English—that made one's life deficient. When it came to Indians writing creatively in English, he felt that it took at least two generations for English to sink in to someone's literary consciousness. What Satchidanandan seemed to believe was that language should not be merely a tool to get ahead in society but a way to be in the world and to know oneself and others. It was the flagrancy with which people abandoned languages that seemed to disturb him.

Listening to Satchidanandan, I got a sense of how he had moved through Ngũgĩ 's position, first toward and then away from English, by putting himself at the center of the Indian literary storm. Moving from his native Kerala to Delhi was certainly a risky endeavor; even his friends were worried for him. There was the economic loss, in that he left behind a house and now had to pay rent in Delhi. But the larger fear was about what the move would do to his writing. He said he would not have been able to make the move as a young man, when his literary sensibility was just being formed. By the time he moved, however, he said, "My idiom was somewhat formed. I was acquainted with the deeper rhythms of the language, the nuances of each word. I was sufficiently trained, I was *in* the language and culture already." And then he surmised that perhaps if he had come to Delhi at a younger age, he might have started to write poetry in English, adding that he had tried some writing in English as a student but then "consciously gave it up."

Satchidanandan's "national" position enabled him to reexamine his now "regional" language in a new context, but it also changed his own linguistic experience. To come to Delhi was to extricate himself from his constant immersion in Malayalam, and eventually to accept Delhi, the city of "cut" tongues. And yet there were new opportunities for Satchidanandan in Delhi in terms of the influence he would have over national discussions of literature. He explained, after years of teaching English in Kerala, "I had a feeling, in fact, I was a little self-critical about what I was doing, and I had a feeling that perhaps I should be doing something for the languages of India and including my own language rather than teaching English, which is of course a colonial legacy with its own problems and its own advantages, definitely, because it has also helped liberate us. It has also created its own special problems for the languages of India."

He also admitted that he would never have written a poem titled "Malayalam" if he had not left Kerala for Delhi. His feeling for his language increased, even as he became open to experiences in Delhi. He wrote a series of poems that came to be known as *Delhi-Dali* that captured this seesaw dynamic. For instance, the middle stanza of one of these poems, "Languages," which he translated from Malayalam into English, goes

> I long to build a palace
> for these refugees among the tombs
> I, who am yet to find my own house.
> I stammer in broken words,
> in distorted sounds from some other body.

Which of the three tongues I use
during the day is truly mine?
Or is it the pure language of mystery
I speak in dream at night?

Being in Delhi seemed to require a new spatial ordering of language, yet one that was not necessarily constant or predictable.

One significant change in Satchidanandan's home life in Delhi was that his family became a space of linguistic familiarity. Even in Kerala the question of the place of Malayalam in his own family's life was negotiated. He sent his children to Malayalam-medium schools rather than English-medium ones, which was to influence the kind of relationship to language—both Malayalam and English—his daughters had. One of them, T. P. Sabitha, went on to complete an M.Phil. in English. She, too, lives in Delhi and writes poetry in both Malayalam and English. She also teaches English literature at Delhi University's Hans Raj College. When we met from time to time in Delhi, it was clear that Sabitha had a breezier attitude to her own multilingual Delhi life as compared to her father's, even if she carried some angst about being the daughter of a literary giant. Being the child of a writer makes you a "late bloomer," she explained one afternoon over tea, and then listed several of her friends who were also the sons or daughters of major writers and who had had similar experiences. She spoke of how she had the perfect mentor at home, yet that meant that she did not look for creative guidance outside her family. This turned out to be something of a struggle, especially when she first came onto the poetic stage when the family was still living in Kerala. She explained that when she was first published at the age of sixteen (in *Kerala Kavita*) people assumed her father had written the poems. The experience "scared" her, and she did not publish again (in the journal *Malayalam*) until she was twenty-four. "It was difficult to take yourself seriously as a writer," she went on to say. "You always feel you have to live up to something."

Now, in Delhi, Sabitha speaks Malayalam with her immediate family and mostly English and some Bengali with her husband, who is from a Bengali-speaking background. Of Malayalam, she said, somewhat sheepishly, "It is good to have a secret language." But she also emphasized that her intellectual discourse was conducted almost exclusively in English. Even when speaking with her father, they seamlessly and unconsciously switch to English when discussing "ideas." She could not pinpoint when it happened, only that it did, and then the switch back to Malayalam might occur, again, without either of them noticing.

Sabitha began writing in English when the family came to Delhi. She remarked that in English the audience or reader is "disembodied." But she didn't seem troubled by this. For her the question of authenticity is an "ahistorical" one. She is "more interested in history and the experiential." This appeared to be the case in her poem, "What he said, what she said," which captures the world of the SMS (Short Message Service), or "texting," a language that is arguably the fastest-growing one among India's (and the world's) mobile-phone-carrying masses:

He said
lts mt
She said
tel me whr
He said
undr da kurinji tree
in ma grans dream
She said
leav da schmltz 2 ur gran
u'll fnd me wid jsmn flwrs
on ma crpd hair, lukin HIDEOUS
He said
da brz wafts in ur smel here,
nw.
She said
u ol' fool, dats GROSS
coz i aint hd a bth 2day
He said
U r grss, no fine flngs,
i pine 4 u n im pale n ma
bangles fall off ma hnd lik mpty
moons
She said
c'mon shw me PINK then.
He said
da moon pierces ma hrt n u
mok me!
cum undr da crzy kurinji tree.[16]

I heard Sabitha read this poem, alongside others of hers in standard English, as well as a few in Malayalam. This poem had a different rhythm and cadence and sounded like an altogether different language. Reading the poem on the page evokes the micro-screen world of mobile phones, yet hearing her read the clipped and compact words aloud was something else entirely, a kind of made-up language that was not spoken anywhere, though instantly recognizable in its digital form.

What might Satchidanandan make of Sabitha's deployment of English? Not surprisingly, it is the relationship and identification with language that is paramount for him. For instance, Satchidanandan sees a distinction between students who learn English in addition to attending mother tongue–medium schools and those who are exclusively educated in the English medium:

> From my experience as a teacher, the more intelligent students were the ones who had come from their own mother tongue–medium schools. . . . It's not a paradox really. The English-medium students acquire a kind of fluency in the language early, but often they don't care for the subtlety and nuances of the language. They can speak very well, fluently, but handling the language with real care, with an aesthetic understanding of the language, that comes to those who have handled the mother tongue very carefully. English-medium schools are now extremely fashionable, and even the ordinary worker would like to send his children to one. He would like to hear them speak English. I would call this a colonial hangover, and partly for practical reasons, to be accepted by high society and for job opportunities.

Like Ngũgĩ, Satchidanandan sees the mother tongue as intimately tied to cultural authenticity in the most intimate sense, in being able to express one's deepest sentiments. In his views about the mother tongue, it seemed that he was speaking not merely about the politics of language, but a politics of intimacy with language. What did it mean—for people and for language—to lose the desire for that kind of intimacy?

In Indian cities especially, one is familiar with the distancing that happens between "the mother tongues" and English. Cities promote and thrive on mixing, whether of caste backgrounds or linguistic ones. New ways of talking, writing, thinking emerge as old ties are broken, new associations are formed, and, in the process, new selves are made. There is much lamenting among some of the higher-profile bhasha writers who are caught between these two worlds. They, too, must make compromises, often in terms of the language they will teach in, and sometimes even about which school they will send their own children to. English-medium or not? They all know that once someone has gone through an English-medium school he or she will never have the same relationship to his or her mother tongue. And yet to not send your child to an English-medium school is to most often deprive him or her of opportunities and access not only abroad, but, most dramatically, in India itself.

Of course, it is not always a compromise for bhasha writers to teach in English; it might widen their horizons and make them better writers, just as learning a new language and perspective on the world would help any artist or individual. But in the Indian context the stance of bhasha writers as being somehow suspicious of literary creation by Indians in English is almost part of their self-definition. They, too, are often molded by the discourses of English and their own participation within those discourses; but the fact that they set their "first" language to paper, rather than their second or third, marks a line in the sand.

When I met Satchidanandan in 2008 he explained why, after his tenure as secretary of the Sahitya Akademi was over, he did not move back to Kerala. All these years he had been making trips to Kerala every few months at the very least and was still very much part of the community of poets there. Yet there was a difference between being there and being in Delhi. "Staying here, in Delhi, meant having the chance to be exposed to more things," he said. But he also said that Delhi is "no more a subject" for his poetry. Being in Delhi, he went on, "protects me from a lot of controversy." In Kerala, "I'm asked to comment on anything and everything—nuclear energy, for instance. Things I know nothing about. Writers are important public figures, especially in Kerala." So Delhi had become a place of exposure but also a kind of refuge.

As for his relationship with the Akademi, Satchidanandan returned to edit its English-language journal in 2008. This time I went to see him in his much smaller, third-floor office. He was surrounded by papers and books and seemed cheerful about being reimmersed in the broader shaping of the literary world. Yet he also had distance from his earlier experience at the helm of the organization. We got into a discussion about the politics of the organization itself and how that had changed in the interim. He talked of how his vision for the Akademi had been to make it more "democratic." He had been interested in promoting the "positional" literatures, of Dalits, women, and tribals but also the young in general, of giving them a space at the national literary table. He seemed happy about some of the strides he had made in these areas and for "sections" of society "who had been kept out previously."

But it was also clear that there were limits to what an organization like the Sahitya Akademi could do for literature. Certainly, the Akademi had been "crucial for the survival" of "minor languages." But the question of translation still loomed, one of the Akademi's primary missions, yet one for which they were continually criticized.

Satchidanandan no longer believes the Akademi working alone can achieve what is necessary in terms of translation. "Translations can be, should be, more selective now; there should be more emphasis on quality," he said. "In fact what is needed is a translation academy." We talked about this a bit. He cited the "good work" that Oxford University Press and Macmillan were already achieving in the world of translation and continued, "An academy that would deal both with theory and practice, a place that put translators and writers together is needed. Part of the problem is how inter-Indian languages are translated to one another. Often it occurs through English, so if the English translation is not good, you can imagine what a translation from a poor English translation might look like. Translating from Oriya to Malayalam, for instance: no one can do it. We have to develop new modes of translation. This is something India could contribute to the world. More work needs to be done on syntax, structure, the way words function." There had been previous attempts at such an academy, he explained, but they "fell apart after a few years due to in-fighting." Meanwhile, the government's National Mission for Translation focused on social science and technical books. It seemed that the key to the literary flourishing of the mother tongues was to find ways for them to speak to each other in a fashion less mediated by, or at least less dependent on, English. And yet the institutional structures created for that fashioning seemed dependent on that very mediation.

CHAPTER 6

Across the Yamuna

For the last ten years of her life, I used to visit my grandmother in Pune. She didn't like living there, even though it was a nice apartment complex, and she lived with her eldest son and daughter-in-law, my uncle and aunt. It had been a compromise; the family had decided that for her to live alone in Delhi was unwise. So she went from son to son to daughter to son in Toronto and Los Angeles and Bombay (as she knew it) and finally, at the age of seventy-six, said no more, she was not leaving India again, and so after my uncle's retirement went with him to Pune. Whenever I visited her I would accompany her on morning and evening rounds in the apartment block garden. She missed gossiping with the ladies in Punjabi, the way she used to in Delhi; she did not speak English and here, they did not chat in Hindi. On those visits to Pune, I only left the apartment complex to check email at the local internet café and occasionally go to a beauty parlour. There I got to know another woman, who over the course of my visits told me about her unsatisfying marriage. It was the kind of talk between women one might expect, but what struck me was that this woman was sure she knew the exact cause of her and her husband's mismatch. They shared the same mother tongue; he, like her, was a Marathi-speaker and of the same family (i.e., class, caste, sub-caste) background, but unlike her, she knew English and he didn't. He lacks the same outlook as me, she said. He doesn't understand me, he sees the world differently. We have grown apart.

The idea of a "mother tongue" has great resonance; it is mythic and suggests origins, and yet it is also the most prosaic of things. It is these intimate associations that are explored in this chapter, where language ideology gets broken down into the very emotions that propel the writing life. No one chooses her mother tongue, just as one does not choose where she is born or into which family. Bharati Mukherjee captures this mythic dimension when she says that for a writer, "the melting of a mother tongue is the madeleine, the way back, and the way in, an early loss with the deepest memory, the mother of all plots."[1] But to what extent is the idea of the mother tongue—that we have one and only one and that it is a primordial attachment throughout our lives—a construction in and of itself?

Lisa Mitchell presents an interesting historical perspective on this question. She argues that in the course of the nineteenth century the whole notion of what it meant to be literate and multilingual in the Indian context changed. Through her study of south Indian linguistic spheres, she shows how languages go from being "task specific"—where the appropriate language is linked to a particular task at hand—to being "separate, but equal." This shift, she claims, opens the way for identity to be linked to one's first, and henceforth, primary language, a process that she calls "the making of the mother tongue." Where at the beginning of the nineteenth century it might have been "perfectly natural to compose an official letter in Persian, record a land transaction in Marathi, study music in Telugu, send a personal note to a relative in Tamil, and perform religious ablutions in Sanskrit," by the end of the century there was a new perception of commensurability among languages. Languages became interchangeable or "parallel" in Mitchell's terms. This description gives a different perspective on the notion of the mother tongue as being singularly identifiable; however, this multilingual world also rests on particular hierarchies—social and emotional—of language, chiefly about what may or may not be done in a particular language and by whom. In this vein, Rita Kothari and Judy Wakabayashi write that at least up until the nineteenth century people moved "within a multilingual structure," not necessarily thinking of the languages and dialects they spoke as different languages, but rather as "different registers of the same language, each with a specific task—almost as if languages had their own caste system and were assigned different jobs."[2]

In contemporary debates about literary language, having a mother tongue rests on the idea that one has a "first" language that may only ever express one's most intimate self. It is also seen as the language that expresses the story of the community. The discourse on "dying languages" is one that sees the vanishing of mother tongues as evidence of globalization and the loss of cultural diversity. In the case of the bhashas as mother tongues, it is their relative position vis-à-vis other languages that is at stake, rather than their existence per se. The mother tongues of many English-educated Indians, for instance, are often relegated to the kitchen. English begins as the medium of instruction and becomes dominant for intellectual and professional discourse. A "kitchen" language, meanwhile, suggests a less cultivated form of language with a restricted vocabulary that one uses to speak to mothers, grandmothers, and domestic help, a language that they presumably speak among themselves. It is not the language of intellectual discourse and "getting ahead" but the language of emotional needs and wants, of "going back." The shift can be seen as a privileging of English over the bhashas, but it could just as well be seen as the privileging of "getting ahead" over "going back."

Yet the notion of the mother tongue is also more than this. It imbibes an inevitable equation between "mother," "language," and "nation," a potent triumvirate cast as primordial attachments, able only to sustain singular notions of identity. What underlies the debate about language and cultural authenticity in the Indian context is not only about the "closer-to-home" bhashas versus the more "flighty" English, but it is the idea that English-educated Indians have given up on their mother tongues, that language is a matter of choice, volition, and will. It is not that these languages, the mother tongues, are dying out—hardly, the vibrancy and bhasha newspaper sales alone are outstripping English ones—but it is that an elite class of cultural producers are relinquishing their mother tongues in certain sectors of their lives.[3] The issue of the mother tongue has instead become one about who has which kinds of power in society, who is expected to cradle the traditions associated with mother tongues, and who will bridge the worlds of English and the bhashas. Chandrabhan Prasad has written in his columns in the *Pioneer* that Dalits are expected to have mother tongue education in government schools, all the while being unable to reap the benefits of private English-medium education. Prasad and others say they should be allowed entry into English, and his own mission has been to instill that desire in Dalit parents themselves, so that they demand English education for their children. The mother tongue thus raises the question of what it means to be multilingual and, most crucially, how different identities are negotiated, based on class, caste, and gender.

A.K. Ramanujan, who has written about the distance between his "mother tongues" (Kannada, Tamil) and "father tongues" (English, Sanskrit), identifies the former as being closer to the earth and common people. In the essay "Telling Tales," he famously maps language onto the architecture of his childhood home by recalling how the house "had three levels: a downstairs for the Tamil world, an upstairs for the English and the Sanskrit, and a terrace on top that was open to the sky where our father could show us the stars and tell us their English and Sanskrit names." He writes of how the "father-tongues distanced us from our mothers, from our own childhoods, and from our villages and many of our neighbors in the cowherd colony next door. And the mother-tongues united us with them." He ends this linguistic architecture with an interesting image, of himself as a young boy on the terrace, looking down to the cowherd colony where festivals and weddings are going on and men are fighting in the street.[4] At which point, then, does language become a way of seeing?

U.R. Ananthamurthy offers a schema similar to Ramanujan's, albeit more polemical, in his description of the "front yard" and "backyard" languages in his childhood home. The backyard refers to life in Kannada, the world of the folk, the rural, the lowest-caste workers, or *shudras,* women, medicinal herbs, subcultures, and "secrets," with the kitchen being "the most private place of all." The front yard, by contrast, is "literate"—a space for readers, writers, and discussants—where discourse occurs in Sanskrit or English. Like the openness of Ramanujan's upstairs "terrace" where, guided by his father, he looks up and beyond, Ananthamurthy's front yard is the male part of the house, where guests are received and news of the world enters. It was a place where his father, literate in three languages, held court but also where "caste was no bar."

Both portraits offer compelling, even moving understandings of how a writer might come to know himself and his place in the world. They are understandings premised on the spatialization not only of language but also of gender and caste. As such, both writers attempt to understand modernity and tradition as a kind of continuum within the household. In both cases the boy-heroes imbibe the meanings of front yard and backyard and upstairs and downstairs; they do not appear to be "split" or even "hybrid" figures but instead find a logical if not always happy medium for themselves. In the case of Ananthamurthy, he moves between the two worlds within the household and explains how it is the stories of the "backyard" that make him a writer and the outlook of the "front yard" that makes him modern.[5] Ramanujan offers a more disquieting vision of the relationship between his two worlds when he describes the goings-on in the cowherd colony he sees from the terrace. Is he connected to what he sees or alienated by it? When, we might ask, does the distancing create a blindness to one's own world?

The claims individuals make about language say something about how they identify with particular languages over time and in space. My argument throughout this book has been that this act of claiming, as much as the actual speaking or writing in a particular language, is a central feature of modern Indian identity. For example, the Marathi and English novelist Kiran Nagarkar, as we will see in the next chapter, claims English as a "second mother tongue," as if to diffuse the notion of inauthenticity inherent in using English for one's literary expression. To call it a second mother tongue is to make a claim for its primacy in one's life. English may be widely spoken by the urban middle and upper classes, but it is technically the "mother tongue" of very few, according to the Indian census. The idea of English as a "second mother tongue" seems at once a riposte to the charge of inauthenticity and a bid for one's own literary nationalism. Nagarkar is not saying that he is only made of English but that English and Marathi are his primary languages and that he sometimes chooses one over the other is a virtue born of artistic necessity, not a dismissal of his mother tongue.

THE PROBLEM OF THE MOTHER'S TONGUE

The Hindi novelist Geetanjali Shree in her first novel, *Mai,* offers a different portrait of the relationship between modernity and tradition, bhasha and English, and the spaces—both mental and physical—of an Indian household. It is Shree's novel as well as her position in the Hindi literary world of Delhi that initially became the focus of my forays to meet her across the Yamuna River where she lived. There the question and problem of the mother tongue became more about what it means to be a bilingual person and writer.

I first met Shree through her husband, the historian Sudhir Chandra. Chandra is a bilingual intellectual who writes scholarly books on colonial history in English as well as regular columns on cultural and political issues in Hindi newspapers. One evening we chatted at the India International Centre, one of the city's cultural venues and known as a watering hole for the Hindi and English literati. Chandra is a lively, outgoing person, and when he heard about my interest in talking to Hindi writers, he penned his wife's name and number on a pad of paper and handed it to me. I had known of Shree but had heard through the grapevine that she was a "private person" and was in the midst of finishing her latest novel. I had thought it would not be the best time to approach her. After meeting Chandra, I reconsidered and gave her a call. Shree said she would be happy to meet me in about a week, after she sent off the manuscript of her latest novel to her publisher, Rajkamal Prakashan. I first met with Shree just after she finished her novel, *Tirohit,* which was published by Rajkamal in 2001.

Early on Shree told me that she was not fully comfortable in Hindi or English, an intriguing admission by a writer, but one that, I came to see, also provided the creative tension in her work. *Mai,* published in Hindi in 1993 by Rajkamal Prakashan, is a working out of that unease; but I also read it as a kind of manifesto for why Shree writes in Hindi. She told me that her publisher, Ashok Maheshwari, had to coax her a bit by saying, "Hindi is your mother tongue." And it would seem, reading *Mai,* that he was on to something, for the novel is precisely about the encounter with the mother tongue as the mother's language. Shree has written four other novels since the 1993 publication of *Mai,* but it is her first novel that is a meditation on the "mother tongue" and how the world of the mother impinges on the consciousness, and conscience, of her two children. The novel also concerns the struggle of "getting ahead" versus "going back." It is a coming-of-age story of a girl who lives not only between Hindi and English but also between the gendered, generational, and emotional worlds that those languages enact in her life. The novel also strikes a contrast. The protagonist, Sunaina, is never able to compartmentalize the languages and the functions they are meant to have in her life; she meanders, unlike her brother, Subodh, who follows a more linear path. The character, mai (mother), understands and accepts these divides, but they do not seem to bother her, unlike her children, who are tormented by this space between them and their mother. Sunaina explains at the start:

> I cannot do anything else until I narrate mai.
>
> I want to narrate 'mai' but the distance between 'mai' and the 'narration' is so troubled, so full of opposition, that one doesn't know how to

> cross that distance or what might happen on the way.
>
> . . .
>
> How to reach 'mai'? How to get her out from this place after finding her? And the shards of mai we manage to get out, will they actually be her? Memory, time, the longing to understand might pierce her image through like a sieve. Mai is somewhere right now, whole, but when we catch her and bind her up in our words, she may be made half.[6]

Language itself is a culprit in Shree's novel. Or as Nita Kumar, the English translator of *Mai,* has put it: "The 'problem' of the mother is also the problem of the 'mother' tongue."[7]

My analysis of *Mai* highlights the dialectical relationship between Hindi and English, for it is only through the prism of a Hindi world that we may come to recognize more meaningfully the place of English. This reading of the text also means to "situate" Shree in the larger linguistic landscape of Delhi and north India.[8] This landscape begins in the small towns of Uttar Pradesh and then moves to Delhi and across the Yamuna River to Patparganj, where an enclave of Hindi and English writers and publishers reside. When I first visited Shree at home, I first stopped in to say hello to her downstairs neighbors, Nirmal Verma and Gagan Gill. I was friendly with Gill from previous visits to Delhi, and though Verma was quite ill by this time (he died in 2005), we had had a few exchanges over the years. Like many middle-class Indians, writers or otherwise, the development of land and apartment blocks in Patparganj allowed for more living space at cheaper rents. People started to sell their flats in central Delhi and move across the Yamuna. Previously Verma and Gill had lived for many years in Karol Bagh, one of the iconic market areas of central Delhi; but once they were able to sell their house, they moved. I remembered the old house since I had visited Gill there some years earlier. The area was vivacious, crowded, busy; whenever I went to Karol Bagh I always did a number of other things as well, like pick up sweets, get a piece of clothing dyed, trip over something or someone. I understood when Gill told me that here in Patparganj their life was more ordered, more organized. Yet she knew and understood why her husband missed their old neighborhood at times. She spoke of others she knew who had also left the old market areas of town, that they had "everything they needed" in their new, less hectic neighborhoods but still went to their old markets to "go shopping" once a month. By that she meant that they went to "walk in a familiar place, where one has not just walked, but gotten one's eggs and milk and stamps." She added, "These are our most important journeys." This poetic understanding of place had become decidedly out of place in Patparganj; yet when I continued upstairs to see Geetanjali Shree, I saw that Patparganj gave her a different kind of space and time that was equally as poetic and necessary for her literary survival and flourishing.

Shree grew up in a Hindi-speaking household. Although she went to Delhi University, she was careful to tell me that Delhi is not where she grew up. She comes from Uttar Pradesh, where the Hindi way of life dominates. Her mother raised five children, and her father served as an Indian Administrative Service (IAS) officer; the family was posted in small and big towns all over Uttar Pradesh. Shree was educated in English-medium convent schools from primary school on. She came to Delhi University in the mid-1970s to do her bachelor's degree in history honors from Lady Sri Ram College. She went on to receive her master's degree in modern Indian history from Jawaharlal Nehru University (JNU) and her Ph.D. in history from the Maharaja Sayajirao (M.S.) University in Baroda. She completed her dissertation on Premchand in 1986, which was later published as a book, *Between Two Worlds: An Intellectual Biography of Premchand*.[9]

Her thoughts about her Hindi and English educations belie the fluidity of her resume as an academic; yet they might explain not only why she writes, but why she had to write: "In a conventional sense I learnt no language well, being unmethodical in Hindi and skewed in English. But that also spared me, and others like me, from the fallout of a formal, orderly, systematic training and purism. It gave us the chance to learn anew, in adventurous and unconventional ways, either or both of these languages."[10]

When Shree was thirty years old she began to write fiction and to write exclusively in Hindi. Thus the two languages—English and Hindi—also mark a division between her scholarly and literary activities. Shree, then, emerges from an English-educated milieu as a Hindi novelist. And yet, like many Hindi writers, she continues to be part of the world of English as well, especially in her urbanized Delhi location. She has described the relationship as follows: "It is almost by accident that some of us chose Hindi and some others English. 'Almost by accident' I say, because it might not be entirely so. The osmosis of the world around, the politics-economics-culture of language and protest, the sound of the Hindi that I heard, over and above the veneer and sophistication of the English that I was taught, may well have had me 'chosen' by Hindi."[11]

She began by writing short stories. She wrote the first one while on a long train journey. After writing several more, she sent them to the Hindi literary journal, *Hans,* which was edited at that time by Krishna Sobti. Sobti commended the stories and asked to see more. Shree's first story, "Bel Patra," was published in *Hans* in 1987. This exchange helped launch Shree's career as a writer, and it began her long association with Sobti, whom she considers her most important mentor.

Shree explained her decision to write fiction as a simultaneous decision to write in Hindi. Although her critical work on Premchand had connected her to the world of Hindi language and literature, Shree's own academic writing and intellectual life had been conducted entirely in English. Despite this immersion and great facility with English, Shree told me, she never thought of writing her fiction in English. Shree educated herself about Hindi literature through and in English, but she maintains that English "was never mine." She described how she felt she could explore and create in Hindi, that there was much to discover within it, whereas she did not have this "expansive feeling" with English. But most significant perhaps is the way she described the relationship to her mother tongue. She said, "My mother only speaks Hindi, so this vital relationship is a Hindi one."

Shree's positioning as an "insider" and "outsider" in the Hindi literary scene is reflected in her location in the city as well as in her self-reflexive relationship to both Hindi and English. Shree sees her community as being not within the *pukka* (fully cooked) Hindiwallah world but as existing within a "cosmopolitan Delhi" literary and intellectual scene. Shree's community is an imagined one in the sense that it is what Delhi stands for that makes the place her literary home as much as the communities and people around her.

Shree stressed to me that although she "can live in Delhi" she doesn't "have to." Instead, it is a place in which she "can imagine" herself. It is accessible to her, linguistically and culturally, but it does not define or limit her experience as a writer. She explained that she needed to be "living in Hindi" but that she also needed an awareness of the non-Hindi world. For her, being "cosmopolitan" meant being able to be "anywhere." She explained: "We can live anywhere as long as we have a certain feeling of community, a feeling that we have what we need." This "need" seemed to refer to a kind of intellectual stimulation and openness, an openness perhaps predicated on acceptance, where an urbanized Hindi exists comfortably in a multilingual city. She said she feels she has this kind of situation in Delhi, as she gestured to the flats around her.[12]

DISTINCTION IN THE FAMILY

Mai demonstrates how different languages—the actual speaking of them and the subject positions created by doing so—are implicated in the social and emotional dramas of a family. The household itself is divided spatially between men and women, between English-knowers and not-knowers, between the young and the old. The Hindi-English binary becomes a shadow of the gendered and generational binaries. And yet those binaries are continually being unraveled and then remade in the course of the text, as interrelationships in the family continually change. The young daughter of the household, Sunaina, narrates as follows:

> When I started going to school and babu tried to speak to me in English, I would be too shy to reply.
>
> 'Come on, speak,' dadi pinched me, 'otherwise in today's times no one will marry you.'[13]

This dialogue illustrates most simply the consciousness that Hindi speakers have of the currency of English and its gendered aspect. Boys and girls learn English, or learn at all, for apparently different reasons. The viability of English is, in this instance, about the exchange of women between families. The novel points to the social mobility inherent in the acquisition of English and how this desire is funneled through the narrator's grandmother, who does not know English herself. For Dadi, it is the sounds of English in the household that she expects, more than any English conversation in which she will take part. The dialogue above points seamlessly to the alliance between linguistic and social capital by foregrounding the way that speaking English, even a few phrases, may be seen as a personal attribute that holds the promise of an important social index: one's marriageability. English is not meant to liberate the young girl but to continue to deny her agency. This conflict will occur again and again in the novel, and the reader becomes witness to how Sunaina internalizes the conflict.

Sunaina has been distanced from her mother (mai) through her own acquisition of English and her entry into the aspiring world of English speakers. It is a discomfort not in the utterance of words so much as in the desires and aspirations associated with knowing English. Knowing

English must mean wanting a different life, but for Sunaina and her brother, it also means wanting a different life for their mother. For Subodh, it is a practical struggle of moving out and moving on; his own emotions get directed toward "saving" his sister by enabling her to move out of the family house and ultimately go to art school in England. For Sunaina, the geographic dislocations only intensify what is an emotional struggle not merely to save her mother, but to understand her. All the while, Shree writes at the unraveling edges of language and forages there. There is an unease not only about speaking different languages, particularly for the novel's narrator, but also about living in different languages and what it means to commit to the life that each language promises. The difference for Sunaina between living a Hindi life or an English one becomes nothing less than a modern existential crisis. Sunaina explores the conundrum of the power dynamics in the family as follows:

> We kept trying to save mai. She is weak, a puppet, she has no one but us. So weak that when we do battle for her she retreats at the very moment of climax and our war cry shatters uselessly to pieces in all directions. For instance, Subodh bought tickets for a play. Mai got ready in a silk sari. Baba commented as he came out, "You are going too? Are you sure?" And mai stopped. Subodh kept ranting, but mai changed her sari and went into the kitchen.

In this passage, we see quite literally how it is assumed that mai's limited worldview will inhibit her understanding and enjoyment of going out to see a play. She retreats to the kitchen in response to her husband's questions, questions that are posed in such a way as to suggest that he might be concerned about her becoming bored in the play. But then in the passage that immediately follows we see another aspect of mai's positioning in the family:

> This is clear enough. This we saw clearly even then. But there was much we did not see clearly. Once dada lifted his hand to strike Subodh who was insisting that I should go to the hostel. Mai entered the sitting room, and met dada's gaze for perhaps the only time in her life. Dada's hand dropped, mai pulled Subodh inside, and he eventually dropped me off to the hostel.[14]

Here it is mai who negotiates the wills of the two remaining men of the household, and in the bargain, her daughter gains a modicum of independence.

Shree's literary language comes not only from her mother, but from the mother's position within the family and within the space of the household. It is this space that is contradictory and elusive in the text of

Mai itself. Shree casts the space of the mother as shrinking, bent over, and marginalized, and mai's many silences create a crater of unease at the center of the text. Mai, in the end, will not be pinned down by the narrator, and in fact, this dynamic could be seen as the main dramatic conflict: the narrator's attempt to narrate. Sunaina tells us from the start that this will be the mountain she must climb: "I cannot do anything else until I narrate mai." From the beginning we see that it is *her* life, Sunaina's, that is precarious and needs mending. She continues: "I want to narrate 'mai' but the distance between 'mai' and the 'narration' is so troubled, so full of opposition, that one doesn't know how to cross that distance or what might happen on the way."[15]

The drama unfolds in moments when Sunaina's frustration with mai is paired with realizations about her own place in the world:

> We had begun to fight with mai. 'Why don't you say something? Don't you have a will of your own? Don't you think? Why are you afraid? Why are you so weak?'
>
> We were getting strong. We were not afraid. Subodh could talk back to dada without fear. I could wander around in front and when dada said, 'Go inside,' at the opening of the gate, I would go inside. But very slowly, lingering there, my head held high, surveying the visitor with a direct gaze.[16]

As Sunaina and Subodh gain linguistic power and bodily assurance throughout the novel, mai becomes more crumpled from the perspective of her children. It is in these moments when Sunaina's conscience is activated, and she is literally torn in two. Lawrence Cohen describes this dynamic in his description of the modern "bad family" that does not care for its elderly by allowing for the erosion of the joint family and the loss of what he calls "known selves." The space of English, as conveyed through Shree's Hindi, becomes the site for individual achievement, independence, and a measure of "freedom" from certain social norms, yet it is precisely a "threat of the loss of self," in Cohen's terms, that the narrator is constantly negotiating and ultimately mourning.[17] In both cases, the family and its fracturing is a poignant site for the wrangling of modern subjects. It is the children who project their increasing power in the world—symbolized through language and education—onto their mother's body, and they are conflicted because they cannot see or decide if this projection leads to mai's greater detriment or satisfaction. The problem, of course, is that the space of English itself is not unified. In this passage, Sunaina explicitly refers to the gendered power struggles in the household that reveal language as a ruse:

> Dada sent me too to the mission school in town which, in our nice, hot country, was misnamed 'Sunny Side Convent.' Dada wanted that I should learn English.
>
> But not speak it. Or Hindi either. That is, not speak at all.[18]

The self-consciousness about language is tied to a self-consciousness about how to be and how to live, and ultimately, for Sunaina and Subodh their struggles diverge. On the one hand, English divides the household on gendered and generational lines, and it is mai who is completely sidelined and whose English-educated children must tell her tale, even if in Hindi. And on the other, mai's children want to save her, but in the narrator's attempt to understand her mother—bent over, subservient, in purdah—she is faced with the futility of her situation more than that of her mother's; for mai, it turns out, does not want to be saved. How can Sunaina move into the world of English and its easy advancements and leave mai behind unsaved and unrealized? One passage near the end of the novel captures this sense of futility well:

> We had been adamant from the beginning that we would not leave mai to be mai. Our experience, our deep thinking, our weighty analysis had taught us that mai was a hollow thing because this society had made her hollow for its own advantage. We would supply the human content, give it the opportunity to grow so that this suffering, this oppressed hollowness of centuries would slip away and mai, now mai no longer, would be come her full self, a not-mai.
>
> The not-mai was the human for us.[19]

AT HOME IN HINDI

The experience and meaning of life in Hindi is the starting point for Shree's fiction. At first, the question that appeared to face her was, how does one imagine from a Hindi perspective, from within a Hindi consciousness rather than an English one? Shree told me that when she first started writing fiction she would use English words and phrases but that "happily those went away after a while." The more she wrote, the more Hindi engulfed her literary voice. After completing her third novel, *Tirohit* (Vanished, 2001), Shree says, she "even thinks and dreams in Hindi now."

Not surprisingly, Shree achieved a fuller submersion in the Hindi language the more she wrote. When I visited her in 2001 we had been chatting for some time in her sitting room when she got up and took me to her study. We stood at the door, and she pointed in toward her writing desk, an almost bare wooden table. I knew she had just finished her third novel, and I imagined that she had some pride showing me her place of work. I expected a desk full of papers, or at least a notebook and pen. There was nothing; it was empty. I thought that maybe this showed that the novel was done, the papers cleared away until the next time. But then why show it to me? And then another feeling came over me: perhaps this was where the struggle within herself happened as she wrote. I realized it was about her and the chair and the desk. The pen and paper came later.

Despite the fact that Shree had finished several novels and was even "dreaming in Hindi," I knew that any battle that was still being waged between her Hindi literary voice and the presence of English was likely to still be an echo at least. What if this reimmersion into Hindi and the necessary, at times forced, marginalization of English were never fully satisfied in her? Perhaps this dialectic would be the tension that would keep her writing in Hindi, even propelling her to write at all. She might always continue to tread in this distance between the two languages, between two worlds, to echo her own thesis title about Premchand, the "father of the Hindi novel" who was actually an Urdu writer.

Mai is an ode both to her mother's language and to her mother's marginal position within the family. Shree became a novelist by returning to her mother *through* the place of her mother tongue, which is to say, through the domestic spaces of her mother's language. This kind of "choice" is really an enactment of one's history and creativity; she turns to Hindi to find the vocabulary and syntactical sentiment of her stories. It is also a return to the language of childhood—there is something to rediscover but also something that must be reconstituted and pushed forward into more complex, adult realms. With *Mai*, Shree told me that she felt that the things she wanted to write about could only be expressed in Hindi. And yet she found herself writing certain phrases in English and then translating them into Hindi. In some ways, this admission turns the question of authenticity on its head by revealing the multilingual registers of many writers.

Shree's literary sensibility has in many respects been informed by the somewhat constricted position of Hindi in the upper-caste and middle-class world of English-speaking India. It is not that Hindi is marginal; how could it be when it thrives in every corner of the North? Yet because of the immense social prestige of English—of speaking it well, of being in command of it, of having been educated in it—Hindi's status is and has been unquestionably diminished. There is an assumption—from the English-language world—that if she can write in English, she should write in English. It is for this reason that she speaks of "the challenge of Hindi," which is to say, the challenge of writing from this position. It is a position Shree herself sees as both part of the colonial legacy and a measure of her own hybrid linguistic background; it is, she has written, "no ordinary bilingualism."[20] English and Hindi are weighted differently, and it is precisely the binary between Hindi and English that she explores in *Mai*.

The following passage illuminates the place of Hindi and English within the household, especially in mai's complicity in her own marginalization, and the young narrator's guilt and resistance as she is placed between the conflicting worlds of her mother, her own self, and that of her brother (Subodh), grandfather (dada), and father (babu):

> When Subodh came home mai would say happily—'Tell your sister everything also, she should also know everything.'
>
> Subodh knew a lot. Even dada's guests would call out for Subodh. He could argue with all of them. About western culture, the ways of a big city, politics, history, all kinds of things.
>
> Babu, too, was impressed, especially with Subodh's knowledge of English. 'Make her English good also.' He wanted that I too should speak at breakneck speed. If I spoke at all. Subodh also took a fancy to being my teacher.
>
> It's true that I had reached a point where I would have won a competition for mixed speech. I could not speak a sentence without jumbling up languages.
>
> The languages were, one of the 'heath', the other of the 'melon', English and Hindi. A whole sentence could be in English but at least one word would have to be in Hindi—'I was saying *ki* . . . '
>
> And if I was speaking in Hindi, the same thing—'*Wah* before *a gayi thi to main tayar* . . . '.
>
> Subodh became critical of this eloquent technique.
>
> There was a remarkable phase when, whether I could speak Hindi or not, he wanted me to speak English. The world has moved ahead rapidly outside this house, he told me. Move with it. Master it.
>
> We sat down to eat and I had only to open my mouth, 'Pass the *dal*', and he would correct me, 'In what language madam?'
>
> I often repeated myself in English but also often kept silent in stubbornness.
>
> He complained to mai, 'You ask me to teach her but . . . ' And mai would persuade me, 'Speak a little, he is only doing it for your own good.' And I would be angry that everyone could forget, including me, that I was the older by two years. Who was Subodh to teach me anyway?[21]

As we see Sunaina's fear about being able to keep up with her brother and her reluctance to distance herself too much from her mother's non-English, unlearned, unconfident world, we see how language is not something neutral passed from one generation to the next. Subodh employs and advocates English to pull his sister out of the house and into the world, a world of achievement and freedom of movement. This sentiment is amplified later in the novel, when we see how Subodh's relationship to English has a more unambiguous meaning in the family:

> Subodh's prestige in our house increased hundredfold because of his leaving. Dada and babu practiced their English on him at every chance. Mai did not know any English. Dadi could not even speak straight Hindi. The corners of our house echoed with many tongues.
>
> . . .
>
> Subodh promised me, 'I will teach you good English, make sure you have a great accent, get you out of here . . . '[22]

Sunaina exists in an uneasy space between that of her mother and that of her upwardly mobile, English-educated brother, even if they have similar expectations of her. It is a space where hierarchies based on gender begin to be rearticulated through those based on language. The discourse on language that is occurring within the Hindi text reveals how language itself becomes character-building and character-depriving. The world of English will take Sunaina to England, and to greater social and physical mobility, yet the conflict in the novel will precisely be about her need to return to and confront the Hindi household of her mother.

English opens doors and creates division and silence at the same time. For Sunaina, it lights the path out of her home and into the world. Yet the world of opportunity and mobility and of being able to "become someone" is fraught for her if she cannot also expand and enliven her mother's world. It is not merely that Sunaina wants to reform her mother, it is that she wants her mother to understand and value the pleasures that she herself experiences as a student, as a traveler, as a painter, as someone's lover. Sunaina cannot be whole in the world until she garners this last affirmation from her mother, who, not surprisingly perhaps, never gives it. Mai is not ready to damn her life or relinquish her past. She stays true to herself to the end. Yet her "truth" is not obstinate. She allows her children to show her the world through their eyes, even if it is just crossing unknown streets not far from home.

BETWEEN TWO LANGUAGES

In one of our conversations in 2008, Shree called her Hindi *"duchasi"*—risky, adventurous, "my 'strange' Hindi." And then she said of the result: "If it works, I don't care." She attributed her confidence in her language, in her Hindi, and what she has to say in it, to the years of writing in it. We started to talk about the relationship between literature, art, and experience. These pastings together of a Hindi this and an English that, is it not all meant to represent experiences that are ultimately beyond language? The languages we know and understand pin down who we are, and yet they are hardly us.

After the publication in 2006 of her fourth novel, *Khali Jagah* (The Empty Space), Shree wondered aloud to me about the cultural moorings of language. Does writing in one language rather than another necessarily change the meaning of the story? Would *Khali Jagah*—the story of a bomb blast in a university cafeteria and its aftermath—be a different book in English? She's not sure. It seems the more she has written in Hindi, the less sure she has to be that what she writes must be written in Hindi, even if she only ever sees herself as wanting to write in that language.

There is most certainly a creative impulse for Shree to write in Hindi, to discover and make the language her own; this journey has essentially been her self-appointed task over the past twenty years. And there is something else, something that I am reluctant to call political or ideological, so perhaps it is also an impulse but then one of a slightly different order. She said that she finds English "more intrusive," though it is unclear if she means intrusive into her consciousness or into society. I saw how both could be true. And then, before I could ask anything more, she continued, "I want to say that English is not the only space where we can know about the world, that this knowing can happen, that it is happening, in Hindi."

It has become easy to understand why people who have been educated in English would write in that language. It is not merely for global recognition or prizes or large advances, which only very few writers attain anyway, but that, for many, English is their "authentic" language. It is also a language that crosses borders more easily, both within India and beyond it. It was only with the publication of Nita Kumar's translation of *Mai,* for instance, that Shree received widespread acclaim for her novel. And yet to create a conversation with the world in Hindi is also a way to fortify that language, to in some measure put the responsibility of worldly concerns onto and into the Hindi language.

When, some months later, I came across the transcript of a paper Shree had given at a Hindi literature conference in the Netherlands, I was surprised to find that she expressed an even more stark version of her own struggle. In that context, she wrote: "I do feel persecuted sometimes by this need to translate in my head. I do not know what chance it is, or design, that a particular thought may choose English words and not Hindi. But once that happens, I know that now the original thought has worded itself in English, to say it in Hindi I can only take recourse to translation! I have lost that thought in Hindi forever! It may not always be a problem. But on occasion, when I am with my writing and something profound and powerful seeks utterance, I wish it to word itself originally in Hindi, and let English come in translation, rather than the other way round."[23] For Shree to be a Hindi novelist is to will the Hindi language into a fuller existence, to cultivate Hindi over English, even as both make up her linguistic consciousness.

Shree is part of both the intellectual world of English and the creative world of Hindi, a common phenomenon for a bhasha writer. But because of her somewhat oppositional stance to the conservative worldview promulgated by Hindi language culture, Shree sets herself apart from the larger Hindi language community. Thus, like many writers, she also faces the problem of trying to identify and relate to a particular audience. While some bhasha writers might pride themselves on having an "organic" audience whose relationship between location and language is more clear-cut compared to the English-reading one, Shree admits that the Hindiwallah "mentality" holds a more limited vision, partly because the language and culture of Hindi has been co-opted by politicians. This state of affairs is especially the case in her home state of Uttar Pradesh, where the promotion of Hindi is often included in political platforms. Here, she echoes the views of Alok Rai in *Hindi Nationalism,* which describes a Sanskritized "Hindi" that casts a pall over the Hindi of the people. Shree is critical of the Hindiwallah world and says the changes within the Hindi community that could happen should be "multipronged," meaning they should come from "different places," not just government initiatives, but alternative sites of Hindi consciousness.

In this regard, being "across the Yamuna" points to a kind of alternative sensibility within and outside the mainstream Hindi world.

Much of this critical perspective within the Hindi world comes from a gendered critique of linguistic space, as we see in *Mai*. Shree also sees herself as at once writing a Hindi that is idiomatic rather than ideologically managed by Hindi nationalists. In an essay published in 2011, she links this idiomatic Hindi to the bilingualism of her generation of writers, and so distinguishes it not only from more Sanskritized Hindi but also the kind of Hindi of older writers such as Nirmal Verma and Krishna Baldev Vaid:

> In this changed bilingualism, the equation between English and the mother tongue is often reversed. Many of us have grown up 'knowing' only English, and possessing just the modicum of Hindi needed for everyday transactions. But it is precisely this bilingualism that writers like me are using for a new kind of eclectic borrowing and literary adventure.[24]

In her description of this "reversal," we may also see how the role of women in the family takes on a pivotal role precisely *because* of the spaces of the kitchen and other realms of "everyday" interiority lived and imagined.

This kind of dual consciousness, where language is mediated through gendered family relations and spaces, is also apparent in the work of the U.S.-based Pakistani writer and scholar Sara Suleri. In her memoir, *Meatless Days*, she presents the dilemma of living in two languages and the incommensurability of experience that each language provides. Suleri grew up in Lahore, nurtured in an elite English- and Urdu-speaking environment; her mother was Welsh and her father Pakistani. But Suleri now lives far from her linguistic roots and the familial relations that engendered them. She recounts that she and her siblings always had Urdu tutors and lived in both languages. She describes the feeling of this dual consciousness, as well as the way each language conveys different metaphysical and cultural meanings for ostensibly the same idea:

> Speaking two languages may seem a relative affluence, but more often it entails the problems of maintaining a second establishment even though your body can be in only one place at a time. When I return to Urdu, I feel shocked at my own neglect of a space so intimate to me: like relearning the proportions of a once-familiar room, it takes me by surprise to recollect that I need not feel grief, I can eat grief; that I need not bury my mother but instead can offer her into the earth, for I am in Urdu now.[25]

For Suleri, the idioms of different languages offer her real alternatives—not merely how to speak but how to feel and exist in the world. To be in Urdu is to experience her body and its relation to the world in a distinct manner. What is possible to express in a particular language and impossible in another—feeling grief versus eating it *(kha gaya hai)*—offers a distinct way of interpreting the sentiment and the actions associated with it. What is unique about a kind of grief that must be chewed, swallowed, and digested? In this relationship between the body and grief, one language offers a distinctive vocabulary of pain, and through that vocabulary different possibilities emerge for encountering pain.

Shashi Deshpande, who writes in English but lives in a multilingual Indian context, puts it simply: "We have a different cultural space for women, and our languages carry this within them." However, Deshpande feels neither guilt nor inadequacy when representing these women's worlds in English. For her, it is part of the challenge and pleasure of writing in English. She tells us that she realizes she cannot "translate" everything from the languages into English the way she might want to but that ultimately she is "the creator" and can come up with different options to get her story across.[26]

Similarly, Shree defined to me her "use of Hindi" by the way in which she writes "up to the limits" of a particular idiom. Her writing, then, is also about, perhaps chiefly about, her own dialogue with the Hindi language, a dialogue that occurs partly in English. When I told Shree that I had read both the Hindi and English versions of *Mai* and found that each gave me a different feeling, she started to describe how English and Hindi offer different emotional registers in her text: "Many people say the English translation [of *Maï*] is better, that it is light and has a bounce to it that the Hindi doesn't have. When you are saying things like 'I love you' in English and compare it to the Hindi—*Main tum se pyaar karti houn*—the Hindi is heavy in comparison. It depends what you are talking about of course. The Hindi I write in is not a learned Hindi but the Hindi I grew up in, the Hindi I spoke to my mother."[27]

She was able to "let go" of her text in the process of its translation into English but spoke of how she also appreciates the way in which certain phrases and ideas translated into English. For example, in her notion of love as something lugubrious (her example in Hindi), as opposed to something carefree (the English version), language offers up two kinds of sensations. If in Hindi her characters can only love in a "heavy" way, in some sense it is this characterization of love that is lost in the translation. The point, however, is not to dwell on what is lost in the English translation but instead to see what it might mean for Shree to have written her text in Hindi to begin with.

CHAPTER 7

"A Suitable Text for a Vegetarian Audience"

In 2000 Kiran Nagarkar's novel *Cuckold* won India's top literary prize for best original work in English, yet the accolade seemed to alienate him further from his most prized readership in his home state of Maharashtra. The novels and plays that had initially established Nagarkar as an acclaimed author were written originally in the Marathi language. He went on to write more Marathi plays but then made the "mistake" of writing two novels in English, *Ravan and Eddie* (1995) and *Cuckold* (1997).[1]

In February 2001 I listened as the winners of the 2000 awards each addressed a packed lecture hall at the Sahitya Akademi. Besides *Cuckold,* twenty-one other literary works (one for each officially recognized Indian language) were given the Sahitya Akademi Award that year. In his address Nagarkar focused his remarks on why the Marathi literary establishment saw his switch from writing in Marathi to writing in English as a kind of betrayal. When his first English novel, *Ravan and Eddie,* was published in Marathi translation, he explained,

> the publisher sent thirty-six review copies to various Marathi newspapers and journals. Not a single review of the book has appeared in the four and a half years that have gone by. No author interviews, etc., were published, even though the interviews were undertaken. . . . It slowly became clear to me that I must have committed an unmentionable crime, a crime that was beyond forgiveness and beyond the imagination of men and women, though I had no idea what it was, and why I was being punished for it. I had

> broken a covenant with my people. . . . [F]or if you don't acknowledge an author's work, it ceases to exist.

Nagarkar's tone was dramatic and somewhat self-righteous. He was clearly unnerved by what had happened, or, more accurately, by what had not. Why shouldn't his Marathi fans be as eager to read his English novel in Marathi translation? He then explained that the "covenant" he had "broken" was an implicit agreement between author and audience: if you are a celebrated Maharashtrian writer, you should be writing only in Marathi. Nagarkar went on to describe an exchange he had had with "a top editor and doyen of Marathi publishing" who had initially congratulated him on his recent award for *Cuckold*. But then the editor added that he had "a grievance": "Why don't you write in Marathi any longer?"

Nagarkar gave the audience at the Akademi a sense of the kind of disciplining an author must endure from critics, readers, and editors, while addressing his apparent "crime" of having written in English. He confronted the question, and seeming incongruity, of his own linguistic and regional identity head-on by explaining that writing in English was a "natural" turn of events for him. He said, "Barring the first four years in a Marathi school, my entire education was in English. My parents were Westernized liberals, and conversation at home was mostly in English. Marathi is then my mother tongue because I was born in a Marathi family, but for better or worse, English is my second mother tongue."[2]

A QUESTION OF AUTHENTICITY

Nagarkar's predicament, and his forefronting of it at the Akademi, is a fairly straightforward example of the way literary writing in English is seen not only as being less authentic than vernacular, or bhasha, literature but also, and more specifically, as a betrayal of a particular linguistic community by one of its own.[3] Writing in two languages raises important questions of readership, audience, and community that ultimately destabilize singular notions of identity and cultural authenticity. Despite his national acclaim, for instance, Nagarkar is not willing to forgo his regionally based Marathi mother tongue readers, critics, and editors. At some level they, too, are the locus of his identity as a writer. And yet from the perspective of most bhasha literary communities, to write in English is to reject willingly (and perhaps willfully) part of one's Indianness. There is a linguistic but also an ideological divide between English and all the other Indian languages. In the balance are various interpretations and permutations of Indian "culture." By saying that "for better or for worse" English is his "second mother tongue," Nagarkar is asserting that it is not a matter of choice to write in English but part of his Indian identity. It is on this point where Nagarkar's reasoning for writing in English diverges, to some extent, from the kinds of critiques of linguistic imperialism that writers like Ngũgĩ have written about. And it is in this context where I believe thinking about language politics in India must go beyond the frame of the postcolonial.

Nagarkar's story typifies the kinds of resentments bhasha writers and literary communities have against the literary use of English by Indian writers, the reasons for which I have also discussed in earlier chapters. But even English has become compartmentalized in the contemporary Indian context; no longer merely imperial or even global, it has different resonances depending on who is using it, where, and to what end. I emphasize "literary" English, since bhasha writers are not anti-English in any general sense. Many of them are fluent in English as well, by virtue of being educated, and some are professors of English.

In the story of Nagarkar's "betrayal" of his Marathi literary community (and, from his perspective, their betrayal of him), literary language is cast as a barometer of cultural authenticity on the public stage of the Akademi. The Sahitya Akademi is often the site where disputes break out, new theories are proclaimed, and a mix of literary gossip and rumor is revealed. It is a space where struggles over cultural authenticity are staged, where linguistic choices are defended, promoted, and derided, where the regional trumps the national and yet is continually subjected to it. In this case, authenticity has to do with the social and economic privileges of the literary Indian English writer who is assumed to be pandering to a global rather than to a regional audience and who is considered to be "less Indian" for doing so. These privileges, at their core, point to questions of social responsibility and obligation. And this kind of literary culpability is nearly always linked to upper-middle-class urban privilege, "Westernization" by Nagarkar's reckoning, and, more broadly, to the perception that English represents a globalized, consumerist culture that hypes its products. It must be noted that each Indian English novel is supported by a marketing apparatus that is simply nonexistent for most bhasha novels. Multinational publishing houses with offices in Delhi, such as Penguin, HarperCollins,

Random House, and, most recently, the French conglomerate Hachette, have budgets that vastly outstrip any bhasha literary publishing house, even if more books are actually sold to Indians by the latter. That the bulk of Indian English novels are marketed and sold to readers outside of India only magnifies the questions of authenticity surrounding using the English language to write Indian literature.

The tension, then, is not only between individual writers and their communities but also in the positioning of one literary apparatus vis-à-vis another in regional, national, and global spheres. These spheres, as this chapter reveals, have distinct sets of authenticity markers that continually intersect. What emerges in this complex of language ideologies, literary production, and overlapping geographies are judgments made by writers, critics, translators, and others as they take part in various forms of literary production and consumption. In the process, accelerated by the greater prominence of Indian English literature since the early 1980s, the terms of literary debate have become less about traditional hermeneutics and more about the relationships individuals have to language and their obligations to different language communities.

Another aspect to keep in mind in light of Nagarkar's sense of betrayal by the Marathi literary critics is that, in the reverse case, it would be rare for an English-language journal in India to print a review of a Marathi novel. It is often only when a bhasha novel has been translated into English that it gets noticed, but even then it may not. So Nagarkar's indignation over being ignored should be seen in this context. If he had not already been part of the Marathi literary scene, he most likely would not have expected his English novels to be reviewed in Marathi journals. Nevertheless, his story shows how a literary establishment closes ranks to discipline authors by refusing to acknowledge their books with reviews. Nagarkar, in turn, uses a national forum on writing, outside the geographic space of Marathi, to justify and perhaps reclaim his regional stature. But it is the loss of regional stature that matters to him.

Nagarkar's predicament also reveals how the manner in which a novel enters the public domain is a process mediated by publishers, book reviewers, and institutions, not to mention booksellers in shops and on the pavement. The meanings and contestations produced in this process frame each printed and published literary work. What is pertinent to literary practices in India, and no doubt elsewhere, is how these positions become complicated in a multilingual literary field, where symbolic attachments and dismissals are rife. It is a field where

Nagarkar's dismissal by Marathi critics is cemented at the precise moment when he wins a coveted national award.

In what follows, I peel away the layers of cultural authenticity that both animate and cloud sociopolitical debates about language, cultural identity, and globalization. As will become clear, the heart of these debates turns out to be about caste, class, and "religious considerations." Through my analysis of several points in Delhi's literary field, I illustrate through one stark case how these authenticities are multiple, contradictory, and often in flux. My second aim is to show how the bartering of cultural authenticities creates repeated opportunities for individuals and communities to assert their own ideological positions, to the point where authenticity becomes a foil for such positions. It is also my intention to show how the individuals and communities I discuss are well aware that it is ideology, not authenticity, that is at stake. That is to say, literature becomes important not just for what it represents but also for how it produces itself and is produced regionally, nationally, and globally. India's cultural production, more broadly, has also come to shape, in part, its intellectual and economic standing in the world. It is yet another stage on which its modernity is tried and tested.[4] Thus my argument is not only that India's literary case is a complex multilingual arena of competing authenticities but also that it marks a new space for fashioning ideological commitments. The contours of this space go beyond questions of language and literary production, and they also go beyond the geographic and national case of India. The issues that I point to here are part and parcel of a new global order of literary production and translation subject to both new and old ideologies of language.[5]

THE HINDI TRANSLATION OF *A SUITABLE BOY*

In 1993 the novel *A Suitable Boy* by Vikram Seth was published internationally. Seth, who comes from Delhi, is one of the best-known and best-regarded (by critics and readers) contemporary Indian English writers. *A Suitable Boy* is set in a fictional north Indian town named Brahmpur, in the fictional state of Purva Pradesh, most closely resembling the Indian state of Uttar Pradesh. The novel is a 1,350-page saga of four interconnected middle-class families and details the social mores and political life of the early 1950s. *A Suitable Boy* was originally written in English but is set in a Hindi-speaking milieu. A Hindi translation of the novel titled *Koi Accha-sa Ladka* was published in 1998 by the Delhi-based publisher Vani Prakashan. Gopal Gandhi, a well-known and respected cultural figure and civil servant, was commissioned to translate the novel.[6]

Arun Maheshwari, who owns and operates Vani Prakashan, explained in a conversation with me why translations of Indian English novels into Hindi were becoming more common. Since Indian English novels and novelists were receiving so much acclaim in the English-language press in India and elsewhere, he reasoned, they had sparked interest among Hindi readers. These readers wanted to know and judge these novels for themselves, especially considering that they were written by Indians and featured Indian locales and characters that would in reality most often be speaking an Indian language other than English. The Hindi- and English-speaking worlds of north India often occupy distinct worlds in terms of class, gender, caste, religious sensibilities, and levels of urbanity, and yet there is also much overlap and bilingualism. What I aim to show is that it is precisely because English and Hindi represent different perspectives on the same place, and reach different audiences living in the same region, that translation becomes a particularly significant cultural transaction. Initially, what is striking about the translation of *A Suitable Boy* is Seth's own authorizing of it. In the preface to the Hindi version, Seth poignantly writes about what is gained in the translation:

> The novel's authority is made by events that have occurred in our country and in the language of our region. For this reason the translator has given the gift of restoring it to its original characters. A big part of the dialogue was reconstituted here in that language, where it had been playing in the ears of my mind. The political debates and arguments in the novel are more real in the Hindi. The Hindi-Urdu poetry that had been put into English in the novel has now returned to itself. Being a writer I am surprised to admit that in contrast to my original, this work in the Hindi translation has come out much stronger.[7]

Having commented on the elevated aesthetic experience of the Hindi version of his novel, Seth then sentimentally identifies the characters in his novel with his actual Hindi readership. What adds weight and complexity to the Hindi translation of the novel, in particular, he goes on to say, is that it is the language that his characters would actually have been speaking. He says that the beauty of the Hindi translation is that those characters of his (whom he projects onto his actual Hindi audience) would now be able to read his novel. But he goes even further than this; he writes that if the Hindi-speaking people he was writing about cannot read the novel, then "all this praise for me has no meaning." It is only with the more linguistically and culturally authentic Hindi appearance of his novel that he should be allowed any praise as an author. His tone is one of reverence and gratitude throughout. It exhibits both tender feelings toward his audience and his own emotional identification with them. In the space of the preface, Seth, step by step, admission by admission, redefines the authorship of his own text. Because he himself and, by his own admission, his psyche are situated between and in the worlds of Hindi and English, it is natural that his text also occupies this space. Seth is, of course, writing this preface to his Hindi, not English, audience. The preface serves to cultivate that audience while creating his own vision of what it means to portray a Hindi-speaking world in English. Seth is not saying that he should not have written the original novel in English or that those copies should now be taken off the shelves, but he is making a value judgment about the worthiness of his own novel and detailing his responsibility to the Hindi-speaking world.

Seth's authorizing of the translation of his novel is remarkable for a second reason. Considering the highly charged literary atmosphere in India, especially between the English and Hindi intellectual constituencies, Seth is willing to give up part of his claim of authorship to the Hindi translation, if not quite to the translator himself. In his rendition of his writing process, it is almost as if he is saying that the Hindi version of his English novel was always out there somewhere. Rather than defend his use of English (Nagarkar's method), Seth raises and then gives in to those who would always question the authenticity of an English novel proclaiming to represent Indian social realities. Seth himself maintains that the Hindi version captures something that he was unable to render. And, as we shall see, his admission did not go unnoticed by the Delhi literary establishment.

AUTHENTICATING AN AUTHOR

In a review of the Hindi translation of *A Suitable Boy* (Koi Accha-sa Ladka), the well-known University of Delhi English and Hindi literary scholar and critic Harish Trivedi takes the opportunity not only to revere the Hindi translation as an act of "cultural recovery" but also to praise Seth for writing a novel that lends itself to being "recovered" in this way.[8] But Trivedi does not leave it at that. His review of the translation, which appeared in the English-language Delhi-based journal

Book Review, is a curious act of authenticating Seth. He writes: "Of all the spectacularly successful Indian novelists in English of recent years, it is *A Suitable Boy* which is the most deeply embedded in the theme and the context which it depicts, and the most intimately complicit in a local language. Seth's English has a doubleness, a twice-born *sanskar* and resonance of cultural heritage, which should be the envy of some other Indian novelists in English such as Rushdie and Roy."[9]

Trivedi implies that Seth's English text carries more cultural weight, and in his use of the phrase "twice-born *sanskar,*" this cultural weight refers to its resonance not only with the Hindi language but also with the Hindu religion, and the connotation of rebirth into upper-caste respectability. For Trivedi, Seth's language has been in effect "reborn" into Hindi. He contrasts this notion of Indian cultural, linguistic, and religious authenticity with what he sees as the dispossessed narratives of "other Indian novelists" like Salman Rushdie and Arundhati Roy, who simply "use" India as their cultural backdrop (read: unembedded, not intimate) and then peddle their wares to Western-based publishers (i.e., make a lot of money, become famous—though Seth has accomplished this, too). One's transnationality then becomes marked by one's use of language (whereby its translatability is an index of its authenticity) and not one's geographic location per se.

It is interesting that the discourse of levels of authenticity among Indian English writers emerges in the discussion of *A Suitable Boy,* since, if Rushdie's *Midnight's Children* (1981) was a watershed in the style of Indian English writing, then Seth's novel was an economic watershed in terms of the kinds of book advances ($375,000) that Indian fiction writers could hope to attain. Since then several other Indian English writers have received even larger advances, fueling the suspicion among many Indian critics and writers that Indian English writers are unjustly rewarded for their first novels and cementing the literary hierarchy that privileges English prose. In 2003 Seth received a £1.3 million advance from Time Warner Books for his memoir, *Two Lives* (2005).[10] These details are relevant since much of the animosity toward Indian English writers from bhasha writers and critics stems from a sense of linguistic injustice over the size of advances possible in English, due to a lucrative Anglophone publishing nexus. Advances from publishers in London or New York become a marker of authenticity and inauthenticity at the same time, depending on the larger ethical terrain of literary production: the writers, their location, their relationship to the language or languages in which they write and, perhaps, in which they think. And it is for this reason that merely garnering a global audience is not always what will secure a writer regional or national acclaim.

But Trivedi does not merely agree with Seth's own admission in the preface. He also denigrates Seth's original English prose in some measure when he writes of the original English version, "It is as if all these icons of our culture, aptly evoked in this exceptionally polyglot and intertextual work, had been to a glittering fancy-dress party where they had had fun, but had not come home to relax and be themselves again."[11]

Trivedi states quite boldly that Seth's language is not culturally authentic enough and that his images were borrowed for an English-language rendition of Indianness that is not only artificial but also second rate. He takes Seth's preface and pushes it to what, for Trivedi, seems to be a logical conclusion: the English language was merely a dressed-up version of the real down-home experience only to be had in Hindi. As we have seen, Seth, too, gives greater cultural validity to the poetry, dialogue, and debates of his novel as they appeared in the Hindi version but not at the expense of his original English text in the way Trivedi does. Trivedi's critique is ideological and reflects Hindi-English language politics in contemporary north India. He appears to see the Hindi translation of *A Suitable Boy* as a kind of restoration of the novel to its "proper cultural context," where culture equals language and, to some extent, religion. It is this kind of claim to cultural authenticity that implies that by admitting that he was thinking in Hindi, Seth allows some to assume that he thinks he should have written it in Hindi. And yet Trivedi takes Seth's preface as evidence that Seth is more authentic and hence "more Indian" (closer to whatever cultural truths Trivedi has in mind) as compared to other Indian English novelists. His review promotes the idea that there is a true Indian identity to be found, that it is to be found in Hindi, and that it *should* be found in Hindi. It is this kind of reasoning through which a cultural hierarchy is promoted within Indian English literature itself.

A TRANSLATOR SPEAKS OUT

The question of authenticity became much more complex when the Bengali translator, Enakshi Chatterjee, relayed her own experience of reading the Hindi translation of *A Suitable Boy*. In her comments, we see yet another logic of authenticity emerging.

Speaking to a packed audience in the Akademi's main lecture hall in January 2001, Chatterjee described translating Seth's novel from English to Bengali. She recounted that she first studied the Hindi translation of the novel to prepare herself to translate Seth's English original into Bengali. She described Hindi as her "second mother tongue" and said that it was therefore a good medium through which to think about her impending task of translation. However, in her reading of the Hindi version, she explained, she noticed that the translator had left out some descriptions of leather processing that appear in the original novel. She said that Seth had apparently lived with a Chamar community outside of Delhi for a few weeks in order to understand their lives and represent them more accurately in his novel. One of the "suitable boys" in the novel, Haresh, runs a shoe factory, so the making of leather, as the primary material component of shoe-making, must have seemed relevant to Seth. Chamars are represented in the novel as people who skin cowhides and tan leather, "polluting" work that places them at the bottom of the Hindu social schema. Chatterjee told the audience that Seth's descriptions do not appear in their entirety in the Hindi translation of the novel. She chalked these deletions up to what she called "religious considerations" the translator must have had for a "largely vegetarian audience."

Chatterjee's comments elicited some chuckles from the audience, which she indulged, but she clearly had a serious point to make. By using the word *vegetarian* to describe the likely north Indian upper-middle-class Hindi readership for Seth's novel, she was pointing to the predominantly upper-caste, Brahminic character of that audience, who pride themselves on their higher religious status and distinguish themselves from lower castes through their vegetarian eating habits. Her comment marked the ways in which class in north India is predicated on caste distinctions as much as by markers such as education, wealth, language, and other social habits and tastes.

Chatterjee framed the act of translating texts as a moral practice based on a series of choices. She began by describing how she herself deleted passages in the novel that described the naming of Brahmpur, where the novel is set. These passages referred to the mythological origin of the name of the town. Chatterjee reasoned that since Brahmpur was such a common name for towns in Bengal, the novel would "lose credibility" if the novelist thought its readers had never heard of Brahmpur before. As a translator, she explained that this deletion was in the service of her Bengali readership. But she strongly condemned the condensation of translations from the original that sometimes occurs so that "they are easier to read and hence sell." She then asked rhetorically, "Are translators meant to dilute and distort the text, to beautify it in order to make it more easily digestible?" She ended her address at the Akademi by asking, "What are the fundamental rights of the translator, the translator's dharma [moral and social duty]?" To abridge the text, she explained, would be an immoral act.

Chatterjee's tale, and the way she told it at the Akademi, was a moral tale of disdain, if not quite outrage. She was also explicitly taking a stand on her own position as a translator into Bengali. She told the audience, with some satisfaction, that she would not make such deletions as the Hindi translator had.

What is at issue for Chatterjee is the deletion by a translator of an author's original fictional details of the skinning of animals and tanning of their hides. The circumstance of Seth undertaking a kind of ethnographic research in a Chamar colony on the outskirts of Delhi raises a key question and reveals the subtext of this entire story: what are the politics of imagination at work in elite portrayals of Dalits?[12] Many if not most Chamars do not work with leather in India today and in fact do a range of other low-skilled work, but the classical representation of this group as "leather workers" has great purchase in Seth's text (which is set not in an ethnographic present but in the historically reimagined 1950s). What, then, is at stake in this portrayal of Dalits in a middlebrow Indian English novel and its Hindi translation? There may be a fine line between superfluous cultural explanations and sociological or ethnographic descriptions, and some may ask: Why not edit out social descriptions to which Indian audiences would presumably already be privy? Why school readers about the very social conditions and relationships in which they live? And it is this reasoning that Chatterjee ascribes to her decision to delete the passages on the origins of the town name of Brahmpur. But, of course, certain descriptions may also be a form of social critique integral to the novel, whether for an English or a Hindi audience. North India has long been the site of upper-caste Brahmin hegemony, especially in the making of a pan-Hindu identity, hence its appellation as not only the Hindi belt but also the Cow belt, referring to the sacred status accorded cows by Brahminic Hinduism. Thus these descriptions of animal skinning and the disposal of carcasses have a very particular meaning and resonance in Hindi that they might not have in English. Their resonance is a question of both language and location. In an example of one of the passages that was deleted when *A Suitable Boy* was translated into Hindi, we see how Seth renders caste privilege by detailing his middle-class characters' (Kedarnath and Haresh) reactions to their visit to a community of Chamars (the italicized portion does not appear in the Hindi translation of the novel):

> Kedarnath and Haresh re-entered the neighbouring lanes; the stench was hardly better. *Just at the opening of a lane, at the periphery of the open, pit-riddled ground, Haresh noticed a large red stone, flat on the top. On it a boy of about seventeen had laid a piece of sheepskin, largely cleaned of wool and fat. With a fleshing knife he was removing the remaining pieces of flesh off the skin. He was utterly intent upon what he was doing. The skins piled up nearby were cleaner than they could have been if they had been fleshed by a machine. Despite what had happened before, Haresh was fascinated. Normally he would have stopped to ask a few questions, but Kedarnath hurried him on.*
>
> *The tanners had left them. Haresh and Kedarnath, dust-covered and sweating, made their way back through the dirt paths.* When they got to their rickshaw on the street they gratefully breathed in the air that had seemed at first unbearably foul. And indeed, compared to what they had taken in for the last half-hour, it was the breath of paradise.[13]

What makes this omission most striking is that the tanners' work is described from the perspective of Seth's middle-class characters. It is their liberal fascination and disgust that is highlighted. The result is a kind of embarrassment about their privilege but also an implicit disdain for the social hierarchy that makes their world a "paradise."

In another example of a passage omitted from the Hindi translation (the italicized portions below), Haresh takes his possible future mother-in-law, Mrs. Rupa Mehra, and possible future wife, Lata, to his place of work. The tension of the scene, almost all of which appears in the Hindi translation, is about the two women's polite but clear disgust with the tannery. Seth's deft social comedy, bordering on satire, contrasts Haresh's cheerful pride in his work with the two women's growing unease. The narrator writes of how "Lata felt a sudden revulsion for his work, and a sense of disquiet about someone who could enjoy this sort of thing. Haresh meanwhile was continuing confidently: 'But once you have it at the wet-blue stage, it's easy enough to see what comes next: fat liquoring, samming, splitting, shaving, dyeing, setting, drying, and then there we are! The leather that we actually think of as leather!"[14] Further down, the narrator continues:

> While taking them back to the car he explained that this was a comparatively odourless tannery. *Not far away, there was a whole locality with*

tanneries on both sides of the road, whose wastes and effluents were left in the open to dry or stagnate. At one time there had been a drain that took the stuff to the river, the holy Ganga, itself, but there had been objections, and now there was no outlet at all. And people were very funny, said Haresh—they accepted what they had seen since childhood—shavings of leather and other offal strewn all around—they took it all for granted. (Haresh waved his arms to support his contention.) Sometimes he saw cart-loads of hides coming in from villages or marketplaces being pulled by buffaloes who were almost dead themselves. 'And of course in a week or two, when the monsoons come, it won't be worth drying these shavings, so they'll just let them lie and rot. And with the heat and the rain—well, you can imagine what the smell is like. It's as bad as the tanning pits on the way to Ravidaspur—in your own city of Brahmpur. There even I had to hold my nose.'

The allusion was lost on Lata and Mrs. Rupa Mehra, who would no more have dreamed of going to Ravidaspur than to Orion.

Mrs. Rupa Mehra was about to ask Haresh when he had been to Brahmpur when the stench once more overpowered her.

'I'm going to take you back at once,' said Haresh decisively.[15]

Once again, it is the most viscerally "polluting" aspects of leatherwork, including animal waste flowing into the holy Ganga River, that do not make it into the Hindi translation.

Chatterjee explained that she did not approve of such deletions in a work of translation and that they were inimical to the integrity of translating a work of art. Her logic of authenticity, then, is about content rather than language. She conceded that the Hindi version of *A Suitable Boy* is "a richer book, due to the speech" (echoing Trivedi's point about "cultural recovery"), but she also adds that "it is a different book." Something may have been recovered, though she never uses that word, but at the same time something was clearly lost. It has become a truism to say that things are "lost in translation," and it may be said that any translation of a book is different in style and often in meaning from the original, but this particular translation sanctions a deletion from the text based on the presumed audiences of Hindi and English novels. It is a willed and deliberate deletion. Meaning and style do not fall away as words are translated from English to Hindi. In effect, the translation never occurs.[16]

Chatterjee's comments make clear that she not only disapproves of the Hindi version of the novel but also wants to point out that the deletion speaks directly to caste politics in the Hindi belt. In this episode, and the way it surfaced in the literary journals and forums of Delhi, we are able to crystallize some of the very real tensions between caste and class at this particular moment in contemporary north India, especially if we consider Chatterjee's appraisal of the Hindi translation of the novel in light of Trivedi's. Her comments suggest that the Hindi translation is in fact not a true rendition of Seth's original, that it, in fact, lacks a certain authenticity that was in the English original; and more troubling for her, it is not a true rendition of Indian social realities as Seth imagines them. Her comments suggest that something new has entered the Hindi literary field: the cultural pressure of Hindu nationalism, or Hindutva. This pressure, which is increasingly becoming a social norm, seeks to at once elide caste differences in order to create a pan-Hindu identity and promote upper-caste Brahminic culture as a hegemonic influence on that very identity. It is succumbing to this pressure that is morally suspect, in her reckoning. Thus Chatterjee's story about the deletion of the descriptions of the leather workers reveals an entirely different perspective on the question of cultural authenticity, which she frames in a wider ethical context. The fact that an Indian English novel being translated into Hindi in the late twentieth century seeks to appease an upper-caste audience points to a particular configuration of the Hindi-English literary field and a particular moment in the linguistic and caste culture wars of the Hindi belt. Alok Rai describes the current power dynamic between Hindi and English elites in the Hindi belt as follows:

> It suits the English elite to accept the "Hindi" elite as the representative of popular democratic energies—since the acceptance demands no radical social transformation. And as for the "Hindi" elite, its politics consists almost entirely of pretending to represent those democratic energies even as they seek to contain them—and so preserve its precarious dominance. The English elite cannot—and will not—call the Hindiwallah's bluff. It is inhibited by its bad conscience, plus the possible recognition that its own long-term interests lie with the Hindi elite. The Hindi elite in turn cannily plays, or retains the option to play, the democratic card from time to time.[17]

Yet there is an alternative reading of Gandhi's omission that has to do with caste and linguistic identity but not in the way that Chatterjee imagines it or Rai frames it. What if, in omitting certain passages of the novel, the Hindi translator was not trying to appease upper-caste vegetarian audiences but instead trying not to offend Dalits? This question was posed a couple of times when I presented this material in Delhi and Baroda in 2008. Some of my interlocutors pointed to the rise of Dalit power, activism, and consciousness and to the rise of the Dalit leader, Mayawati, as chief minister of Uttar Pradesh—the heart and soul of the Hindi and Cow belts—as being reason enough for the translator to have made these kinds of deletions.[18] This perspective seemed to turn everything on its head, and certainly adds to the complexity of the issues outlined here. Most of all, it shows the extent to which consciousness about Dalits in middle-class society is changing. And it offers up once again the issue and problem of reality and representation itself. As the critic James Wood reminds us, literary realism is not the same thing as social reality.[19]

Part of the problem, then, is precisely that in his depiction of the Chamars Seth is implicitly critiquing the social distinctions of caste society. It is a mild-mannered critique, but it is there, and more significantly, it is coming from an elite English-language writer. My point is that writing in English imparts a moral stance on its Hindi audience, even once translated into the Hindi language. If Seth had originally written the novel in Hindi, his critiques might resonate differently. In addition, the political situation in India today has to a large extent pitted Hindi as a regressive nationalist language (where Indian equals Hindu) and English as a liberal secular language (where Indian identity encompasses diverse religious traditions equally).[20] Translating ideas and imaginaries has a political import that would be missing in two languages that had little political relationship with one another. It is at this juncture that we recognize how literary languages import their ideologies, especially during the process of translation, whereby a text and its audience is being evaluated in social, political, and linguistic terms. One might argue, in this case, that this omission from the Hindi translation in fact makes the Hindi version culturally inauthentic in terms of hiding caste and caste relations of production as described in the novel. This omission speaks to yet another aspect of linguistic authenticity, dictating whose stories belong in which language, and which authors and translators are authorized to tell which stories. In this case, so-called cultural authenticity, in Trivedi's sense, takes a backseat to the obfuscation of caste hierarchies.[21]

In recounting these episodes and debates, my aim has been to illustrate how I see literary texts, literary production, and the politics of language, caste, and class as integral to the workings of a multilingual literary field. A focus on literary production enables us to see how the politics of language (and the way those politics intersect with those of class, caste, religion, and gender) at once informs and is made by literary institutions and practitioners. It enables us to see literary production not only as the creation of literary texts (which is why I am less concerned with authorial intention per se) but also as sites of production of social difference (in terms of debates instigated and how they contribute to the larger discourse—to which this chapter also contributes). In the example I have delineated here, this social difference has to do with belonging to different status groups based on language, class, and caste. In the writings and public reactions of Vikram Seth, Harish Trivedi, and Enakshi Chatterjee on the topic of the Hindi translation of *A Suitable Boy* we see how the translation of literary texts from one Indian language to another is not a simple act of literary exchange but a set of discursive maneuvers in a dense multilingual field.

My aim also involves the analysis of the text itself and the question of competing logics of authenticity in the production of a Hindi translation of an Indian English novel. In this regard, I have attempted to expand the question of literary language and authenticity in India beyond the usual parameters of an author's loyalty to his regional language or his reason for writing in English, as in the example of Kiran Nagarkar switching from writing his novels in Marathi to writing in English. The focus on loyalty alerts us to the ethical undertones implicit in the questioning of a writer about which language he writes in, but it also reinforces a dichotomization of English and bhasha languages. In fact, the multilingual literary field in India is more complex than this dichotomy allows.

Choosing which texts to translate and how to translate them—what to include and what to omit from the original—makes translation a measure of what is deemed authentically "Indian." The Hindi text, by omitting these descriptions, could be viewed as an implicit chastisement of an upper-caste Hindu author (Seth) for his attempts at social and cultural authenticity as much as it is censoring the novel for the supposed benefits of a "vegetarian" (upper-caste) audience. Hence, we may ask, what does English allow that Hindi apparently (in this case) does not, and what might this have to do with Seth's writing the novel in English in the first place?

If the Hindi language is able to render a more culturally authentic story, as Trivedi suggests, it also makes the subject matter of the story more potent when translated into the local language. In Hindi, it is the supposed offensiveness of polluting work that must be deemphasized for the reading benefit of "vegetarian" audiences. English, on the other hand (for Trivedi), is seen as an artifice ("a fancy-dress party"), pointing to a different sort of privilege—one based on class and urbanity.

But are these not competing privileges? The question is not merely which text—the English original or the Hindi translation—is more culturally authentic, since, after all, Seth authorizes both texts. He writes the English one but then writes in the preface to the Hindi version that it contains another kind of subliminal authenticity. Both are true to his creative aim, he tells us. But if the meaning of a text is also in the hands of the reader, in this case Chatterjee, it would appear that she sees something inauthentic in the deletion of key passages about low-caste labor in the Hindi version of the novel, just as Trivedi sees an inauthenticity in Seth's originally English-speaking Indian characters.

What is at stake in these divergent notions of the culturally authentic and inauthentic? For one, the "realness" of what is deemed authentically Indian does not lie in the opposition of English and bhasha literature. Indeed, the question of and quest for authenticity in the literary realm employ and deploy language and cultural authenticity as foils for ideological debates. The process of translation demands a new interpretation and social reckoning not only with a text but also with an entire literary field of writers, translators, and publishers, as well as audiences and booksellers. Language ideologies emerge from different positions within this field. What is further revealed are the contested places and roles of English and Hindi, languages that compete for national authority and political legitimacy. In literary representation, what is authentic is not merely a question of the literary language being employed by a writer or translator, but a larger question concerning the politics of imagination and whose imaginings become legitimate in which language. More dramatically, the question posed in these debates is not only which language should be used to create literature but also what ought to be thought or imagined at all.

In this "cross-cultural" translation, what is being crossed are not oceans or even national or regional boundaries but instead language ideologies within the same "national culture" and regional space. These ideologies do cross boundaries, but most stridently those of religion, class, and caste. The cultural competition among languages in north India and the constituencies those languages represent make ideological stances out of literary poses and critiques. Thus the real debate underlying the perspectives outlined here is not about which text is more authentic but about the kinds of social and political privileges that each language assumes and subsumes.

CHAPTER 8

Indian Literature Abroad

In chapter 5, "At the Sahitya Akademi," the idea of literary nationality meant bringing in but also equating numerous region-based languages into a central framework. In that schema the English language was a mediator between other Indian languages, making it integral to forging a contemporary literary field as well as helping to define literary modernity itself. As we move beyond Delhi to the centers of Indian English literary production "abroad" one might ask, What happens to the pursuit of literary nationality outside of India? In this chapter, an alternate aspect of this concept emerges as authors and critics define "India" with a view to the "outside." This act of defining resonates both within the nation and beyond its borders, and requires us to ask: What are the literary borders in an age when publishing is multinational, increasingly digital, and writers often move between two or more nations and sometimes languages?

The publication of Salman Rushdie's *Midnight's Children* in 1981 is seen as a literary watershed, an almost universally accepted "start date" for the transnational "boom" in Indian English writing and, more generally, for the opening of Anglo-American literary markets and audiences to postcolonial immigrant writing. After Rushdie, Indian novels in English are often understood as having emerged from a global or diasporic culture rather than a national one. This characterization is most often framed as a narrative of success for Indian novels in general and, as Amit Chaudhuri writes, has a particular resonance with the professional-class, immigrant success narrative: "And so the Indian writer in English must be co-opted into this narrative of success and record growth; anything else, during this watershed, is looked upon with anxiety. The writer mustn't cause anxiety; in our family romance, he's the son-in-law—someone we can be proud of, can depend on, who is, above all, a safe investment."[1]

At the same time, the themes of these post-Rushdie novels are often perceived as being nationalistic, or at least about national concerns, paradigms, or narratives. The language of these novels, English, is the language of global mass communication, and as a result, these novels have become a form of transnational mass communication. All the while, there is an assumption that English is politically neutral, but might English, at times, also be actively neutralizing? Might it stamp out the very politics that it wishes to forge, the things, we are told, that can only be said in English?

Here, through an analysis of how Indian literature was staged in England in the 1980s versus New York in the late 1990s, I consider how Indian English fiction has gone from being grounded in the politics of particular places to being framed as a deterritorialized literary flourishing, thereby denuding its political relevance in an era of transnational literary production. This chapter explores several facets of the discourse on the globalization of Indian literature and some of the spoken and unspoken questions that underlie the politics and aesthetics of books that are published across borders and read by transnational audiences. As books and authors "travel," the question of place does not become less important; rather, a new set of ethics emerges regarding the idea of place itself.

STAGING LITERATURE

Chapter 1 of Salman Rushdie's *Midnight's Children* first appeared in 1980 as an excerpt in the British literary magazine *Granta*. The theme for the issue was "The End of the English Novel," a bold pronouncement for a new publication edited by an American from a garage in Cambridge, England. In his editorial preface, Bill Buford characterized the emergence of novelists like Rushdie as nonwhite former colonial subjects, many of whom were now British citizens, who were "writing back" in a style and language and with an imaginary scope that seemed to be surpassing English (read: white) writing. Buford went on to describe the English novel as having become parochial, of looking inward and to past glories; of being timid, not inventive enough, and not exhibiting or containing something *new.* As for the new British writers, who were not necessarily white, Buford wrote:

> The fiction of today is . . . testimony to an invasion of outsiders, using a language much larger than the culture. . . . Today, however, the imagination resides along the peripheries; it is spoken through a minority discourse, with the dominant tongue re-appropriated, re-commanded, and importantly re-invigorated. It is, at last, the end of the English novel and the beginning of the British one.[2]

In his manifesto-like prose, Buford posits "English" as the culture of Old Britannia (the dying empire prone to colonial nostalgia and racism against its black citizens and new immigrants), as opposed to a new "British" ethic of cultural and racial inclusion. Buford was claiming a literary stake in the new liberal, multicultural ethic in England that had arisen in the face of Margaret Thatcher's anti-immigrant stance, partly fueled by riots in some of England's urban industrial centers. This inclusion gave new signification to the term "British," one that came to imply a wider notion of citizenship based on race and ethnicity. Buford notably placed *Midnight's Children* firmly in the sociopolitical milieu of Britain and not India. On the one hand, Buford was saying that "English" writing was a white citadel even if not a very interesting or profitable one. On the other hand, he heralded a new opening for the commercial viability of nonghettoized writing by nonwhite Britons.[3] However, Buford's larger point was to make the connection between the politics of race in Britain in the 1980s and the historical relationship between Britain and its former colonies. In the Rushdie moment, there was a dovetailing of the colonial past and the immigrant present.

Seventeen years later, in 1997, the *New Yorker*'s annual summer fiction issue featured Indian fiction as its theme, coinciding with the fiftieth anniversary of India's independence. The issue was edited by the same Buford, now in his role as fiction editor of the magazine. By the time Buford left the now London-based *Granta,* the magazine had already become an imprint of Penguin Books, and Buford had moved closer to the center of the transatlantic literary establishment. His appointment at the *New Yorker* solidified this shift. Buford introduced the Indian fiction issue of the *New Yorker* with a reflection on a new group of writers whom he saw as having been descended from Rushdie. In Buford's essay, subtitled, "Why Are There Suddenly So Many

Indian Novelists?" he did *not* refer to Indian English writing as having reinvigorated the *British* novel, as he had in 1980. Nor did he connect these writers (Vikram Chandra, Anita Desai, Kiran Desai, Ardashir Vakil, Amitav Ghosh, Rohinton Mistry, Arundhati Roy, Vikram Seth, Amit Chaudhuri, and the Sri Lankan Romesh Gunesekera) to cultural or political trends in American society or its fiction. What linked these writers was that they all originally hailed from the Indian subcontinent and that they were able to render India in the English language. Buford seemed almost tickled by the fact that the group of writers featured in the magazine had never met each other and that they all lived in different cities and often different countries. He wrote, "What's happening among Indian writers must be unprecedented: they work, some of them in an adopted language, and often in isolation, even thousands of miles from their homeland."[4] Significantly, there was no talk of peripheries and centers, the old postcolonial trope, but there was also little reference to the South Asian societies described in the novels. By 1997 transnational publishing and English-language fiction from South Asia had been allied with tropes of migrancy and dislocation to such an extent that, in the process of celebrating and promoting this literature, it had become deterritorialized and thereby delinked from the social and political contexts of the novels themselves. In the move from a postcolonial moment to a transnational one, the politics of race, language, and ethnicity seems to have disappeared. This characterization is not entirely surprising since those politics often emerge in national contexts, where people actually live (which is not to say that there are not shared politics across national borders). There are also, of course, many postcolonial moments and many transnational ones, and they are not necessarily contiguous; they might be and often are coexistent. What I want to identify here is how the politics of the framing of Indian writing in English changes over time. Indian writing in English gains more prominence in the Anglo-American publishing world at the same time that it is seen as being less political and more of a multicultural literary phenomenon that almost, as it were, comes from nowhere.

What does the trend of depoliticization and deterritorialization, symbolized by Buford's framing in the *New Yorker* as compared to *Granta*, portend? While postcolonial criticism has emphasized the relationship of colonizer and colonized, transnational literary markets seem to be focused on how Western readerships might understand the political and social conditions of the so-called third world. What these two models of reading and framing Indian English literature have in common is their promotion of a literary axis that posits knowledge of and from India flowing to Western metropoles. The English language becomes a convenient medium by which this knowledge is transferred. What gets lost between the politics of the colonial encounter and newer transnational frameworks is the way in which English has been transformative for Indians, how the language has been about their modernity, as well as how English has been transformed by Indians and their other languages in the process. English exists in the world differently now that it is also an Indian language.

If we return to Buford's postcolonial and transnational framings of Indian English literature, we see how the intricate and complex meanings of English, infused with the politics and practices of Indian society that I have delineated, get diluted if not nullified. The politics of ethnicity, religion, gender, age, and language in India—with their competing nationalisms and regionalisms—get sidelined by the politics of postcolonialism as well as transnationalism, a concept that, in most respects, still makes peripheral the non-Western world. Those frameworks, almost by definition, chart literary meanings based on circuits of knowledge between "East" and "West" and carry the implicit assumption that India is peripheral to the English-language-speaking and publishing centers of the United Kingdom and the United States.

The place of English in India ultimately means much more than the postcolonial or transnational frameworks allow. And it is the localization of English that in fact should infuse any transnational meanings of its literature. How else to forge a politics in an increasingly globalized world? Emphasizing the universal themes of great literature should not be seen as somehow opposed to the understanding of local contexts, affective ties, and political meanings of great texts. It may be true that a writer's home address does not matter to literature, but the language, content, and form of his or her text surely do.[5] Indian English writing does not come from "nowhere," but the social contexts from which it emerges offer a way into a critical understanding of Indian English literature, no matter how transnational its writers or the sale and packaging of their fiction. Even more centrally, it is the locations of English in India that change both the character of the language—its speakers, writers, and readers—and the other languages in its midst. This way of reading texts, focusing on place and linguistic context, illuminates a process of indigenization of the English language itself. And it is this process that tells us something essential not only about society and politics but also about the creative process and impulse. What is required, therefore, is a new politics of reading Indian English literature that is grounded in the very languages that it seeks to represent, and the places where those languages come from. To do so is to understand the politics of where English itself resides.

To recognize that English emerges and exists alongside other languages in an intensely multilingual society is to repoliticize and reterritorialize Indian novels rather than read them merely in their transnational "isolation." To reterritorialize is not to make Indian writing in English parochial but instead to see the work that English does and has done in Indian society; it is also to recognize the "centers" of the discourse on Indian languages in India rather than merely in the commercial, transnational context of London and New York, places that create viable but limited meanings for this literature. This kind of reterritorialization, then, is both a hermeneutical strategy (a way of reading texts) and a theoretical claim.

THE VIEW FROM SOMEWHERE

In 2009, while checking in for a flight from Hyderabad—where she was living in retirement—to Delhi, the literary scholar, Meenakshi Mukherjee, suffered a fatal heart attack at the age of seventy, but not before publishing her last book; in fact, she was to take that flight to attend her book launch in the capital city. As a professor of English and a literary critic, Mukherjee was a part of Delhi's literary field not only because of her pioneering studies in "Indo-Anglian" (as it was once called) literary criticism but also because she wrote about so many major authors—who wrote in English, Hindi, and Bengali especially—sometimes debating directly with them. As a professor in Delhi, she also taught students English literature for twenty-five years and edited the journal *Vagartha* from 1973 to 1979.[6] Her location in Delhi was significant since much of her own work is about location and language. Also significant is that in the long and important trajectory of her criticism, we see a shift in her perception of Indian English novels that is linked directly to how a writer's location is perceived and the extent to which his or her literature is "globalized." What happens, she seems to ask, when Indian writers go abroad and stay for too long? When does an Indian English text—its concerns and its language—become too distanced from "India"? How are these changing aesthetics, which go into how places are imagined, customs described, characters developed, to be understood?

Mukherjee's critique speaks to the transnational experience of many writers who live and work outside of India. Writers from many societies have long been known to spend time abroad; it is almost part of the writerly vocation to widen one's experience through exposure to different places and people. As the world has become smaller through transportation and communication technologies, more writers have been able to achieve this mobility, not only within their own national borders, but often outside them as well. In the case of Indians abroad writing in English, however, there is a double distancing from what is seen as being "authentic." Not only are these writers representing Indian social realities in English, but they are doing so from north London, Toronto, and Brooklyn. And often they do not only go for edifying stints abroad but to work and settle.[7] Where one lives became an ethical question in the Indian literary context, but did it change the books being produced, the meanings they convey, and the aesthetics being forged by them?

Mukherjee was one of the first scholars to analyze the "themes and techniques" of Indo-Anglian fiction in *The Twice Born Fiction,* whose title, she explains in the preface, points to this fiction as having had "two parent traditions." When the book was first published in 1971 there was still an argument to be made for the validity of what was then called "Indo-Anglian" literary criticism. Mukherjee prefaced her book by saying that she hoped it would be "the first step towards granting the Indo-Anglian novel its proper place in modern Indian literature." At that time, Mukherjee writes, it was assumed, for instance, that regional-language novels would always be seen as being superior to those having been written by Indians in English. By bringing a critical focus to Indo-Anglian fiction, she was asserting that this literature had a rightful place in discussions of Indian literature. The book marked an important moment in literary criticism but also in the changing place of English in Indian society. In the early 1970s, though English was firmly entrenched in academic and political life, it was not seen as being or having been central to Indian cultural life, especially in the realm of literary and other culturally elite pursuits. English could not, for instance, claim to be part of the variety of Indian "traditions" that had been "rediscovered" during the anticolonial nationalist period as a way to create India's national pride and unity. English was a medium through which Indians could contribute and get ahead but not excel. There was also a sense that Indian cultural production in English was derivative; it imitated rather than expressed something original, and so was yet to "come into its own."

In Mukherjee's assessment of Indo-Anglian novels (there had been about two hundred, she tells us) from 1930 to 1964, she identifies common themes such as nationalism, the East-West encounter, search for self, and renunciation, but she is careful to frame Indo-Anglian fiction as being part of Indian fiction and not "English" fiction, which at this time was still exclusively associated with England. This distinction was important, as is her explanation that one should make such a categorical distinction because this literature was "rooted in the social and cultural ethos of India."[8] Interestingly, the opposite of this claim becomes her main line of critique for later Indian English novels from the 1980s to the present. She often argues that post-Rushdie novels are in fact not sufficiently rooted in India. What caused the shift in her perception of many of these texts?

THE POLITICS OF LOCATION

It is important to note that when Mukherjee began writing about Indian novels in English, most of the authors of this literature lived in India, even if they were being published abroad. By the 1980s and 1990s many Indian English authors were living abroad, or mostly based there, but still writing about Indian society. In fact, Indian English literature was beginning to be seen as a transnational literature, part of a kind of "literature-scape," to draw on Arjun Appadurai's notion of a variety of "ethnoscapes" in the era of globalization.[9] However, even as cultural objects become less fixed to local contexts, as Appadurai argues, those local contexts still inform, even if in a more diffuse manner, the politics of the global. My concern in this chapter is to track a new politics of location for literature within these broader global movements or "scapes."

What is today commonly referred to as the South Asian diaspora did not exist previously as a cultural locus of production. With the increasing globalization of Indian literary production, Mukherjee began to see Indian English novels as stemming from that tide and changing the nature of the literature being written in English by Indians. The politics of location had changed, but what about the novels being produced?

In Mukherjee's essays from the late 1980s on, she expounds on and sometimes reduces Indian literature to belonging to two camps: Indo-Anglian and bhasha. While bhasha writers have a wealth of cultural influences and resonances at their behest, she argues, the Indian English writer is at a cultural disadvantage and often cannot even figure out whom he or she is writing for. This is the case, she says, because it is unclear who or where his or her audience is. Mukherjee begins to argue that bhasha writers have a more organic relationship to whichever more authentically Indian language they write in because they are part of a living and thriving society in which they may literally dip their pens before writing; their own hierarchical positioning regarding their use of often upper-caste language and idioms, however, is largely unremarked upon.

The critic G.N. Devy, a contemporary of Mukherjee's, makes a similar assessment in his description of what is lacking in the space of English in India: "English does not have its independent sociological space in India; it lives like a subtenant in the consciousness of the bilingual Indian community of English speakers. . . . [T]he sociology of Indian English literature is inevitably that of marginalization and seclusion." Devy gives critical space to English while socially and culturally cordoning it off. He takes this line of critique even further when he writes, "In the case of the post-colonial Indian English writers, fiction precedes language; it is as if these writers are trying to create an Indian English through their fictions rather than creating fiction out of a living Indian English."[10] Devy's perspective is a nativist one, and he in fact recommends that Indian English fiction look inward and take a nativist turn.

Devy and, in a more nuanced manner, Mukherjee, and as we saw in the last chapter, the critic Harish Trivedi, are all responding to a moment in Indian English writing when English becomes the only literature that is seen as national. Moreover, the fact that the process of being recognized as a national cultural production takes place through and on the global literary stage only heightens the anxieties of cultural authenticity for Indian critics who write in English as much as for the writers.

Mukherjee's critique gains steam as more and more Indian English novels and novelists become celebrated on the global literary stage. By the early 1990s she bemoans the cultural authenticity of Indian English writers, their motivations for writing, and the texts they produce. She describes the "predicament" of Indian writing in English as evidence of the "anxiety of Indianness," a state that she posits as Indian English writers' interminable desire "to explain India" as a subject in their fiction. In the process, she argues, "a homogenization of culture" occurs in their texts, whereby "Indianness" may become a mere metaphor and "India less a place than a topos, a set of imaginative references." The lack of this organic connection does not preclude

Indians writing in English from producing high-quality literary texts, she says, but they are plagued with the idea of having to incorporate or explain (to their ambiguously defined audience) "India," thereby leading to "a certain flattening out of the complicated and conflicting contours, the ambiguous and shifting relations that exist between individuals and groups in a plural community."[11] Mukherjee is arguing that literary aesthetics themselves change based on which audience one is writing for, and she has no qualms about taking individual writers to task for succumbing to what she sees as a cruder portrayal of Indian society. And in various ways, some of them have responded, not only to her, but also to the wider society. For writers, it becomes necessary to locate oneself, but as we will see, in the younger generation who tend to assert new, more globalized identities, there is less patience with these questions.

When their novels are not being held up as cultural emblems to be bartered at traffic lights, Indian English writers are often, in the pages of Indian magazines and newspapers, criticized for selling their country for personal glory and gain, often by peddling exotic portraits of "home" for consumption "abroad." This line of critique played out in some India-based reviews of Kiran Desai's first novel, *Hullabaloo in the Guava Orchard* (1998), a work that was derided for having exoticized India, with its abundant references to tropical fruits and monkeys. That the novel is a comic and somewhat fantastical parable was less remarked upon, and instead the book was criticized for not taking on serious social problems and realities. That Desai is the daughter of Anita Desai, who seems only to take on weighty topics, may have had something to do with the criticisms of the younger Desai. The onslaught of bad criticism from "back home" led the younger Desai, a decade later in a public discussion in New York City, to assert that it had become "impossible to find a ground where you will be safe in our part of the world," that part of the world being India. "No patch of land," she said, goes uncontested. She then explained how she resented having been made "more self-conscious" about her writing (referring to the hullabaloo over her first novel) and called the literary debates in India an attempt to dictate "how we should behave as Indians in the world."[12] Her next novel, *The Inheritance of Loss,* "won" on both accounts by being taken more seriously for writing about the plight of immigrant workers in a harsh, globalized world and by going on to win the 2006 Man Booker Prize.

In 2001 I had gone to Jawaharlal Nehru University in south Delhi to meet Meenakshi Mukherjee. That day I sat with her and a few of her students at a wooden seminar table discussing the marginal space of Indian English novels in the larger Indian literary imagination. Mukherjee was discussing some of her well-known views, that the English prose of Indian novels, for instance, has an extra layer of fabrication or artifice that she finds cumbersome, and that this layer is not meant for Indian audiences but for audiences abroad. Rushdie's language is a case in point for the kind of writing that she and other critics lambast. In a 1983 interview published in the Pune-based journal, *New Quest,* Rushdie explained that his invented idiom was just that, an invention. Of the characters in *Midnight's Children,* he said that in reality they would be "talking some curious mixture" of languages, and creating another idiom became his way to "just leap over that problem":

> In Bombay you can understand these various kinds of Bombay English that might have a mixture of English and Gujarati or English and Marathi or English and Hindi or English and Urdu. But I couldn't get into that problem because that would have been a terrible tangle.[13]

Rushdie is not making an excuse for writing in English—hardly—but instead describes his literary solution to "that problem." For him, any debate on the question of linguistic authenticity ends there. Mukherjee meanwhile became known for making these kinds of critiques of Rushdie-esque and post-Rushdie "boom" fiction in her lectures and writings. In 2000, she was roundly vilified by the novelist Vikram Chandra in his widely circulated "The Cult of Authenticity," an essay that some saw as being a kind of manifesto for Indian writing in English. In her critique of Chandra's work, Mukherjee had called the mythic names (Dharma, Bhakti, Kama, Shakti, Shanti) of the five chapters of Chandra's collection of interconnected stories, *Love and Longing in Bombay,* "disembodied signifiers for India that promise to live up to the unambiguous alterity of the title," and so evidence of the cultural homogenizing and defining tendencies of Indian English novelists.[14] Chandra, in turn, chastised Mukherjee for calling for a kind of literary purity and for seeming to ignore the inherent heterogeneity of every aspect of Indian cultural life, including his own English, a language that he calls his "father tongue." He taunts her, and critics like her, for being part of an English-speaking Delhi literary establishment whose own guilt about their social privilege makes them lionize "the regional" as the "real India."[15] He turns the question of ethics to being about *their* location. More interestingly, Chandra challenges the notion that he writes from a position of being "abroad" and instead argues for his own "regional" Indian identity:

> I must respectfully submit that I too am a "regional writer." I will not presume to claim Maharashtra or even the entire city of Bombay as my region. I will only claim part of the western suburbs, let us say north from the highway junction at Mahim causeway, roughly an area containing Dharavi, Bandra West, Khar, Santa Cruz, Juhu, Andheri West, and Goregaon West. This is my region. I live in it, in the locality of Andheri, in the colony called Lokhandwalla.

Chandra then stakes a relativistic claim for regional cosmopolitanism:

> My region is a hugely cosmopolitan place. Every single person who lives in my region is a cosmopolitan. I am of course a cosmopolitan; I travel away from my region every few months to make a living. My neighbors do also. There are the Gujarati diamond merchants who spend three weeks out of every four travelling from Africa to Belgium to Holland; flight attendants who fly to Beijing; businessmen who sell textiles in Australia; mechanics and welders and engineers who keep Saudi Arabia running; merchant navy sailors who carry cargo to Brazil; nurses who give care and nurture in Sharjah; and gangsters who shuttle between Bombay and Indonesia and Dubai as part of their everyday trade.

This last example is especially apt since Chandra's novel *Sacred Games* (2007) is based on his experience with those very gangsters. And this is really his point in equating his time abroad with those of his neighbors: Who is to say whose experience is or is not authentically Indian?

Chandra's tirade, or "rant," as he has called it, is powerful insofar as it articulates his position on the making of art and the integrity of artistic practice.[16] He succeeds in showing how ridiculous it is to say that one Indian identity is more authentic than another, an exposition that he carries off with literary flourish. He is also careful to mention the in-built inequities of language on the question and position of the English language and the unequal literary dispensation of global prizes to English-language writers. Still, the implicit and often explicit cultural relativism in his diatribe is not always convincing. Writers should certainly write about what they want and where they want, and Chandra is right to highlight the intricacies of his own language and location. Where Rushdie sees the use of the English language as a "problem" that can be fixed through the creative process itself, Chandra delves more deeply, and perhaps hazardously, into the politics of identity in order to authenticate himself more fully. It may not, after all, be about the titles of his chapters, the size of his advances, or the level of his American university salary. It may have more to do with how success is defined, often through a hierarchy of languages, what that hierarchy means in the society he writes about, and how this affects the literary realm more broadly. By making his response acutely personal, he offers an admirably spirited response, yet does little to take on these broader social and political questions. At some level, it may be precisely because these questions are seemingly impossible to resolve that younger generations of writers are dismissing them. Or it could also be that in a more liberalized India and globalized world, where identities are even more fluid and flexible, these debates seem quaint at their best or even regressive.

THE POX OF MODERNITY

Chandra's response becomes more interesting if we compare it to an exchange between two writers in the generations preceding his, writers who were also dealing with the issues and ethics of location. In his 1986 essay, "Being There: Aspects of an Indian Crisis," the Mumbai-based, English-language poet Adil Jussawalla describes a conversation he had with the Hindi writer Nirmal Verma in the early 1980s. Both men had returned to India around 1970 after having been abroad for some time. Verma had been living in Prague for almost a decade, while Jussawalla had been living mostly in London from the late 1950s through the 1960s. In his essay Jussawalla narrates an incident when he is admonished by Verma for not having a sense of the real divides in their country. What is interesting is that Jussawalla at first wants to dismiss the politics of place, as informed by language, but then reconsiders.

> When I met him three years ago, he held the Nirala Chair for Literature in Bhopal—a city in India's Hindi-speaking belt—and he offended me a little by saying that I couldn't possibly have any idea about any kind of young Hindi writer who came to him with his work and what his problems were. I replied with some heat that I didn't see why that writer should be any different from young writers in Bombay and why his problems should be so very different either. Verma came back with great vehemence. "They are different because they write and talk only in *Hindi*," he said. "They don't know a word of *English*!"

Soon, however, Jussawalla explains how he comes to understand Verma's point. He goes on to reflect on the positionality of Hindi, with the lack of good translations into the language, among other things, thereby giving the (hypothetical) young Hindi-only writer a different position in the world. It is important to remember that Verma is not talking about the established Hindi or other bhasha writers, most of whom speak English and many of whom are professors of English, but he is talking about a young writer who lives exclusively in the world of Hindi. Yet Verma is not identifying the Hindi-only writer as being from a more "real" India or being more authentically Indian; instead, he is pointing out that he is at a disadvantage in terms of his ability to access the outside world. His emphasis on this writer not knowing a word of English refers to the kind of education, family, and community he comes from. However, the lack of certain privileges may also, of course, be a marker of a certain kind of authenticity; and Verma may very well be pointing to an authentic position in that regard, a position that is less corrupted, let's say, by commercialism. And in this regard, Verma's recognition of the Hindi-only speaker refers to a preliberalized India, before the numerous changes in cultural production and their dissemination through new technologies. Today it is unlikely a Hindi-speaker would not know at least a few words of English and share more of the "world-awareness" that his English-language counterpart in India would. The class and caste divide persists, but its contours have changed. Jussawalla and writers like him must, in their turn, confront how much their own modernity, informed by the Western literature they have made part of their own intellectual and literary background, divides them from other Indian modernities. It is this divide that Jussawalla speaks of below as he refers to an essay Verma had written about his return to India after having lived for many years abroad:

> I hope it's clear to you now that the crisis I've been attempting to describe all along is a crisis of identity. We have so far touched on two causes for it and they have both to do with distrust. I mentioned Nirmal Verma's distrust of himself as an observer when he returned to India, but it's a familiar enough malaise among writers who have never left India too. And then there's a distrust of the English language and English literature. But what if you begin to distrust your whole being, distrust your modernity and everything that's made you modern? Can you write anything at all then when it was the very force of modernism that compelled you to write a certain kind of literature in the first place?[17]

He then considers the issue of relativism more starkly, again in relation to Verma's essay:

> The poor peasant, the trapped young writer in Bhopal, the contracted tribal breaking stones on a city street—they aren't figments of an Indian writer's imagination but indelibly part of his consciousness. Blanking them out can only be momentary. He doesn't have to go far in India to see them or people like them. So Nirmal Verma, on returning to his native land, steps out of the brief embrace of a cinema hall and is appalled at the obscenity he was subject to—a commercial which shows 'smooth-faced healthy children being fed corn-flakes by their smiling mother'—nothing he'd get too worked up about if he were in London—but in India he can't reconcile the children he sees on the screen with the children outside it—'wilted faces under a merciless sun.' It's the context which makes the commercial obscene; there's a wide gap between the streets and the screen—just as there is a wide gap between me and the peasant, the young writer and the tribal.[18]

If we compare Jussawalla (b. 1940) to Chandra (b. 1961) on their notion of where they belong, two interesting points emerge, first a convergence, and the second, a divergence. The first is that the divides in Indian society have not only to do with English and the bhashas, but with urban versus rural privilege and access to power, or more specifically, rich versus very poor; it is about how those cultures exist side by side but also about how, by being "here," one still has a choice about whether to notice and respond to them. The second is about questioning one's own modernity, and in this regard I would say that we see a divergence in Jussawalla's and Chandra's perspectives that perhaps has mostly but not completely to do with a generational difference, and hence perspective on one's relationship to modernity and, perhaps, definition of it. It just might be that Chandra has the post-Rushdie "confidence" in his modernity that Jussawalla doesn't or chooses not to have. Whether it is actually a choice is not my concern but rather how each of them portrays it in their respective essays. Chandra makes an unambiguous claim to write from the position of English by making relative his position vis-à-vis his neighbors in Bombay (the diamond merchant, the flight attendant, the mechanic, the nurse, etc.); further he does not raise the issue of having to contend with an alternate or Westernized modernity that has compromised or fractured him in the way that Jussawalla does. Jussawalla, for his part, speaks of an awareness of how that modernity has become naturalized and how he is troubled by that. This difference in the two writers' perspectives on the questions of authenticity, identity, and location is informed by the different moments in the recent Indian past that they reference, but it is of course not only a generational difference; it is also about the particular genealogies a writer imagines and creates for himself or herself.[19]

The clouds were becoming darker and heavier as the afternoon at JNU wore on; it was humid and about to start raining. Mukherjee offered me a ride out of the sprawling campus to a nearby auto-rickshaw stand. As I stepped down from her car, she turned to me and said with some resignation, "You know, ever since Arundhati Roy, most of my students tell me they have fiction manuscripts sitting in their top desk drawers. They all think it might happen to them."

What really irks Mukherjee is that these students with English manuscripts in their desks aspire "to be part of a global league" without having an "acquaintance" with bhasha literatures. This charge—of Indian English writers' apparent disinterest in the worlds of bhasha writing—was one I heard many times in Delhi.[20] Mukherjee finds it paradoxical that "if they achieve any fame abroad, it will be on the basis of their relationship with India and their ability to find new modes of representing the complex reality of their own culture."[21] This charge brings an ethical dimension to the question of a writer's location and to the issue of place within a creative work. Do writers have a responsibility to engage in the societies they represent in their fiction? Who sets the terms of this engagement?

In Mukherjee's last set of published essays, she is suspicious of the increase in the number of English translations of bhasha books.[22] Although one might presume that more translations of bhasha works into English would make it more possible for writers and others to acquaint themselves with those literatures, that, in Mukherjee's reckoning, misses the point, since more translations into English would be another instance when English is privileged as the language of cultural transmission. It is in this sense that it is important to think of translation as a cultural zone, one that exerts a power field of its own, depending not only on which languages are in question but also on whether they are being translated into or out of. It is due to these larger power imbalances that Mukherjee favors intra-bhasha translations and has done some of those herself (from Bengali to Hindi). She might agree that more translations into the bhashas *and* into English would be a good idea, but her point, again, is to call attention to the power imbalance between English and the bhashas and the directionality in which creativity flows. In her view, this imbalance continually privileges English as the mediating language between other languages, and this fact leads to the impoverishment of the literary and cultural dialogue among Indians and between other Indian languages. It would appear that her critique has gone beyond select authors and their texts and has come full circle, back to the place of English in Indian society—a place that has changed significantly from the one where she first had to legitimize her critical interest in Indo-Anglian fiction.[23]

SOME NOTES ON THE ART OF REFUSAL

Indian literature abroad and the globalization of literature more generally is another way of talking about the perennial relationship between politics and literature. It is a relationship that necessarily highlights issues of place and history. In my reading of the refusals of prizes by two leading Indian English authors, I see an "art" in how audiences are cultivated across borders, but with reference to specific kinds of politics. I see them as an example of how writers may intervene in what is really a discussion about the ethics of location.

The awarding of prizes has become a central staging ground for global literature. In the examples below we see how two Indian novelists who write in English—Amitav Ghosh and Arundhati Roy—affirm their loyalty to "bhasha worlds" as a way to assert their own politics. In both cases, refusing a prize enables an author to "locate" himself or herself on a particular stage, whether regional, national, or international, but also to assert loyalty to particular causes, people, or ideas. Both of these writers associate themselves with Indian causes no matter where they actually reside, yet the fact that they are so well known abroad impinges on their identities as writers. The association with causes, thus, becomes a way for authors to explicitly claim the moral and intellectual ground on which they stand. Refusals are often politically charged statements that now get transmitted across the world over the Internet in minutes. The refusal of a prize may thus also be seen as another genre of writing.

In 2001 Ghosh politely but unequivocally asked that his novel, *The Glass Palace,* be taken out of competition for the Commonwealth Writers' Prize. The prize was instituted in 1987 and is administered by the Commonwealth Foundation, an intergovernmental organization based in London that represents forty-six Commonwealth nations. Its Board of Governors consists of representatives from the member states, most of which were at some point part of the British colonial empire. The Commonwealth Writers' Prize works on a two-tier system whereby each year four regional prizes and one overall prize are given in two categories: best book and best first book. Ghosh refused the prize at the regional level when he was informed that his novel had won the Eurasia prize for best book, making him eligible for the overall prize for best book, which was to be announced the following month.[24] Ghosh explained that his publisher, HarperCollins, had put forward his name without his knowledge.[25] He used the occasion of his refusal to make a political statement, which went on to be featured on his personal website. His refusal also became a feature story in the leading Indian English magazines and was covered in all the major English-language daily newspapers and news magazines, including the *Times of India* and *India Today.* Ghosh's original letter to the Commonwealth Foundation Prizes Manager was reprinted in *Biblio,* along with an analysis by the journal and responses by Delhi writers and publishers. Ghosh's refusal became part of postcolonial discourse itself, as he used the occasion to broadcast his views more widely.

In his letter to the foundation, Ghosh cited three specific reasons for his refusal: it was an outdated, hierarchical, and imperial mapping of the world; it ignored the literatures of non-English writers who formed the majorities of these postcolonial societies; and the historical inflection of the term "Commonwealth" speaks only of the "brute facts of time" (colonial domination) rather than a more nuanced view of how people, societies, and nations have developed over time. He cited his agreement with Salman Rushdie's well-known 1983 essay, "'Commonwealth Literature' Does Not Exist," and wrote that the grouping of Commonwealth Literature was outdated and harking back to imperial days and hierarchies. However, in Rushdie's case, it would appear that his own critique was not of the prize per se (since he did not object to being short-listed for it twice) but of the notion of "Commonwealth" writing more generally. It was the pigeonholing of writers that Rushdie disapproved of.[26]

Ghosh's second reason for refusing the prize had to do with the privileging of English over other languages. He writes that by including only Commonwealth writers writing in English, the Commonwealth was privileging a very select and tiny minority of writers, considering that the vast majority of people living under the Commonwealth umbrella write and speak in other languages.

Fellow Indian writers (of English and bhasha literatures) lauded Ghosh's action, though several publishers commented that only a writer of his stature could forgo the prize money and the boost in book sales. As James English has written in *The Economy of Prestige,* prizes are "the base camp of canon formation" and for writers, "their richest and most reliable source of publicity."[27] In Ghosh's case, he was already a well-established, canonized writer, and refusing the award garnered him more, not less, publicity. As for book sales, it is also possible that they may have been increased by his refusal or stayed the same. He was clearly in a position to refuse the award without being in danger of hurting his career.

Some bhasha writers were especially heartened by Ghosh's refusal of the award since it is precisely the English-language infrastructure of press events and international awards that often relegates their works to being "regional literature," as opposed to the implied global reach of English-language works. The "world stage," as symbolized by the postcolonial grouping of former British colonies as the Commonwealth, is simply not open to their languages. Ghosh's refusal not only of the award, and the possibility of winning overall in the Best Book category, but also of the £10,000 in prize money, as well as the presumed increase in book sales if he had won the overall prize, was seen as an almost heroic gesture by many India-based authors. It appeared he was not only acting in his own interest but also trying to make a broader political point.

Ghosh's actions are another example of making a claim to "literary nationality" as defined by specific extratextual literary practices. To a large extent, location is defined by the political debates in which one inserts oneself, and in his refusal, Ghosh took a moral stand on issues of location, language, and history. His actions authenticated him as an Indian writer because he was able to take critical stances that are felt to be genuine in the Indian literary world.[28]

If we compare Ghosh's refusal to Roy's refusal of the Sahitya Akademi award in 2006, we see another way in which literary nationality lends meaning to a book and its author. In her refusal letter, Roy wrote, "I have a great deal of respect for the Sahitya Akademi, for the members of this year's Jury and for many of the writers who have received these awards in the past. But to register my protest and re-affirm my disagreement—indeed my absolute disgust—with these policies of the Indian Government, I must refuse to accept the 2005 Sahitya Akademi Award."[29] Like Ghosh, it is not that Roy refuses all literary prizes but that she made a particular choice by refusing a prize based on its funders. In this case, she used the refusal to restate her well-known diatribes against the Indian government. Some would say her action is anti-national by being anti-government; others would say she is showing her loyalty to her nation by critiquing the government in the hope that it would change its policies and ultimately improve conditions for her fellow Indians.

Again, in his book on the symbolic meanings of prizes, James English notes a shift in the meaning of why artists refuse prizes, a shift that in his analysis points to changes in the globalization of art. He argues that writers who refuse prizes today are no longer perceived as acting within "the long tradition of sincere animosity between artists and bourgeois consecrations," what used to be recognized as the "artistic freedom fighter on the old model of art versus money." If we consider earlier refusals of the Sahitya Akademi award, for instance, we may get a sense of a different kind of logic that animates these refusals, one that has to do more with literary pride than political purpose. In a book the Akademi commissioned and published, *Five Decades: A Short History of the Sahitya Akademi*, there is a listing of several other authors who have refused the award, and these refusals are presented as a list of curiosities, citing statements from the authors such as "I should have been given it earlier," or "I didn't deserve the award for these stray essays, and winners are usually spent forces anyway." Another stated that the Akademi had taken "too long to recognize the genre of the short story" (for which the claimant had won the award).[30]

Artists today, writes English, are instead "more likely to be seen as players in a newer cultural game whose 'rules' and 'sides' are rather more obscure."[31] What he is suggesting is that the reasons for refusing a prize might be more specific to a particular cultural or political situation than previously. Not surprisingly, the bigger the prize, the more of a statement an author may make as he or she has more of the prize's own cultural capital to work with. English shows that "traditionally" for a writer to benefit from such a refusal, he would have to have "already accumulated a wealth of symbolic capital." Roy and Ghosh both were already well known at the time of their refusals. For Roy, this fact is partly due to the widespread acclaim for her novel *The God of Small Things* and partly due to the political activism she has undertaken since winning the Booker Prize in 1997. This work has led to her winning many awards (including the 2002 Cultural Freedom Prize from the Lannan Foundation), participating in international events such as the World Social Forum, and giving lectures around the world. So her refusal must be seen in the context of her position as a global figure. Like Roy, it is not that Ghosh refuses all literary prizes but that he has made a particular choice in this case. In Ghosh's refusal it is not the funders whom he maligns but the idea of the Commonwealth itself, which he takes as a literary, linguistic, and historical insult. However, neither author is opposed to prizes in general. Nor has either refused corporate or establishment values in light of the other awards they have won and accepted or shortlists on which they have let themselves stand. Instead, their refusals are more precisely political.

In 2010, it was Ghosh's *acceptance* of a prize that became controversial, in part because of his earlier refusal. Some wanted him to act similarly (that is, refuse) when he won the Dan David Prize, which is bestowed by a private foundation at Tel Aviv University in Israel. To justify his acceptance, Ghosh precisely detailed his political stance about his recognition of the legitimacy of the state of Israel, the reasons why he did not want to boycott its cultural and academic institutions (even though he supports the cause of Palestinians and deplores the violence against them perpetrated by the Israeli state), and how he thought a two-state solution negotiated with the help of President Barack Obama holds the best hope for ending the conflict in the region. In one letter, he responds to those who questioned why he refused the Commonwealth Prize and not the Dan David Prize. First, he clarifies that he did not turn down the Commonwealth Prize but "withdrew" it from the competition. He then states that he was against "the specific mandate of that prize" and the framework in which it placed authors.[32]

As James English sees it, writers and artists today are already implicated in a broader cultural field where the refusal of a prize is merely one move in a larger game; it may no longer be seen, he says, as "a refusal to play." Instead, English writes, "they must pursue the game more tactically."[33] The "game" for many Indian authors, I would suggest, is precisely about their own identities and cultural authenticity, one that recognizes the language politics of their own writing. In Ghosh's refusal of the Commonwealth Prize, he lambasts the old colonial categories and draws attention to the international neglect of the bhasha literatures. It is not that Ghosh is going to stop writing in English, but he is going to call attention to the structural injustices against writers who do not write in English. In Roy's case, by refusing the Sahitya Akademi Award, she is underlining the critiques in the book for which she won, *The Algebra of Infinite Injustice* (2002); the injustices she writes about are linked to the causes of the rural poor, for instance, those impacted negatively by the nuclear program, the building of dams, or the violence between the armed forces and the Maoist insurgency. She may write in English, but her moral compass points toward the concerns and problems of those living in non-English milieus. In this regard, she said in a 2011 interview:

> I've spent the last six months traveling across the country, speaking at huge meetings in smaller towns—Ranchi, Jullundur, Bhubaneshwar, Jaipur, Srinagar—at public meetings with massive audiences, three and four thousand people—students, farmers, laborers, activists. I speak mostly in Hindi, which isn't my language (even that has to be translated depending on where the meeting is being held). Though I write in English, my writing is immediately translated into Hindi, Telugu, Kannada, Tamil, Bengali, Malayalam, Odia. I don't think I'm considered an "Indo-Anglian" writer any more. I seem to be drifting away from the English speaking world at high speed. My English must be changing. The way I think about language certainly is.[34]

Here, language becomes imbricated with place and social activism. Her description seems to suggest that the locus of authenticity is small towns and specifically the causes and the people, the English have-nots, whose lives are most affected by them. In an increasingly globalized world, where authors regularly travel and win awards across borders, it becomes necessary to assert one's loyalty and affirm one's politics of location, whether or not it is the actual ground on which one stands.

CHAPTER 9

Conclusion

In early 2011 I attended a party at Navayana, a small, independent publishing house devoted to Dalit writing and caste politics. It was Navayana's first event since setting up shop in Shahpur Jat, a gentrifying "village" in the heart of south Delhi, not far from the pavement booksellers with whom I began this book. That evening the city's literary intelligentsia was eating rolled-up kebabs and drinking rum or beer, each carrying a red paper bag of books bought. If there were any doubts about there being a literary scene in Delhi, that evening at Navayana might diminish them. Arundhati Roy moved in a quiet pack at the back; the columnist Chandrabhan Prasad held forth in a louder circle up front. A young poet, Meena Kandasamy, read from her collection of poems that Navayana had just published. Dalit writing originally in English is still rare, and when I ask Prasad about it that evening, he tells me that Meena represents the hope for the future.

Outside, on the main road adjacent to Shahpur Jat, traffic is heavy and boys are selling more magazines than books. I pass them as I am traveling south most days to the Indian Institute of Technology (IIT), where I am teaching. It is the institution about which Chetan Bhagat wrote his first novel—*Five Point Someone: What* Not *to Do at IIT!*—an English-language best-seller on a scale not previously seen in India; it, along with his subsequent novels, has sold millions of copies.[1] What is generally acknowledged about Bhagat's books is that his huge readership is most eager to consume the places and experiences his narratives offer—an ease with the idioms of Anglicized urban middle-class life; newly liberalized spaces such as call centers; and entry into institutions such as the IIT and the Indian Institutes of Management. The life young people imagine possible with English. His novels offer them a kind of passport that links to their own desires and connects them to a cultural shorthand that is already familiar but that they may not quite possess.

Bhagat's novels are remarkable, not for putting Indian literature on the world stage in the way other novelists have, but for relating to and inspiring a vast readership within India itself. His works exist in a different world, a less literary one most certainly, but a world that marks a new kind of writing and sensibility in English. The sentences are short, clear, and not overly expository. There are few if any novelistic passages, where people, ideas, or places are described in any kind of depth. And yet whatever is described, even if brief and mostly in the form of dialogue, is compelling enough and moves the story along. Bhagat's novels are not only sold to people who already read English novels, but to thousands upon thousands who might never have read one before. Moreover, Bhagat has also become something of a public intellectual, promoting liberal secular values, such as meritocracy and government accountability, in newspaper columns and on television news programs. The fact that his novels are not literary means most critics dismiss them, but what cannot be dismissed is that his novels represent a new readership whose relationship to English and to their own class identities is markedly different from before.

Throughout this book, I have been interested in understanding how Indians—primarily those involved in some aspect of literary production—relate to the languages they speak and write in. How, for instance, K. Satchidanandan balances his own politics of language, formed through his life as a Malayalam-language poet and English-language intellectual, with the institutional demands of the Sahitya Akademi and of Delhi itself. His is a personal reckoning, as it is for Geetanjali Shree, who moves between Hindi and English. Both wrangle with the limits of place, despite the artistic spaces and opportunities they have created for themselves in Delhi. I have also meant to show the interplay of cultural, linguistic, and affective practices that produce the everyday world of English as it lives among other Indian languages. This interplay was dramatized in the debate over the Hindi translation of Vikram Seth's *A Suitable Boy*, while also inherent in the professional life history of Ravi Dayal. In these examples and others, English mediates the everyday, and does so through time, in the very constitution of classes, castes, genders, and languages themselves. To this end, I have been insisting on a closer attentiveness to what languages signify as they travel through contemporary society; and I have argued that this signification undercuts the thorny questions of identity formation and cultural authenticity. Moreover, I have also foregrounded an attachment to and habitation of language partly to present the political life of literature as being more than just about the elitist position of English vis-à-vis the more "authentic" bhashas. Instead, I have attempted to show how English becomes defined, molded, and nuanced by its often complex relationships to other Indian languages, especially Hindi. I have also pointed to the ways in which Hindi itself has multiple social and political meanings, as its own literary practitioners such as the Maheshwari brothers attest to. Both languages are deployed in the pursuit of literary nationality, which, I have argued, has more to do with the politics of language than it does with the creation of literature. These pursuits are often rearticulations of regional identities and loyalties. They are deployments by individuals and institutions that reveal the constructed nature both of the idea of the national and of positions within the literary field.

My rendering of this multilingual literary world has not been merely to illustrate how English has an Indian accent. Rather, it has been about the indigenization of English in institutions, through livelihoods, careers, and class formation, and through the act of creative expression. In the process, I have tried to show the density of the literary field, its complex layers of meaning that surround seemingly simple topics such as Indian fiction in English and rubrics like cultural authenticity. It has also been my aim to resist a simple mapping of the oppositions and binaries of the colonial period—however illusory those might be—onto to the postcolonial one. In doing so I am not suggesting that there is no longer any "resistance" that is played out in the linguistic realm. What I am emphasizing is that forms of resistance are much more complex than previously imagined and involve strategic uses of different languages and what they stand for depending on regional, national, and transnational contexts. In this regard, I have meant to detail how social and political hierarchies between languages create a particular intellectual and literary discourse in India precisely because of the place of English, and how these have changed in the decades after independence. I have been arguing that the "postcolonial," as a theoretical term, does not do this social and literary reality enough justice, since it does not explain why and how English has played both a liberating and a confining role—and much in between—for so many bhasha and English writers, publishers, and others. That is to say, the postcolonial framework does not let us see all that is produced not just in English but *by* English. More significantly, the postcolonial frame does not allow for how the way English is imagined and lived on a day-to-day basis intersects in myriad ways with the other Indian languages, and the politics and ideological frameworks therein. Understanding these ideological frameworks is important, since they illustrate how elite privilege itself changes, the fact that there are new elites and new aspirants but also new sets of politics—most often having to do with shifting class and caste alliances, and relating, as always, to religious and gendered notions of identity. These alliances, in turn, show us something about the nature of contemporary Indian society, in terms of the morals being promulgated and the social distinctions being set forth.

By way of closing, it might be useful to consider a novel such as Upamanyu Chatterjee's *English, August* (1988) alongside Chetan Bhagat's *Five Point Someone* (2004). They both involve college-aged, pot-smoking youth, albeit in Chatterjee's novel the characters are situated firmly in an ironic, preliberalization India, caught in a bureaucratic haze, and in Bhagat's works, they exist in a comic, postliberalization one, working at call centers or negotiating corporate salaries. *English, August* is a literary novel and became a cult classic as compared to the easy-reading, plot-pulsating *Five Point Someone.* Both English-original texts were made into movies, the former, a small independent film in English and some Hindi that toured the world's festivals and won a number of awards, the latter, a wildly popular Hindi movie—the hit of 2009—renamed *3 Idiots* and starring Aamir Khan, one of Hindi cinema's biggest stars.

Not much happens in *English, August* as the protagonist, Agastya, languishes in a civil service posting in a small town far from his native Delhi. The reader languishes with him, in long, meandering scenes that mimic the nowhere-ness of his own existence. His posting in the highly prestigious Indian Administrative Service is the most lucrative and powerful position he could hope to attain as a middle-class person in those years. Yet his English credentials, if anything, remind him of just how out of touch he is with the rest of India. The narrator describes

Agastya's journey to the small town of Madna as follows: "Glimpses of Madna *en route;* cigarette-and-paan dhabas, disreputable food stalls, both lit by fierce kerosene lamps, cattle and clanging rickshaws on the road, and the rich sound of trucks in slush from an overflowing drain; he felt as though he was living someone else's life."[2]

By the time we get to Bhagat, and the phenomenon of Bhagat, we realize that those towns are filled with lower- and middle-class aspirants, and their relationship to English has changed in the intervening fifteen to twenty years. More people are "in touch" with a kind of English than ever before and, as a result, have a new consciousness about their own social mobility. This awareness does not take census numbers away from the bhashas but in fact creates more porous boundaries between languages, and the thoughts and ideas contained in them.

Notes

PROLOGUE

1. For instance, in the classic critiques of imperialist ideology by Aimé Césaire (1950), Frantz Fanon (1961), Edward Said (1978, 1993), Gayatri Spivak (1985, 1987), and Ngũgĩ wa Thiong'o (1986), as well as a host of other foundational studies delving into the nature of colonial rule and colonial and postcolonial discourse, including Ashis Nandy (1983), Gauri Viswanathan (1989), Ashcroft, Griffiths, and Tiffin (1989), Sara Suleri (1992), Homi Bhabha (1994), Mrinalini Sinha (1995), Ann Stoler (1995), and Robert Young (2001).

2. The following works enabled me to think more imaginatively about the study of texts and society, the relationship between academic disciplines, and the relationship between literature and society in India: Bernard Cohn (1987, 1996), Nicholas Dirks (1993), Brinkley Messick (1993), Stefania Pandolfo (1997), Lawrence Cohen (2000), and the volumes edited by E. Valentine Daniel (1996) and Jonathan Boyarin (1993) in the realm of anthropology; and in regard to Indian literary and political modernities, the volumes edited by Svati Joshi (1991) and Rajeswari Sunder Rajan (1992) and essays by Sudipta Kaviraj (2010).

CHAPTER I

1. The novel had already won the Commonwealth Prize for First Novel in the "Eurasia section" in 1998, which might have been why it became a question on the show to begin with, but I avoided this chicken-and-egg intervention.

2. *The Inheritance of Loss* sold 2,000 copies when it was first published in India, and 70,000 more soon after winning the Man Booker Prize in 2006.

3. Which books make it to the pavements is perhaps the best indicator of what people are reading (as this snapshot from 2007 indicates) or what is

considered of enduring or iconic value, such as Khushwant Singh's 1956 novel about partition, *Train to Pakistan*. Print runs for most novels or other general interest books in English are usually about 2,000 copies, with sales of 1,000 to 2,000 being typical. Ravi Singh, when he was editor in chief at Penguin India, said that he considered a best-seller to be any book selling more than 5,000 copies, while Urvashi Butalia, publisher of Zubaan, cited the figure of 10,000 on the "We the People" television program, "Will books survive the digital age?" (23 January 2011). Other booksellers and publishers told me they also considered 10,000 copies to be the new best-seller threshold. In an interview in 2001 with bookseller K.D. Singh, he told me that when he first opened The Bookshop in Jor Bagh (one of Delhi's exclusive colonies) in 1970, he sold one hundred copies of Eric Segal's *Love Story*, an event that for him was the birth of the "best-seller reading public" in English.

4. Universal primary education in India is far from having been achieved; however, it has been a government mandate for some time. Even though more and more Indians from different class backgrounds are having access to some kind of nongovernment, English-medium education, it is often of dubious quality. India's overall rate of literacy—which varies according to gender and region—is 74 percent, according to the provisional results of the 2011 census.

5. See Krishna Kumar's *Learning from Conflict* (1996), which analyzes the symbolic value of post-independence English education and especially the psychological advantages such an education gives.

6. Anjali Puri, "English Speaking Curse," *Outlook*, 24 March 2008.

7. States in the "Hindi belt" include Bihar, Delhi territory, Haryana, Himachal Pradesh, Uttar Pradesh, Madhya Pradesh, and Rajasthan. The big Hindi newspapers have long had English-language advertisements, so what is significant here is that smaller publications reaching less urbane and educated audiences are also now using some English. The other reason this trend is surprising is that in Uttar Pradesh the politics of Hindi have been such that the purity of the language has long been considered by the Hindi intelligentsia (including newspaper editors) a central point in political platforms. Nivedita Menon and Aditya Nigam, in *Power and Contestation: India since 1989* (2007), chalk up these changes to the postliberalization-era media explosion, and more generally to the forces of cultural globalization that have allowed newspaper editors to break free from the control and policing of Hindi over the last century (89–91).

8. Anjali Puri, "Jab They Met," *Outlook*, 12 November 2007.

9. Author interview in Delhi in 2001 with Maya Sharma, who is from Rajasthan and writes in English. Sharma is an example of someone who did not come from an urban background yet had an elite command of English; she is closer to this other world where English was not as readily available.

10. My entry into thinking about language politics came from my study of colonial histories and postcolonial literatures, where language is already socially and culturally embedded in particular ways—many of which I unravel in this book; however, for many anthropologists, the theorization of language is located within or comes out of the study of linguistics. For instance, the volume *Regimes of Language: Ideologies, Polities, Identities* (2000), edited by

Paul V. Kroskrity, featuring some of anthropology's most important linguists, sought, in the early 1990s, to address larger political questions of ideology by opening up the "microanalysis" of language to "political-economic macroprocesses." Whereas linguistic anthropologists tend to look at the relationship between verbal practices and larger social facts, my work forefronts literary language, production, and discourse, which are then put in relation to larger sociopolitical questions. Starting within the postcolonial paradigm, my questioning begins with the ideological and political. In this regard, see Benedict Anderson's *Language and Power: Exploring Political Cultures in Indonesia* (1990) and Patrick Eisenlohr's *Little India: Diaspora, Time, and Ethnolinguistic Belonging in Hindu Mauritius* (2006).

11. Arjun Appadurai, "Global Ethnoscapes: Notes and Queries for a Transnational Anthropology," in *Modernity at Large* (1996), 58.

12. Bourdieu's notion of the literary field is developed in *Distinction: A Social Critique of the Judgement of Taste* (1984) and *The Field of Cultural Production: Essays on Art and Literature* (1993) and elaborated in *The Rules of Art: Genesis and Structure of the Literary Field* (1996). His trenchant analysis of Parisian publishers, writers, and related institutions and individuals focuses on the production of French-language texts as always emerging from within a set of struggles played out in a field of power. I find his rendering of the literary field overly deterministic for India's literary case and hence limited in terms of applicability as well as in its scope. However, it is very useful for thinking about how the meaning and value of a work of literature are produced. I use "field," "sphere," and "realm" somewhat interchangeably throughout this book precisely because I see the network of associations and attendant relationships of power and influence as being more elastic than Bourdieu's concept of field would allow for.

13. See Wendy Griswold's *Bearing Witness: Readers, Writers, and the Novel in Nigeria* (2000) for another work on postcolonial literary fiction and publishing. Her book impressively categorizes and analyzes the themes of dozens of Anglophone Nigerian novels with reference to publishing and reading networks.

14. The novel as a genre and cultural form has of course long been implicated in processes of modernity, especially in relation to issues of class, nation, race, religion, and imperialist ideology, as illustrated by Georg Lukacs (1920/1971); Ian Watt (1957); Rabindranath Tagore (1907/1998), Raymond Williams (1973), Walter Benjamin (1936), Gilles Deleuze and Felix Guattari (1986), Edward Said (1975), Firdous Azim (1993), Benedict Anderson (1993), and Meenakshi Mukherjee (1995)—to name some of the authors whose works first stimulated my thinking on this topic.

15. Shashi Deshpande, "The Hornet's Nest," in her *Writing from the Margin and Other Essays* (2003), 67.

16. Using the unscientific example of myself, I attempted to gauge the language worlds of daily life by keeping track of my language usage during the course of one day in north Delhi, where I was living in 2001 and again in 2008. The result was as follows: When I was at home, I spoke Hindi to the milkman, the part-time cook, the sometime house cleaner, the housewife across the

hallway and her two school-age children, the *istri-wallah* who came to collect wrinkled clothes, the electrician, and the guy from the phone company who came to fix the broadband connection. I spoke English at various points in the day to the friend (a Kannada mother-tongued, Hindi- and Marathi-speaking, English-educated academic from Bombay) whose flat I was staying in, and it should be said that my most involved and lengthy conversations that day were with her, ranging from which vegetables I should buy from the market to the structure of one of my chapters. I also spoke English, mostly chitchat, to the other professors in our complex. When I left home, I spoke Hindi to the guards at the front gate, the cycle rickshaw driver who took me to the Vishwavidyalaya Metro Station, to the metro station security who searched my bags, and later to an auto rickshaw driver and to shopkeepers and vegetable sellers in Kamla Nagar market.

17. Shashi Deshpande, "The Hornet's Nest," 71.

18. Shashi Deshpande, "Where Do We Belong: Regional, National, or International?," in her *Writing from the Margin and Other Essays* (2003), 32.

19. This reaction was most obviously apparent when *Slumdog Millionaire* won the Best Picture Oscar at the Academy Awards in 2009. Indian film critics and public opinion—as gleaned from a variety of newspaper reports, television commentary, and blogs—did not like the film for its negative portrayal of slum life, which they said promoted stereotypical views of India. Rather than see the film as yet another example of India reaching the world cultural stage, many Indians saw it as yet another Westerner's attempt (in this case the film's British director, Danny Boyle) to portray India as backward and horrific. Some were also critical of the film's aesthetics, but most of the reaction to the film had to do with its subject matter.

20. As reported in the *Outlook* Web Bureau profile, "The Dark Horse," 14 October 2008, www.outlookindia.com/full.asp?fodname=20081014&fname=Books&sid=1.

21. Amitava Kumar, "On Adiga's *The White Tiger*," *The Hindu*, Literary Review section, 2 November 2008. A longer version of the review was published as "Authenticity and the South Asian Political Novel," in *Boston Review*, November–December 2008.

22. Aravind Adiga, *The White Tiger* (2008), 1–2; 14.

23. Even in areas of the world where English was *not* a colonial language—such as Indonesia and China—the language today is an emblem of advancement and a marker of the formation of a globalized elite class.

24. For instance, during an author event in Berkeley (Cody's Books, 9 August 2002) for his novel, *The House of Blue Mangoes* (2002), then Penguin India publisher David Davidar began the reading by telling his American audience that for many Indians, "they write in English by default." There is some truth in this statement, and yet it ultimately obscures more than it reveals.

25. Sheldon Pollock makes the important point that the Indian vernaculars were linked with geographical and ecological features of a place, rather than with a particular people, as European languages had been. He writes, "Languages never made peoples, and were never linked with particular kin groups in narratives of vernacular beginnings." See his *Language of the Gods in the*

World of Men: Sanskrit, Culture, and Power in Premodern India (2006), 510. See also Lisa Mitchell's *Language, Emotion, and Politics in South India: The Making of a Mother Tongue* (2009), for a compelling ethnohistory of the Telugu language that, among other things, details how the terms "bhasha" and "mother tongue" are constructed categories whose contemporary connotations become naturalized in the twentieth century.

26. Estimates vary as to how many Indians are literate in English, but the official number from the 2001 Indian Census is 1 to 3 percent of the total population. Because the Indian Census figures on language record individuals' mother tongues as their primary language (less than 250,000 Indians said "English" was their mother tongue in 2001), those statistics do not take into account the large number of Indians from the middle and upper classes and castes, who attend private, English-medium schools and become fluent in the language, so a figure of 5 percent is more accurate.

27. Sisir Kumar Das, *History of Indian Literature, 1911–1956* (1995), 39.

28. Pascale Casanova, *The World Republic of Letters* (2005), 255.

29. B.R. Ambedkar reveals how the vote on Hindi was tied 78 to 78, and then when a revote was called, it was 77 to 78. See his *Thoughts on Linguistic States* (1955/1989), 14.

30. *Report of the Official Language Commission, 1956*, 31.

31. *Report of the Official Language Commission, 1956*, 33.

32. These figures are from the 2001 Census of India, which recorded the numerical strength of each language by counting those listing a particular language as their mother tongue. See Susan Gal's "Language and Political Spaces" (2009) for an important genealogy of the mapping of languages by modern nation-states, which, she says, creates "a vision of what ethnolinguistic diversity should look like from the eye-view of a nation-state" rather than "a picture of actually existing linguistic practices" (37).

33. In November 2008, Malayalam-speaking scholars and writers from Kerala voiced their dismay after the central government of India awarded "Classical Language" status to Telugu and Kannada, spoken largely in the neighboring states of Andhra Pradesh and Karnataka respectively. Tamil (as well as Sanskrit) had already been accorded this status, so that left Malayalam as the only south Indian language not so designated. The government began the "classical language" designation in 2004, even though bodies such as the Sahitya Akademi advised against it, saying it only created more linguistic hierarchies.

34. The numerical contours of this competition in the literate public sphere have most often been calculated in terms of newspaper sales. Hindi trumps English here with the number of newspapers with circulations over 100,000. Hindi has fifteen, whereas English has eleven. See Sevanti Ninan, *Headlines from the Heartland: Reinventing the Hindi Public Sphere* (2007), 18. It has often been noted that Hindi newspapers are read by many more than circulation numbers suggest since they are often read by more people in joint families and in public places, whereas English papers tend to go to nuclear households. Also see Robin Jeffrey's *India's Newspaper Revolution: Capitalism, Politics, and the Indian-Language Press, 1977–99* (2000).

35. Although the numerical strength of Hindi seems today like an obvious

reason for its place in the linguistic hierarchy, Francesca Orsini documents the somewhat artificial construction of Hindi by campaigners in the early twentieth century, as they framed and bolstered it through public campaigns as the only possible and legitimate national language. She explains that "the linguistic identity constructed in the present is projected backwards in history for the sake of one, national community," with the cost being that the "multilingual past, an essential feature of India, was denied, downplayed, and misrepresented in the triumphant majoritarian drive for one national culture." See *The Hindi Public Sphere, 1920–1940: Language and Literature in the Age of Nationalism* (2002), 132, 135.

36. These debates regarding Hindi being the national language began in the 1920s and 1930s when leaders in the anticolonial Indian National Congress and others were already envisioning what post-independence India would look like. The classic analyses of this topic include Robert D. King's *Nehru and the Language Politics of India* (1997), Jyotindra Das Gupta's *Language Conflict and National Development: Group Politics and National Language Policy in India* (1970), and the firsthand account of B.R. Ambedkar in his *Thoughts on Linguistic States* (1955/1989).

37. By "Hindi," Gandhi actually was in support of Hindustani, the mix of Hindi and Urdu spoken in north India. Most significant, Hindustani is rooted in Sanskrit and Persian vocabularies, hence it represents the shared cultural ethos of Hindus and Muslims. This mapping of religious identities onto Hindi and Urdu is discussed in chapter 2.

38. Rajeswari Sundar Rajan describes this dynamic well: English in India may be both antinational (by opposing Hindi) and pan-Indian (by not being fixed to any particular region within India). See her "Fixing English: Nation, Language, Subject," in *The Lie of the Land: English Literary Studies in India*, ed. Rajeswari Sundar Rajan (1992), 14–15.

39. For more on the imposition of Hindi in Tamilnadu, see V. Geetha and S.V. Rajadurai, *Towards a Non-Brahmin Millennium* (1999), 487–506; and Sumathi Ramaswamy's *Passions of the Tongue: Language Devotion in Tamil India, 1891–1970* (1997), 168–78.

40. Aijaz Ahmad, *In Theory: Nations, Classes, Literatures* (1992), 75.

41. Alok Rai, *Hindi Nationalism* (2001), 2. See also Vasudha Dalmia's review essay of *Hindi Nationalism*, "The Locations of Hindi," in *Economic and Political Weekly* (5 August 2003), where she specifically questions why contemporary literary production in Hindi, which especially in consideration of women's writing and Dalit writing in the language is more varied than the educational and governmental realms of standardized Hindi, is not able (or, as she sees it, no longer able) to affect policy-making.

42. English is not only connected to one's job prospects, but has a social quality whereby in some communities that have "less English," anyone who has mastered it is erroneously considered the most intelligent member of that community. It is hard to quantify the rampant falseness of this association, but it is widely prevalent. Someone who speaks English may very well have had a better education than someone who does not speak English (though not always so or necessarily so); however, what is being valorized in their mastery of

the language is not educational opportunity but intelligence as a more general attribute. The idea that English speakers are smarter also feeds into a trend among aspiring classes not only to make sure their children speak English but also to see to it that they are not heard speaking "dialects" spoken at home and in their communities. One student from the outskirts of Delhi told me her father had simply told her, in regard to the Haryanvi language the rest of the family spoke, "I won't let you learn it."

43. See Kancha Ilaiah, *Why I Am Not a Hindu: A Sudra Critique of Hindutva Philosophy, Culture, and Political Economy* (1996). Ilaiah writes in the tradition of Bhimrao Ramji Ambedkar (1891–1956), Dalit activist, scholar, and drafter of the Indian constitution. Ambedkar believed English to be one of the few equalizing forces for Dalits, partly because knowing the language and attending British government schools in colonial Maharashtra enabled him to attend college, and then, with a scholarship from the liberal maharaja of Baroda, attend Columbia University, where he received a Ph.D. in economics in 1916. Ambedkar completed a second Ph.D. at the London School of Economics in 1923.

44. M. N. Srinivas first coined the term "vote bank" to refer to voting along caste lines in the Indian context; see his "The Social System of a Mysore Village" (1955). The term now refers not only to caste but also to votes garnered through linguistic and religious groupings. For more detail on the political coalition building that went into the making of the Hindu vote in the 1990s, see Christophe Jaffrelot's *The Hindu Nationalist Movement in India* (1998).

45. See Vasudha Dalmia's *The Nationalization of Hindu Traditions* (1997) for her now-classic exposition on the social and literary construction of the Hindi language in the nineteenth century, resulting in the consolidation of Hindu identity.

46. Kancha Ilaiah, "Tryst with English Medium," *Deccan Herald*, 15 July 2008.

47. Thomas B. Macaulay's (1800–1859) infamous 1835 "Minute on Education" argued that an elite class of Indians should learn English so that they could become like the English "in matters of taste and opinion" and, most important, so that they could serve the interests of the colonial administration. Macaulay did not support English instruction on a larger scale primarily because he believed it would be administratively and financially impossible. Instead, he thought elite Indians should learn English and then introduce scientific vocabulary into the vernaculars. Macaulay is remembered today for having denigrated Indian culture, so he is usually a negative figure; however, many Indians also believe he was right in advocating English education and credit him with that fact.

48. See Vrinda Gopinath, "Happy Birthday Lord Macaulay, Thank You for 'Dalit Empowerment,'" *Indian Express*, 26 October 2006; and Gail Omvedt, "Why Dalits Want English," *Times of India*, Opinion, 9 November 2006.

CHAPTER 2

1. See Robert Darnton's essay, "Literary Surveillance in the British Raj: The Contradictions of Liberal Imperialism" (2000).

2. Partha Chatterjee, *The Nation and Its Fragments: Colonial and Postcolonial Histories* (1993), 25–26. I first heard Chatterjee mention this story about *Amrita Bazar Patrika* in a course lecture at Columbia University in 2004 and thank him for that; I have taken the liberty to interpret the story, and any fault therein is my own.

3. In Chatterjee's schema, the differing rules are also about the construction of "civil society," a space for "rights-bearing citizens," as opposed to "political society," a space for those—the majority—without rights but who are nonetheless monitored by government agencies and institutions.

4. Mohandas K. Gandhi, *Harijan,* 25 August 1946. It was later reprinted in *Evil Wrought by the English Medium* (1958), a political pamphlet that brings together many of Gandhi's columns on the question of a national language.

5. M.K. Gandhi, *Hind Swaraj and Other Writings* (1997), 103, 104.

6. Dipesh Chakrabarty, *Provincializing Europe: Postcolonial Thought and Historical Difference* (2000), 155.

7. Franco Moretti, "The Novel: History and Theory," *New Left Review* 52 (2008): 113.

8. See, for example, Harish Trivedi's discussion of the novel's Urdu intonations and form: "Ahmed Ali: *Twilight in Delhi,*" in *Major Indian Novels* (1985), 41–73.

9. Ahmed Ali, *Twilight in Delhi* (1994), xvi.

10. In *An Imperial Vision: Indian Architecture and Britain's Raj* (2002), Thomas Metcalf documents the import of the architectural history of Delhi in this precise period and points to many of the same tensions between urban space and political and cultural power that are subjects in *Twilight in Delhi.*

11. Ahmed Ali, *Twilight in Delhi,* 3.

12. Ahmed Ali, *Twilight in Delhi,* 28.

13. Ahmed Ali, *Twilight in Delhi,* 5.

14. Ahmed Ali, *Twilight in Delhi,* 176.

15. Priya Joshi, *In Another Country: Colonialism, Culture, and the English Novel in India* (2002), 226–27.

16. The process whereby Hindi takes on more Sanskrit-based vocabulary and Urdu more Persian begins in the eighteenth century. See Christopher King's *One Language, Two Scripts: The Hindi Movement in Nineteenth-Century North India* (1994); Christopher Shackle and Rupert Snell's *Hindi and Urdu since 1800* (1990); and Amrit Rai's *A House Divided: The Origin and Development of Hindi/Hindavi* (1984).

17. Urdu, like English, has no regional affiliation in India but was a lingua franca in north India and a language of urban sophistication, and only later in its history so exclusively associated with Muslim identity. Gail Minault ("Delhi College and Urdu," *Annual of Urdu Studies* 14 [1999]: 119–34) has shown how Urdu itself had been a mediating language for the later Mughal emperors, when Persian had been the language of the court and officialdom. During that time (the seventeenth century), Urdu become a "mediating language between Persian and regional Indian languages, and between the imperial court and various regional powers" (121). Urdu retained its place as the language of everyday discourse in large parts of north India until the beginning of the twentieth century.

18. Ahmed Ali, *Twilight in Delhi,* 10.
19. Ahmed Ali, *Twilight in Delhi,* 132–33.
20. Two excellent accounts of partition with special relevance to the violence that occurred in Delhi are Gyanendra Pandey's *Remembering Partition: Violence, Nationalism, and History in India* (2002) and Urvashi Butalia's *The Other Side of Silence: Voices from the Partition of India* (2000). On the question of the post-partition relationship between religious identity and language—especially Punjabi, Hindi, and Urdu—see Paul R. Brass's classic analysis *Language, Religion, and Politics in North India* (1974).
21. Anita Desai, *In Custody* (1984), 14.
22. Anita Desai, *In Custody,* 15.
23. Anita Desai, *In Custody,* 23–24.
24. Anita Desai, *In Custody,* 24.
25. Anita Desai, *In Custody,* 155–56.
26. Anita Desai, "Various Lives," in *Lives in Translation: Bilingual Writers on Identity and Creativity* (2003), 15–16.
27. Describing this "refraction," A.K. Ramanujan has interestingly written about literature's "special contribution" being "its vision, its intuitive grasp of structure, its perspective; not the facts themselves so viewed, but the facts as seen by the imaginative accuracy of a mind that is not merely factual." For him, literature offers "patterns" and "hypotheses" rather than "facts." See his essay, "Towards an Anthology of City Images" (448–62) in *The Collected Essays of A.K. Ramanujan* (1999). I find his perspective—with its emphasis on analyzing the symbolic values created in literary texts—especially pertinent to my reading of Desai's and Ali's novels.
28. In her example, she discusses the Sanskritization of Bengali. See Gayatri Spivak, "Translating into English," in *Nation, Language, and the Ethics of Translation* (2005), 93–110.
29. Aijaz Ahmad likens the split of Hindi and Urdu to a collapsing bridge and sees the split as a watershed in terms of both literary production and the way writing communities themselves (those of Hindi, Urdu, and Punjabi) were fragmented and then reconstituted. See "In the Mirror of Urdu: Recompositions of Nation and Community, 1947–65," in his *Lineages of the Present* (1996), 103–28.
30. Harish Trivedi, "The Progress of Hindi, Part 2: Hindi and the Nation," in *Literary Cultures in History: Reconstructions from South Asia* (2003), 966.

CHAPTER 3

1. Nirad Chaudhuri, *The Intellectual in India* (1967), 73.
2. Nirad Chaudhuri, *The Intellectual in India,* 81.
3. The full list appears in Joseph Slaughter's *Human Rights, Inc: The World Novel, Narrative Form, and International Law* (2007), 270. Also see his interesting discussion of the politics of publishing in "developing" societies. He shows how literacy in particular becomes "bound with the other responsibilities delivered through the international legal formulation of a right

to development" linked to a notion of "personal development" that he goes on to argue is part of the post-Enlightenment human rights discourse (273).

4. Philip G. Altbach, "Publishing in the Third World: Issues and Trends for the 21st Century," in his edited volume, *Publishing and Development in the Third World* (1992). Important works on language politics and print culture in the colonial period include: Veena Naregal's *Language Politics, Elites, and the Public Sphere: Western India under Colonialism* (2001); *Print Areas: Book History in India* (2004), edited by Swapan Chakraborty and Abhijit Gupta; Rimi B. Chatterjee's *Empires of the Mind: A History of the Oxford University Press in India under the Raj* (2006); Ulrike Starke's *An Empire of Books: The Naval Kishore Press and the Diffusion of the Printed Word in Colonial India* (2007); and Farina Mir's *The Social Space of Language: Vernacular Culture in British Colonial Punjab* (2010).

5. His books that came out prior to this one were all published in New York and include *The Autobiography of an Unknown Indian* (1951), *Passage to England* (1959), and *The Continent of Circe* (1965).

6. Author interview with Vidya Rao in Delhi in 2001.

7. When Orient Longman became an Indian company in 1968, the British educational publisher, Pearson, took over the name "Longman" globally, but Orient Longman continued to be used in India until 2006, when Pearson Education, the owner of the Longman name worldwide, filed a suit against Orient Longman in a British court to assert its right to the Longman brand. Under the terms of the 2008 settlement that was reached, Orient Longman agreed to stop using the Longman brand by November 2008. The company's new name is Orient Black Swan.

8. This was also the period in which Purushottama Lal (1929–2010), working out of Calcutta, was fostering literary production in English through the Writer's Workshop, which provided a forum for numerous poets and some fiction writers, including Vikram Seth and Anita Desai. He published around 3,500 slim volumes from the 1960s until his death in 2010. See Meenakshi Mukherjee's tribute to his work in her article, "Writer's Workshop@ Fifty," *The Hindu*, 1 March 2009, www.hindu.com/lr/2009/03/01/stories /2009030150010100.htm.

9. This chapter is based on author interviews with Ravi Dayal in Delhi in 2001.

10. Ravi Dayal, "New Writing in English: The Problem," *Seminar* (August 1991): 12–14.

11. Rukun Advani, "Irreplaceable Pioneer," *Telegraph* (Calcutta), Sunday, 11 June 2006.

12. Madhu Jain, "Sujan Singh Park," in *City Improbable: An Anthology of Writings on Delhi* (2001), 212–13.

13. Khushwant Singh, "The Romance of New Delhi," in *Khushwant Singh's India: A Mirror for Its Monsters and Monstrosities* (1969), 207–8.

14. It also might explain why Singh, somewhat more infamously, decided to support Indira Gandhi's Emergency (1975–77) and allow the *Weekly* to be censored rather than shut it down, as many other periodicals had. In his essay, "Why I Supported the Emergency," reprinted in *Why I Supported the*

Emergency: Essays and Profiles (2009), Singh doesn't really say why he supported it, except for citing his opposition to the leader of the anti–Indira Gandhi movement, Jayaprakash Narayan, when he called for the police and army to revolt against the government. He felt Narayan had gone too far. Most of the very short essay mentions how others responded and then cursorily explains that the government censorship was haphazard and not seriously enforced anyway. He ends the essay by noting how bad the Emergency turned out to be and that it shouldn't be allowed to happen again. For more on the Emergency as experienced in Delhi, see Emma Tarlo's *Unsettling Memories: Narratives of the Emergency in Delhi* (2003).

15. The scholarship on Indian secularism is vast. For a range of important perspectives see Rajeev Bhargava's edited volume, *Secularism and Its Critics* (1998), and *The Crisis of Secularism in India* (2007), edited by Anuradha Dingwaney Needham and Rajeswari Sunder Rajan.

16. In *The Great Indian Middle Class* (1998), Pavan Varma describes the moral values of the English-speaking middle class since independence as being inspired by the nationalist struggle and the high moral stance of leaders such as Gandhi and Nehru. However, he says that this class of people was spurred on by their self-interest even then. The book argues that in the decades after independence, this class lost their moral perspective on society and governance, one that had at least rhetorically took the uplifting of the poor as its chief aim. What this political rhetoric achieved was a constant awareness of middle-class privilege and responsibility to the poor; as a result, it reined in the social acceptability of acquiring and showing off one's wealth.

17. Author interview with Naina Dayal and Mala Dayal in Delhi on 23 April 2008.

18. The Mathurs also consider themselves "Dilliwallahs par excellence," as Dayal himself notes in his short essay, "A Kayastha's View of Delhi" (2010), even as he laments how "the city is now barely aware of them" (178). And then, commenting further on the increasingly amorphous and anonymous identity of Delhi, he writes, "Even the Mathurs have stopped calling themselves Dilliwallahs. How can it be otherwise if you live in GK II, your spouse perhaps a Sikh, your son an investment banker in New York, your daughter-in-law an Italian and your grandson unable to digest a decent, spiced kebab made of goat meat?" (181).

19. Homi Bhabha, *The Location of Culture* (1994). See especially the essay, "Of Mimicry and Man: The Ambivalence of Colonial Discourse."

20. See Sheila Dhar, *Raga'n Josh: Stories from a Musical Life* (2005).

21. Ravi Dayal Publisher, put out a collection of remembrances by writers (including Amitav Ghosh, I. Allan Sealy, Khushwant Singh, Upamanyu Chatterjee, Gopal Gandhi, Rukun Advani, and Mukul Kesavan) who had gone to St. Stephen's. The book makes a somewhat tongue-in-cheek connection between Indian English writing and the college. For some, it also confirmed a "boy's club" mentality among this group of writers. See *The Fiction of St. Stephen's* (2000), ed. Aditya Bhattacharjea and Lola Chatterjee.

22. The Mandal Commission report was one of the defining events of the early 1990s and continues to be at the center of one of the most pressing social

debates: "reservations" (quotas) for low-caste groups. For a detailed discussion, see chapter 13 of Nicholas Dirk's *Castes of Mind: Colonialism and the Making of Modern India* (2001).

23. When Dayal retired in 1987, his official successor was Santosh Mookerjee, who himself retired in 1992. Mookerjee was succeeded by Neil O'Brien, who retired in 1995. At that time Advani was officially made the director of the OUP Academic Division. Advani stayed in this position until February 2000, when he left to start (with Anuradha Roy) Permanent Black, an academic publishing house.

24. Author interview with Rukun Advani in Delhi in 2001. Advani's own telling of how the journal got started is humorously recounted in his "Introduction: Civility, Civilisation, and Chivas Regal," in *Written for Ever: The Best of* Civil Lines (2009). He chalks up the journal's demise to the fact that writers are now so dispersed that an Indian journal doesn't quite make sense the way it might have previously. However, he doesn't mention the import of editorial location, which, as I argue, does matter. Editorial will and funding appear to be the real reasons (dutifully explained in Advani's introduction) the journal did not survive. What is also true is that the journal never caught on beyond a very limited readership, possibly not much beyond the confines of Civil Lines–type localities. Today there are other India-based literary journals that publish quality writing in English, including *Little Magazine* (featuring many translations from the bhashas into English), *Caravan* (focusing on long form journalistic essays), *Pratilipi* (an online journal in Hindi and English), and *Almost Island* (an online journal of Indian and international writing).

25. Introduction, *Civil Lines* 2 (1995), 2.

26. Penguin India (part of the larger U.K. Penguin Group) began publishing in 1985 (under the editorship of David Davidar) and soon became the country's largest seller of literary fiction in English. Urvashi Butalia, who cofounded Kali for Women and now runs Zubaan, describes the partnerships between "indigenous publishers" and multinationals such as Penguin, HarperCollins, and Random House as being a strength in Indian publishing today. One does not necessarily have to replace or stamp out the other, as is the fear among some small, independent publishers. Butalia's point is that small publishers are thriving in many of the Indian languages, not only English, so the diversity of publishers is increasing, not decreasing. She cites Ravi Dayal Publisher, and Zubaan as being examples of small, independent publishers who have linked up with multinationals. See her article, "New Horizons, New Challenges," *The Hindu*, Literary Review, 4 January 2009, 1.

CHAPTER 4

1. My interviews and discussions with Ashok, Arun, and Ameeta Maheshwari occurred in Delhi in 2001.

2. As spoken by newscasters on Doordarshan, the national television channel. Alok Rai, in discussion with Shahid Amin and Palash Krishna Mehrotra, identifies this standardized (Sanskritized) Hindi or "Manak Hindi," as it is called in Hindi itself, as sterile and devoid of emotions. Rai makes the point

that even if some creative writers can avoid or bypass standard Hindi, their audiences have been subject to an educational apparatus that supports it. See "A Debate between Alok Rai and Shahid Amin Regarding Hindi" (2005), 194.

3. The translation of Valmiki's *Joothan* into English has also been significant for the way it has raised the profile of Dalit writing more generally. See Valmiki's *Joothan: A Dalit's Life* (2003), Arun Prabha Mukherjee's English translation from the Hindi, which includes a fine introduction by the translator to the text and to Dalit literature more generally. See also *Touchable Tales* (2003), in which S. Anand, cofounder of the first Dalit publishing house in English, Navayana, corrals a number of commentators to reflect on the idea of Dalit writing and the politics of publishing. Sharmila Rege's introduction to her book, *Writing Caste, Writing Gender* (2006), has an especially good discussion of the pitfalls of the reappropriation of Dalit writing and politics using the interviews collected in Anand's volume as a launching pad.

4. What has changed is that Indian publishers now bid for some books, so some Indian writers are for the first time able to garner lucrative book advances in India. A cover story in *Outlook*, "Books & Bucks: The Big Fat Advance Finally Arrived in Indian Publishing" (11 February 2008), reported that Indians "no longer have to knock on foreign doors" and that the leading English-language publishers in India are now ready to pay for books first and worry about recouping their investments later. The advances range from 3 to 6 lakhs ($7,500–$15,000) for first-time writers to 44 lakhs ($110,000) for the veteran writer Amitav Ghosh's Ibis trilogy (Penguin India). Since that article was published, my informal conversations with publishers lead me to believe that the advances are lower (in the 1–2 lakh range) except for the top-rung, already well known writers.

5. Sheila Sandhu recounts that her husband bought majority shares in Rajkamal Prakashan in the 1960s, and how she soon after became involved and took over running the publishing house. She was literate in English and Punjabi, and reminisces about her Hindi, "I began to work a twelve-hour day in an office that published in a language I did not know, in a script I could hardly even read." However, she soon schooled herself in the *Nayi Kahani* (New Short Story) movement that sought to portray urban realism and featured writers such as Nirmal Verma, Mohan Rakesh, Bhisham Sahni and Rajendra Yadav; and she travelled to Banaras (Varanasi), Allahabad, Lucknow, and Patna to meet authors. Over the years, she stayed devoted to publishing high-quality literature and nurtured at least a generation of writers by hosting literary salons at her home on Ring Road in Delhi. The Hindi poet Kailash Vajpeyi described (in an author interview in 2009) the scene at Sandhu's to me as "evening after evening of good food, poetry, and gossip." In her own recollection, Sandhu says of that time, "Our home began to fill . . . with voices, poems, quarrels, songs, jokes and arguments. Not a month passed without a mushaira or celebration for yet another Sahitya Akademi Award—of which Rajkamal authors had over twenty odd to their credit. . . . Punjabi, Urdu and Hindi began to rub shoulders with each other. In the beginning they sat together formally, ill at ease like distant cousins who have reason to mistrust the other. Then they began to speak, I daresay to even converse, if not enjoy

the company and work of each other." See the transcript of her interview in *Women Who Dared,* ed. Ritu Menon (2002), 8–24.

Sandhu also prides herself on not having given in to more lucrative English-language publishing, especially, at that time in nonliterary realms such as textbooks. Interestingly, today, Rajkamal *is* considering publishing some titles in English; however, the reasoning for doing so is not only monetary, but instead shows how the literary field and the relationships between languages are changing. These changes are also reflected by the fact that most MNC publishers in India today, including Penguin, are beginning to publish select bhasha titles in the original languages.

6. The first Bengali edition of *Lajja* was published in Bangladesh in 1993. The novel was published in its English translation by Penguin India in 1994 and in Hindi translation by Vani Prakashan in 1998.

7. Author interview with Amar Varma in 2001.

8. Varma went on to become chair of the Export Marketing Council of the Federation of Indian Publishers.

9. See, for example, Patrick Eisenlohr's *Little India: Diaspora, Time, and Ethnolinguistic Belonging in Hindu Mauritius* (2006). In his study of language politics in Mauritius, Eisenlohr gives the interesting example of the outcry among Tamil-ancestry Mauritians when there was a move by the government of Mauritius to change the vertical order of languages as listed on the nation's banknotes from English-Tamil-Hindi to English-Hindi-Tamil. Tamil-ancestry Indo-Mauritians were protecting their place vis-à-vis the more dominant Hindi-ancestry Indo-Mauritians; however, most Mauritians (including those who are part of the Indian diaspora in Mauritius, whether of Tamil or Hindi ancestry) speak the more neutral and locally derived Creole language. Eisenlohr's study shows how ancestral linguistic attachments nevertheless persist as emblems of group identification and symbolic domination in the context of contemporary politics in Mauritius.

10. Vijay Mishra, *The Literature of the Indian Diaspora: Theorizing the Diasporic Imaginary* (2007), 245–55.

11. Multibody Fact Finding Committee, MGAHV, Wardha, 1 June 2006.

12. Author interview with Ravikant in November 2008.

CHAPTER 5

1. The Jaipur Literature Festival is a perfect example of the hype associated with Anglophone Indian cultural production, eliciting praise or disdain depending on one's feeling about the commercialism of such events, and often, position in them. The festival is organized each year by William Dalrymple and Namita Gokhale, and funded by DSC, a large Indian infrastructure corporation aiming to do good works in the cultural realm. DSC is partnered with a range of corporate sponsors (and supporters, including the Sahitya Akademi) that finance the lavish event, and as of 2011 began to award a best book prize that comes with an award of US$50,000. The festival is held every January for five days in the city of Jaipur, which is a half-hour flight, five-hour car journey, and twelve-hour bus ride from Delhi; how you get there says something

about your standing at the festival. Invited writers stay in five-star hotels, yet the festival is also open to all free of charge, and so you see local groups of school students alongside socialites, celebrities, and swarms of aspiring writers, author admirers, and others. Largely because of Dalrymple, the festival has featured some of the biggest names in world literature, from V.S. Naipaul and Ian McEwan to J.M. Coetzee and Orhan Pamuk. Gokhale, meanwhile, is responsible for integrating bhasha writers—such as Alka Saraogi, Girish Karnad, and K. Satchidanandan—in a significant way into the festival proceedings; however, the vast majority of Indian and Indian-origin authors at the festival are English-writing ones. The festival feels like a big party in that each year the numbers get bigger—from several hundred to over 50,000 at last count—and there is an array of literary events interspersed with music, dancing, and evening banquets. In terms of the density of writers from different backgrounds in India, for these few days at least it has become a fecund literary space. The panels are crowded and substantive discussions do occur amid the book signings, videotapings, and photo flashes. After the 2007 event, the festival was criticized for having excluded bhasha writers and succumbing to the celebrity of writers such as Salman Rushdie and others who were in attendance; in 2008 a prefestival event was organized, called "Translating Bharat," with the promotional tag line "Language, Globalisation, and the Right to Be Read." It focused on the literature and discourse of bhasha writers, though no one seemed to appreciate the segregation of their event from the main festival. By 2009 the bhasha writers were invited for panels as part of the Jaipur Literature Festival itself. In 2010 the festival included a number of panels on Dalit issues, featuring writers such as Omprakash Valmiki, Kancha Ilaiah, and Chandrabhan Prasad. A second festival, the Hay Kerala, produced by the same production company as Jaipur's (Teamwork Productions) and drawing on most of the same networks of writers, though on a much smaller scale, has also started to be held in India as of November 2010. Unlike the Jaipur Festival, which is a homegrown production, the Hay is a British literary festival franchise that happens in numerous cities around the world. What is significant is that Indian literature in English has become a window—albeit a small one—into other Indian literatures through these festivals. What is being debated now is to what extent Indian letters wants to be defined through these festivals and the parameters for cultural and literary engagements they set.

2. *Crore* means 10 million, and in monetary terms, 100 lakhs; one lakh equals 100,000 rupees.

3. The Akademi also used to publish a half-yearly journal titled *Samsrkita Pratibha* devoted to contemporary writings in Sanskrit. I was told that its publication had been suspended due to issues of funding but that it may be reinstated.

4. K. Satchidanandan, *Sahitya Akademi General Information Bulletin* (2002), 97.

5. The question of refusals of awards might also have much to do with the kind of "stage"—regional, national, or global—on which one finds oneself. This aspect of Roy's refusal is explored in chapter 8.

6. Satchidanandan, *Sahitya Akademi General Information Bulletin*, 1.

7. Sujit Mukherjee, "New Literary History" *Explorations in Literary History* 8, no. 2 (Winter 1977): 225–34; 226.

8. Sujit Mukherjee, "New Literary History," 228.

9. There had also been a complaint by the Marathi advisory board about granting language status to Konkani (which is spoken in Goa and parts of Karnataka and Kerala), which it claimed was a "dialect of Marathi." Both incidents are described by D.S. Rao in *Five Decades: A Short History of the Sahitya Akademi* (2004), 36 and 54.

10. *Encyclopedia of Indian Literature,* vol. 1, ed. Amaresh Datta (1987), xv.

11. M.M. Bakhtin, *The Dialogic Imagination: Four Essays* (1981), 295.

12. Salman Rushdie, "Damme! This Is the Oriental Scene for You!" *New Yorker,* 23 and 30 June 1997, 54. Subsequently reprinted as the introduction to *Mirrorwork* (1997), an anthology of Indian writing (all of which was originally written in English, except for Saadat Hasan Manto's Urdu short story, "Toba Tek Singh").

13. Orhan Pamuk, in response to his garnering a worldwide readership through the many translations of his novels from Turkish, describes the opposing assumptions in the authenticity debate well, even if his conception of "national" is more easily aligned with the European notion of one nation representing one language. In "non-Western nations," Pamuk writes, "novelists who do not write for national audiences are [seen as] exoticizing their country for 'foreign consumption' and inventing problems that have no basis in reality." But then he points out that there is "a parallel suspicion in the West, where many readers believe that local literatures should remain local, pure, and true to their national roots." There is, he says, a desire for an authentic version of Otherness whereby these readers' "secret fear is that becoming a 'world' writer who draws from traditions outside his own culture will cause one to lose one's authenticity." "Who Do You Write For?," in his *Other Colours: Essays and a Story* (2007), 243. What we see, then, following Pamuk, is a cultural suspicion for writers and their audiences, and in many ways, the desire of the "Western" reader vindicates the charge of the nativist. Both, it seems, are suspicious of literature that would presume to go beyond the "natural" experience and "national" location of the writer, whereby there is a simple equation between nation and culture and the expectation of a literary portrayal based on this equation.

14. Ngũgĩ wa Thiong'o, *Decolonising the Mind: The Politics of Language in African Literature* (1986), 9.

15. Ngũgĩ wa Thiong'o, *Decolonising the Mind,* 11–12. Chinua Achebe, who is from Nigeria, has an altogether different take on the question of linguistic justice in the postcolonial African context. Of English, he writes, "I have been given this language and I intend to use it." At the same time, he notes that he hopes there will always be others who "choose to write in their native tongue and insure that our ethnic literature will flourish side by side with the national ones." See "The African Writer and the English Language," in his *Morning Yet on Creation Day* (1975), 103.

16. Sabitha T.P., "What He Said, What She Said," *Little Magazine* 7, no. 1–2 (2007): 197. I heard the author recite the poem at the Prakriti Poetry Festival in Chennai on 27 December 2008.

CHAPTER 6

1. Bharati Mukherjee, "The Way Back," in *Genius of Language: Fifteen Writers Reflect on Their Mother Tongues* (2004), 24.

2. Lisa Mitchell, *Language, Emotion, and Politics in South India: The Making of a Mother Tongue* (2009), 159; Kothari and Wakabayashi, *Decentering Translation Studies: India and Beyond* (2009), 12.

3. See, for instance, Sugata Srinivasaraju's *Keeping Faith with the Mother Tongue: The Anxieties of a Local Culture* (2008). In this collection of reportage, the author laments the increasing dominance of English and the knowledge it creates as a global language in the Indian context and elsewhere, and advocates for the mobilization of minority languages as a kind of antiglobalization movement.

4. A.K. Ramanujan, "Telling Tales," in *The Collected Essays of A.K. Ramanujan* (1999), 449–50.

5. See his essay, "Towards the concept of a New Nationhood: Languages and Literature in India," and others in *U.R. Ananthamurthy Omnibus* (2008).

6. Geetanjali Shree, *Mai,* translated from the Hindi by Nita Kumar (2000), 3. Shrilal Shukla's classic, *Raag Darbari* (1968), is another Hindi novel that contains a discourse on English and its relationship to Hindi; it is a satirical take on politics and bureaucracy, also set in Uttar Pradesh.

7. Nita Kumar, afterword to *Mai,* 204.

8. I am sometimes persuaded by such positions as Roland Barthes's, in which "the death of the author" necessarily precedes the text, but I am also compelled by the way Indian literary modernity has been premised on an author's self-consciousness about language and its relationship to power and history. I would not go so far as to claim that there has been a "rebirth of the author," but I would question the timeliness of her death. See Barthes, "The Death of the Author," in *Image, Music, Text* (1988), as well as Foucault's "What Is an Author?" (1977).

9. Published originally in English in 1989 by Manohar Publishers in Delhi under the name Geetanjali Pandey; Shree is her pen name.

10. Geetanjali Shree, "Hello, How Are You, I Hope," *Pratilipi,* December 2008. http://pratilipi.in/2008/12/hello-how-are-you-i-hope-geetanjali-shree/.

11. Geetanjali Shree, "Hello, How Are You, I Hope."

12. When I first visited Shree at home in 2001, her downstairs neighbors were Nirmal Verma and Gagan Gill. Her upstairs neighbor was the Hindi translator Girthi Rathi. Later, in 2008, she and her husband had moved to another flat in the same complex.

13. Geetanjali Shree, *Mai,* 34.

14. Geetanjali Shree, *Mai,* 44.

15. Geetanjali Shree, *Mai,* 3.

16. Geetanjali Shree, *Mai,* 67.

17. Lawrence Cohen, *No Aging in India: Alzheimer's, the Bad Family, and Other Modern Things* (1998), 104.

18. Geetanjali Shree, *Mai,* 30.

19. Geetanjali Shree, *Mai,* 141–42.

20. Geetanjali Shree, "Hello, How Are You, I Hope."

21. Geetanjali Shree, *Mai,* 53.

22. Geetanjali Shree, *Mai,* 36.

23. Geetanjali Shree, "Hello, How Are You, I Hope."

24. Geetanjali Shree, "From the Polyphonic World of Hindi Fiction," *Caravan* 3: 2 (February 2011).

25. Sara Suleri, *Meatless Days,* 177.

26. Shashi Deshpande, "The Hornet's Nest," in *Writing from the Margin and Other Essays,* 71.

27. The question of what can and cannot be said or expressed in different languages came up with several bilingual writers I spoke to. Mrinal Pande, a well-known bilingual writer and, when I met her, the editor of the Hindi edition of *Hindustan Times,* told me a story (in Delhi on 12 May 2008) about how a translation from English to Hindi of a public health pamphlet on sexually transmitted diseases caused an uproar when it was passed out to villagers in Uttaranchal. The Hindi used was crude and vulgar and deeply offended its target audience; a scandal ensued. For Pande, this experience pointed to the fact that there was no everyday vocabulary with which to discuss sexuality in the vernaculars. She explained that she also met with activists working among sex workers in Tamil- and Kannada-speaking regions who reported similar incidents, saying "talking about sex means either using the gutter language used by school boys [in the vernaculars], or [using] English, since ordinary Indians do not talk about sexuality in public." This made Pande reflect even further (in an email to me some days after I'd met her): "I realize Indians have not talked about sex in vernaculars of day-to-day use variety, for decades! As a result you can discuss sex in English or in Sanskritized Hindi (borrowing terminology from the Kamasutra and Ganika Shastra) but not in conversational Hindi, Bangla, Kannada or Tamil." Pande's point was that even if there had once been a vocabulary for love and sex in Indian literature, it was now so far removed from everyday life and conversation that it would not be a recognizable language for most people. For authors like Geetanjali Shree, finding a language in Hindi for such realities is precisely to confront the disjuncture between social lapses in the language and the desire for literary expression.

CHAPTER 7

1. The Sahitya Akademi considers any work published in the preceding five years for its annual awards; hence, *Cuckold* (1997) was still eligible to win in 2000.

2. Kiran Nagarkar, presentation at Writers' Meet, "We might as Well Be Living on Different Planets," Annual Festival of Letters, Sahitya Akademi, New Delhi, 21 February 2001. He went on to write an essay based on his speech, titled "The Worlds of India," which appeared in the 12 March 2001 issue of *Outlook.*

3. The poet Dilip Chitre explained to me, when I met him in Chennai in 2008, how there were four Maharashtrian writers—Nagarkar, Arun

Kolatkar, Vilas Sarang, and himself—who wrote in Marathi and English and who were all vilified by the Marathi literary establishment for doing so. He suggested that, as a result, in many ways they formed their own literary enclave, where all four writers forged their own self-styled modernist works. The poet Arvind Krishna Mehrotra describes what he calls this "dual citizenship in the world of letters," from Vilas Sarang's perspective, in his Introduction to *A Concise History of Indian Literature in English* (2008), 26–29.

4. In this regard, Arjun Appadurai and Carol Breckenridge have written that "what is distinctive about any particular society is not the fact or extent of its modernity, but rather its distinctive debates about modernity, the historical and cultural trajectories that shape its appropriation of the means of modernity, and the cultural sociology (principally of class and state) that determines who gets to play with modernity and what defines the rules of the game." See "Public Modernity in India," in *Consuming Modernity: Public Culture in a South Asian World,* ed. Carol Breckenridge (1995), 16. In my reckoning, it is precisely through defining the "rules of the game" that literary practice and language ideologies intersect.

5. As Kathryn Woolard writes, "Ideologies of language are not about language alone. Rather, they envision and enact ties of language to identity, to aesthetics, to morality, and to epistemology." See her "Introduction: Language Ideology as a Field of Inquiry," in *Language Ideologies: Practice and Theory* (1998), 3.

6. Gandhi has long held both political and cultural posts. He was a member of the Indian Administrative Service from 1968 to 1992, served as the first director of the Nehru Centre in London, and served as the governor of West Bengal. He has also written two novels in English and writes columns on social and political issues for *The Hindu.*

7. Seth, *Koi Accha-sa Ladka* (1998), preface to the Hindi edition; my translation from the Hindi.

8. Harish Trivedi, "Translation as Recovery: *A Suitable Boy* as *Koi Accha-sa Ladka,*" *Book Review* 22, no. 9 (1998): 30–31.

9. Harish Trivedi, "Translation as Recovery," 30.

10. Hasan Suroor, "Vikram Seth Strikes It Rich," *The Hindu,* 18 July 2003, www.hinduonnet.com/2003/07/18/stories/2003071804270100.htm.

11. Trivedi, "Translation as Recovery," 30.

12. This question arises in a number of novels, most notably in Rohinton Mistry's *A Fine Balance* (1995) and Arundhati Roy's *The God of Small Things* (1997). Novels by non-Dalit writers are often criticized for empathetic portrayals that are either apolitical, portraying Dalits mostly as pitiable characters, or give them no function other than their interaction with the narratives of more complexly rendered, high-caste characters' lives. For a good discussion of the topic, see S. Anand's, "Lighting Out for the Territory: The Arduous Journey of Modern Dalit Literature," *Caravan* 3, no. 2 (February 2011).

13. Vikram Seth, *A Suitable Boy,* 203; emphasis added. The omission occurs on page 248 of the Hindi translation.

14. Vikram Seth, *A Suitable Boy,* 575.

15. Vikram Seth, *A Suitable Boy,* 576–77. The omission occurs on page 629 of the Hindi translation.

16. In an e-mail correspondence with me (15 June 2006), the translator, Gopal Gandhi, wrote that Seth had given him the "liberty to skip portions" of the text but that Gandhi did not discuss any specific deletions from the translation with Seth. Gandhi brushed off Chatterjee's comments on his translation as being "a flight of fancy," but he did not provide an alternative reasoning for the specific deletions regarding animal waste and skinning practices, except to say that he had "no agenda" other than to render effectively the story "in the *zubaan* [language] of its first *khayaal* [utterance]." It should be noted that I take his comments at face value; my interest is in how Enakshi Chatterjee presents the issue of Gandhi's translation to her audience at the Sahitya Akademi.

17. Alok Rai, *Hindi Nationalism,* 9.

18. Mayawati, who heads the Bahujan Samaj Party (BSP), became the first Dalit to serve as chief minister of an Indian state. She was first elected to that office in 1995 and has since been reelected three times.

19. See James Wood, *How Fiction Works.*

20. There is much gray area in the everyday reality and identifications of these characterizations. Many so-called liberals in the Anglicized urban middle classes, for instance, support Hindutva politics in the form of the BJP (Bharatiya Janata Party); whereas there are progressives who live more firmly in the world of Hindi.

21. Nicholas Dirks describes the politics of caste that enable these kinds of obfuscations as follows: "Caste has the dubious advantage of signaling class privilege, highlighting sociohistorically determined modes of access to and exclusion from resources and opportunities, and calling attention to the differentiated and particularistic forms of relationship to other social collectivities and religious beliefs and practices. In many ways like the category of gender, caste both interrogates and acknowledges difference." See his *Castes of Mind: Colonialism and the Making of Modern India* (2001), 295.

CHAPTER 8

1. See Amit Chaudhuri's "Beyond 'Confidence': Rushdie and the Creation Myth of Indian English Writing," in his *Clearing the Space* (2008). He continues his characterization of the Indian writer in English as follows: "He is solvent; preferably settled abroad. He's capable of addressing questions consonant with our emerging prestige. He is not a failure, a daydreamer, a misfit. . . . The triumphal narrative of Indian writing in English bores me; personally speaking, as a reader and writer, I feel almost no connection with it" (309–10).

2. Bill Buford, "The End of the English Novel," *Granta,* no. 3 (1980): 16.

3. Though, Paul Gilroy reminds us with his phrase "the art of darkness"—in reference to black British cultural production—that this "inclusion" is premised on the dubious notion that race enters Britain for the first time. Gilroy therefore argues that there is an inherent falsity to this celebration of black

arts in a new multicultural framework. See his *Small Acts: Thoughts on the Politics of Black Cultures* (1993), 74–85.

4. Bill Buford, "Declarations of Independence: Why Are There Suddenly So Many Indian Novelists?," *New Yorker,* 23 and 30 June 1997, 8.

5. Salman Rushdie has written, "Literature has little or nothing to do with a writer's home address" ("Damme, This Is the Oriental Scene for You!," 56).

6. *Vagartha* contained fiction, poetry, and critical works and was a well-regarded forum in the 1970s. The best of its creative work was published in the anthology *Another India* (1990), edited by Meenakshi Mukherjee and Nissim Ezekiel.

7. The societal perception of NRIs (nonresident Indians) by Indians has also changed. In the 1970s and 1980s there was a sense, especially in intellectual and literary circles, that NRIs had sold out for having settled abroad, that they were not doing enough for India, for its development, social or otherwise, and instead were contributing to "the brain drain." This perception started to change in the 1990s, largely because the forces of liberalization and new communication technologies made the connections and back-and-forth movements of people, capital, and ideas more fluid. Nivedita Menon and Aditya Nigam write that from the 1990s NRIs started to be seen as "resources to be harnessed for the new economic model." Further, they became "brain banks" able to invest their skills and knowledge in India's development. See their *Power and Contestation,* 10.

8. Meenakshi Mukherjee, *The Twice Born Fiction: Themes and Techniques of the Indian Novel in English* (1971), 23.

9. Arjun Appadurai, "Global Ethnoscapes: Notes and Queries for a Transnational Anthropology" in his *Modernity at Large,* 48.

10. G.N. Devy, *In Another Tongue: Essays on Indian English Literature* (1993), 116.

11. Meenakshi Mukherjee, *The Perishable Empire: Essays on Indian Writing in English* (2000), 181–82.

12. Kiran Desai, in conversation with Vikram Chandra, moderated by Rachel Donadio, at a Pen American Center event at the Morgan Library and Museum, New York City, 27 April 2007.

13. Rani Dharker, "An Interview with Salman Rushdie," *New Quest* 42 (November–December 1983): 351–60; quoted passages from 358–59.

14. Meenakshi Mukherjee, *The Perishable Empire,* 197.

15. Vikram Chandra, "The Cult of Authenticity," *Boston Review,* February–March 2000.

16. Vikram Chandra, in conversation with Kiran Desai, moderated by Rachel Donadio, at a Pen American Center event at the Morgan Library and Museum, New York City, 27 April 2007.

17. Adil Jussawalla, "Being There: Aspects of an Indian Crisis," *Bombay Review,* no. 1 (1989); reprinted in the Monsoon 2010 issue of *Almost Island,* http://almostisland.com/essay/being_there.php.

18. Jussawalla, "Being There: Aspect of an Indian Crisis," 24 (in original). Verma's essay that Jussawalla quotes from was originally written in Hindi,

"Apne Desh Wapasi," and then translated by Meenakshi Mukherjee as "Returning to One's Country" and published in *Vagartha* 13 (April 1976).

19. Amit Chaudhuri (b. 1961), a writer who comes from the same generation as Chandra, is at pains to describe his "alternate" sense of modernity in a number of essays that, in part, seek to outline a trajectory that runs parallel to and often in contrast to that of Salman Rushdie and the writers associated with the "boom" in Indian fiction in English—of which Chaudhuri sees himself "at an angle" to. It is a space he defines as composed of a critical humanism emerging from "high" cultural traditions of Bengali humanism and European modernity; yet he is careful to say that he does not pine for some lost "utopian" paradigm, but instead locates his interest in "the elisions that direct the binaries (East, West; high, low; native, foreign; fantasy, reality; elite, democratic)" (*Clearing a Space,* 11–12). This exploration occurs most interestingly when Chaudhuri writes about poetry and, in particular, in an essay linking Walter Benjamin's *flâneur* to the urban explorations in the poet Arun Kolatkar's *Jejuri;* see "Arun Kolatkar and the Tradition of Loitering," in *Clearing a Space.*

20. For instance, Ashok Vajpeyi told me that his only gripe with Indians who write in English is that most of them are "illiterate about other Indian languages." Author interview in Delhi on 18 November 2008.

21. Meenakshi Mukherjee, *The Perishable Empire,* 175.

22. Meenakshi Mukherjee, *Elusive Terrain: Culture and Literary Memory* (2008), 102.

23. Geeta Dharmarajan, the founder of the Katha series specializing in translations from the bhashas into English, regards these questions of power and cultural transmission as a set of compromises, but ones that must be made. She explained to me one afternoon at the Katha office in Delhi in 2001: "Multiple meanings are frozen when you have to choose one English word to stand in for the original word that carries many meanings, resonances." The point was to "avoid" the freezing of words. For a range of interesting examples relating to issues of power and translation, see Emily Apter's *The Translation Zone* (2006) and Rita Kothari and Judy Wakabayashi's edited volume, *Decentering Translation Studies: India and Beyond* (2009).

24. The story appeared on the front page of the *Times of India* on 20 March 2001, with the headline, "Amitav Ghosh Withdraws Book." Another story about Ghosh's decision appeared in *Outlook* on 19 March 2001, titled "The Conscientious Objector."

25. In 2002 the guidelines for the prize as stated on the Commonwealth Writers Prize website had added the following sentence: "Publishers must obtain the author's consent before submitting their book."

26. Salman Rushdie, "'Commonwealth Literature' Does Not Exist," in his *Imaginary Homelands* (1991), 61–70. Rushdie won the Commonwealth Writer's Prize for Best Book in the Eurasia section twice: in 2000 for *The Ground Beneath Her Feet* and in 2006 for *Shalimar the Clown;* in neither case did he go on to win the overall prize. In 2000, he attended the awards function for the prize, which was held in Delhi that year.

27. James English, *The Economy of Prestige: Prizes, Awards, and the Circulation of Cultural Value* (2005), 245, 246.

28. In 2008 Ghosh's novel *Sea of Poppies* was shortlisted for the Man Booker Prize, a £50,000 prize given exclusively to authors who are citizens of Britain, Ireland, or any one of the Commonwealth nations. The Man Group, which took over sponsorship of the prize in 2002, is a publicly traded investment company and hedge fund, and the eligibility for the prize is based on the author's citizenship. In this case, Ghosh did not ask that his novel be removed from the competition.

29. Arundhati Roy, Letter, dated 13 January 2006, to the Chairman of the Sahitya Akademi, as published in *The Hindu,* 16 January 2006.

30. D. S. Rao, *Five Decades: A Short History of the Sahitya Akademi,* 43.

31. James English, *The Economy of Prestige,* 218.

32. For the letter by one activist group asking Ghosh to refuse the prize, see U.S. Campaign for the Academic and Cultural Boycott of Israel (USACBI), "Boycott Israel? Amitav Ghosh and the Dan David Prize," www.usacbi.org/2010/05/boycott-israel-amitav-ghosh-the-dan-david-prize/. For Ghosh's outline of his political stance toward Israel and his reasoning for accepting the prize, see "'Writers Have No Armies,'" (cowritten with Margaret Atwood, with whom he shared the prize, it is a published version of their acceptance speech), *Outlook,* 10 May 2010 and "'It Would Have Been Completely Contrary to My Beliefs,'" *Outlook,* 17 May 2010. For Ghosh's explanation of why he accepted the Dan David Prize but not the Commonwealth Prize, see "'It Is Not Awarded by the State of Israel,'" *Outlook,* 20 April 2010.

33. James English, *The Economy of Prestige,* 222 and 223.

34. Arundhati Roy interviewed in Amitava Kumar, "The Un-victim," *Guernica* 15 (February 2011), www.guernicamag.com/interviews/2356/roy_2_15_11/.

CHAPTER 9

1. Chetan Bhagat, *Five Point Someone: What* Not *to Do at IIT!* (2004).

2. Upamanyu Chatterjee, *English, August* (1988), 5.

Bibliography

Achebe, Chinua. *Morning Yet on Creation Day.* New York: Anchor Press/Doubleday, 1975.

Adiga, Aravind. *The White Tiger.* New Delhi: HarperCollins, 2008.

Advani, Rukun, ed. *Written for Ever: The Best of Civil Lines.* New Delhi: Penguin Books and Ravi Dayal, 2009.

Ahmad, Aijaz. *In Theory: Nations, Classes, Literatures.* London: Verso, 1992.

———. *Lineages of the Present.* New Delhi: Tulika, 1996.

Ahmed, Ali. *Twilight in Delhi.* New York: New Directions, 1994.

Altbach, Philip G. "Publishing in the Third World: Issues and Trends for the 21st Century." In *Publishing and Development in the Third World,* edited by Philip G. Altbach. New Delhi: Vistaar Publications, 1992.

Ambedkar, Bhimrao Ramji. *Thoughts on Linguistic States.* Aligarh, U.P.: Anand Sahitya Sadan, 1989. First pub. 1955.

Amin, Shahid, and Alok Rai. "A Debate between Alok Rai and Shahid Amin Regarding Hindi," edited by Palash Krishna Mehrotra. *Annual of Urdu Studies* 20 (2005).

Anand, S. "Lighting Out for the Territory: The Arduous Journey of Modern Dalit Literature." *Caravan* 3, no. 2 (February 2011).

———, ed. *Touchable Tales: Publishing and Reading Dalit Literature.* Pondicherry: Navayana, 2003.

Ananthamurthy, U.R. *U.R. Ananthamurthy Omnibus.* Edited by N. Manu Chakravarthy. Gurgaon: Arvind Kumar Publishers, 2008.

Anderson, Benedict. *Imagined Communities: Reflections on the Origin and Spread of Nationalism.* London: Verso, 1991.

———. *Language and Power: Exploring Political Cultures in Indonesia.* Ithaca, NY: Cornell University Press, 1990.

Appadurai, Arjun. *Modernity at Large: Cultural Dimensions of Globalization.* Minneapolis: University of Minnesota Press, 1996.

Appadurai, Arjun, and Carol Breckenridge. "Public Modernity in India." In *Consuming Modernity: Public Culture in a South Asian World,* edited by Carol Breckenridge. Minneapolis: University of Minnesota Press, 1995.

Apter, Emily. *The Translation Zone: A New Comparative Literature.* Princeton: Princeton University Press, 2006.

Ashcroft, Bill, Gareth Griffiths, and Helen Tiffin. *The Empire Writes Back: Theory and Practice in Post-Colonial Literatures.* London: Routledge, 1989.

Azim, Firdous. *The Colonial Rise of the Novel.* London: Routledge, 1993.

Bakhtin, M.M. *The Dialogic Imagination: Four Essays.* Translated by Caryl Emerson and Michael Holquist. Edited by Michael Holquist. Austin: University of Texas Press, 1981.

Barthes, Roland. "The Death of the Author." In *Image, Music, Text.* Essays selected and translated by Stephen Heath. New York: Noonday Press, 1988.

Bhabha, Homi. *The Location of Culture.* London: Routledge, 1994.

Bhagat, Chetan. *Five Point Someone: What* Not *to Do at IIT!* New Delhi: Rupa & Co., 2004.

Bhargava, Rajeev, ed. *Secularism and Its Critics.* New Delhi: Oxford University Press, 1998.

Bhattacharjea, Aditya, and Lola Chatterjee, eds. *The Fiction of St. Stephen's.* New Delhi: Ravi Dayal, 2000.

Bose, Ashish. *Population of India: 2001 Census Results and Methodology.* New Delhi: B.R. Publishing, 2001.

Bourdieu, Pierre. *Distinction: A Social Critique of the Judgement of Taste.* Translated by Richard Nice. Cambridge, MA: Harvard University Press, 1984.

———. *The Field of Cultural Production: Essays on Art and Literature.* Edited and introduced by Randal Johnson. New York: Columbia University Press, 1993.

———. *The Rules of Art: Genesis and Structure of the Literary Field.* Translated by Susan Emanuel. Stanford, CA: Stanford University Press, 1996.

Boyarin, Jonathan, ed. *The Ethnography of Reading.* Berkeley: University of California Press, 1993.

Brass, Paul R. *Language, Religion, and Politics in North India.* Cambridge: Cambridge University Press, 1974.

Buford, Bill. "Declarations of Independence: Why Are There Suddenly So Many Indian Novelists?" *New Yorker,* 23 and 30 June 1997, 6–8.

———. "The End of the English Novel." *Granta,* no. 3 (1980): 7–16.

Butalia, Urvashi. *The Other Side of Silence: Voices from the Partition of India.* Durham, NC: Duke University Press, 2000.

Casanova, Pascale. *The World Republic of Letters.* Translated by M.B. Debevoise. Cambridge, MA: Harvard University Press, 2005.

Chakrabarty, Dipesh. *Provincializing Europe: Postcolonial Thought and Historical Difference.* Princeton: Princeton University Press, 2000.

Chakraborty, Swapan, and Abhijit Gupta, eds. *Print Areas: Book History in India.* Ranikhet: Permanent Black, 2004.

Chandra, Vikram. "The Cult of Authenticity." *Boston Review,* February–March 2000.
Chatterjee, Partha. *The Nation and Its Fragments: Colonial and Postcolonial Histories.* Princeton: Princeton University Press, 1993.
Chatterjee, Rimi B. *Empires of the Mind: A History of the Oxford University Press in India under the Raj.* New Delhi: Oxford University Press, 2006.
Chatterjee, Upamanyu. *English, August: An Indian Story.* London: Faber and Faber, 1988.
Chaudhuri, Amit. *Clearing a Space: Reflections on India, Literature, and Culture.* Ranikhet: Black Kite, 2008.
Chaudhuri, Nirad C. *The Intellectual in India.* New Delhi: Vir Publishing House, 1967.
Cohen, Lawrence. *No Aging in India: Alzheimer's, the Bad Family, and Other Modern Things.* Berkeley: University of California Press, 1998.
Cohn, Bernard. *An Anthropologist among the Historians and Other Essays.* New Delhi: Oxford University Press, 1987.
———. *Colonialism and Its Forms of Knowledge: The British in India.* Princeton: Princeton University Press, 1996.
Dalmia, Vasudha. "The Locations of Hindi." *Economic and Political Weekly* 38, no.14 (5 April 2003): 1377–84.
———. *The Nationalization of Hindu Traditions: Bharatendu Harischandra and Nineteenth-Century Banaras.* New Delhi: Oxford University Press, 1997.
Daniel, E. Valentine, and Jeffrey M. Peck, eds. *Culture/Contexture: Explorations in Anthropology and Literary Studies.* Berkeley: University of California Press, 1996.
Darnton, Robert. "Literary Surveillance in the British Raj: The Contradictions of Liberal Imperialism." *Book History* 4 (2000).
Das, Sisir Kumar. *A History of Indian Literature.* Vol. 8: *1800–1910. Western Impact: Indian Response.* New Delhi: Sahitya Akademi, 1991.
———. *A History of Indian Literature.* [Vol. 9:] *1911–1956. Struggle for Freedom: Triumph and Tragedy.* New Delhi: Sahitya Akademi, 1995.
Das Gupta, Jyotindra. *Language Conflict and National Development: Group Politics and National Language Policy in India.* Berkeley: University of California Press, 1970.
Datta, Amaresh, ed. *Encyclopedia of Indian Literature.* Vol 1. New Delhi: Sahitya Akademi, 1987.
Dayal, Ravi. "A Kayastha's View of Delhi." In *Celebrating Delhi,* edited by Mala Dayal. New Delhi: Penguin Books and Ravi Dayal, 2010.
———. "New Writing in English: The Problem." *Seminar,* August 1991, 12–14.
Deleuze, Gilles, and Felix Guattari. *Kafka: Toward a Minor Literature.* Translated by Dana Polan. Minneapolis: University of Minnesota Press, 1986.
Desai, Anita. *In Custody.* New York: Penguin Books, 1984.
———. "Various Lives." In *Lives in Translation: Bilingual Writers on Identity and Creativity,* edited by Isabelle de Courtivron. New York: Palgrave, 2003.

Desai, Kiran. *The Inheritance of Loss.* New York: Atlantic Monthly Press, 2006.

Deshpande, Shashi. *Writing from the Margin and Other Essays.* New Delhi: Penguin Books, 2003.

Devy, G.N. *In Another Tongue: Essays on Indian English Literature.* London: Peter Lang, 1993.

Dhar, Sheila. *Raga'n Josh: Stories from a Musical Life.* Ranikhet: Permanent Black, 2005.

Dharker, Rani. "An Interview with Salman Rushdie." *New Quest* 42 (November–December 1983): 351–60.

Dirks, Nicholas B. *Castes of Mind: Colonialism and the Making of Modern India.* Princeton: Princeton University Press, 2001.

———. *The Hollow Crown: Ethnohistory of an Indian Kingdom.* Ann Arbor: University of Michigan Press, 1993.

English, James. *The Economy of Prestige: Prizes, Awards, and the Circulation of Cultural Value.* Cambridge, MA: Harvard University Press, 2005.

Eisenlohr, Patrick. *Little India: Diaspora, Time, and Ethnolinguistic Belonging in Hindu Mauritius.* Berkeley: University of California Press, 2006.

Foucault, Michel. "What Is an Author?" In *Language, Counter-Memory, Practice: Selected Essays and Interviews by Michel Foucault,* edited by Donald F. Bouchard. Ithaca, NY: Cornell University Press, 1977.

Gal, Susan. "Language and Political Spaces." In *Language and Space,* edited by P. Auer and J.E. Schmidt. The Hague: Mouton de Gruyter, 2009.

Gandhi, Mohandas K. *Evil Wrought by the English Medium.* Edited by R.K. Prabhu. Ahmedabad: Navajivan Trust, 1958.

———. *Hind Swaraj and Other Writings.* Edited by Anthony J. Parel. Cambridge: Cambridge University Press, 1997.

Geetha, V., and S.V. Rajadurai. *Towards a Non-Brahmin Millennium: From Iyothee Thass to Periyar.* Calcutta: Samya, 1998.

Ghosh, Amitav. *The Shadow Lines.* New Delhi: Ravi Dayal, 1988.

Gilroy, Paul. *Small Acts: Thoughts on the Politics of Black Cultures.* London: Serpent's Tale, 1993.

Griswold, Wendy. *Bearing Witness: Readers, Writers, and the Novel in Nigeria.* Princeton: Princeton University Press, 2000.

Hobsbawm, Eric. *Nations and Nationalism since 1780: Programs, Myths, Realities.* Cambridge: Cambridge University Press, 1990.

Ilaiah, Kancha. *Why I Am Not a Hindu: A Sudra Critique of Hindutva Philosophy, Culture, and Political Economy.* Calcutta: Samya, 1996/2005.

Jaffrelot, Christophe. *The Hindu Nationalist Movement in India.* New York: Columbia University Press, 1998.

Jain, Madhu. "Sujan Singh Park." In *City Improbable: An Anthology of Writings on Delhi*, edited by Khushwant Singh. New Delhi: Penguin Books, 2001.

Jeffrey, Robin. *India's Newspaper Revolution: Capitalism, Politics, and the Indian-Language Press, 1977–99.* London: Hurst & Co., 2000.

Joshi, Priya. *In Another Country: Colonialism, Culture, and the English Novel in India.* New York: Columbia University Press, 2002.

Joshi, Svati, ed. *Rethinking English: Essays in Literature, Language, History.* New Delhi: Trianka, 1991.

Jussawalla, Adil. "Being There: Aspects of an Indian Crisis." *Bombay Review,* no. 1 (1989).

Kapur, Manju. *Home.* New Delhi: Random House India, 2006.

Kaviraj, Sudipta. *The Imaginary Institution of India.* Ranikhet: Permanent Black, 2010.

King, Christopher R. *One Language, Two Scripts: The Hindi Movement in Nineteenth-Century North India.* New Delhi: Oxford University Press, 1994.

King, Robert D. *Nehru and the Language Politics of India.* New Delhi: Oxford University Press, 1997.

Kothari, Rita. *Translating India: The Cultural Politics of English.* Rev. ed. New Delhi: Cambridge University Press India, 2005.

Kroskrity, Paul, ed. *Regimes of Language: Ideologies, Polities, and Identities.* Santa Fe, NM: School of American Research Press, 2000.

Kumar, Amitava. "Bad News: Authenticity and the South Asian Political Novel." *Boston Review,* November–December 2008.

Kumar, Dharma, et al., eds. *Civil Lines: New Writing from India.* New Delhi: Ravi Dayal, (vol. 1) 1994–(vol. 5) 2001.

Kumar, Krishna. *Learning from Conflict.* New Delhi: Orient Longman, 1996.

Lelyveld, David. "The Fate of Hindustani: Colonial Knowledge and the Project of a National Language." In *Orientalism and the Postcolonial Predicament: Perspectives on South Asia,* edited by Carol Breckenridge and Peter van der Veer. Philadelphia: University of Pennsylvania Press, 1993.

Lukacs, Georg. *The Theory of the Novel: A Historico-Philosophical Essay on the Forms of Great Epic Literature.* Translated by Anna Bostock. Cambridge, MA: MIT Press, 1971.

Minault, Gail. "Delhi College and Urdu." *Annual of Urdu Studies* 14 (1999): 119–34.

Mitchell, Lisa. *Language, Emotion, and Politics in South India: The Making of a Mother Tongue.* Bloomington: Indiana University Press, 2009.

Mehrotra, Arvind Krishna. Introduction to *A Concise History of Indian Literature in English,* edited by Arvind Krishna Mehrotra. Ranikhet: Permanent Black, 2008.

Menon, Nivedita, and Aditya Nigam. *Power and Contestation: India since 1989.* London: Zed Books, 2007.

Menon, Ritu, ed. *Women Who Dared.* New Delhi: National Book Trust, 2002.

Metcalf, Thomas R. *An Imperial Vision: Indian Architecture and Britain's Raj.* Berkeley: University of California Press, 1989.

Mir, Farina. *The Social Space of Language: Vernacular Culture in British Colonial Punjab.* Berkeley: University of California Press, 2010.

Mishra, Vijay. *The Literature of the Indian Diaspora: Theorizing the Diasporic Imaginary.* London: Routledge, 2007.

Mistry, Rohinton. *A Fine Balance.* New York: Knopf, 1996.

Moretti, Franco. "The Novel: History and Theory." *New Left Review* 52 (July–August 2008): 111–24.

Mukherjee, Bharati. "The Way Back." In *Genius of Language: Fifteen Writers Reflect on Their Mother Tongues,* edited by Wendy Lesser. Westminster, MD: Knopf Publishing Group, 2004.

Mukherjee, Meenakshi. *Elusive Terrain: Culture and Literary Memory.* New Delhi: Oxford University Press, 2008.

———. *The Perishable Empire: Essays on Indian Writing in English.* New Delhi: Oxford University Press, 2000.

———. *Realism and Reality: The Novel and Society in India.* New Delhi: Oxford University Press, 1985.

———. *The Twice Born Fiction: Themes and Techniques of the Indian Novel in English.* New Delhi: Oxford University Press, 1971.

Mukherjee, Meenakshi, and Nissim Ezekiel, eds. *Another India.* New Delhi: Penguin Books, 1990.

Mukherjee, Sujit. "New Literary History." *Explorations in Literary History* 8, no. 2 (Winter 1977): 225–34.

———. *Translation as Discovery and Other Essays on Indian Literature in English Translation.* New Delhi: Allied Publishers, 1981.

Nagarkar, Kiran. *Cuckold.* New Delhi: HarperCollins, 1997.

Nandy, Ashis. *The Intimate Enemy: Loss and Recovery of Self under Colonialism.* New Delhi: Oxford University Press, 1983.

Naregal, Veena. *Language Politics, Elites, and the Public Sphere: Western India under Colonialism.* New Delhi: Permanent Black, 2001.

Ngũgĩ wa Thiong'o. *Decolonising the Mind: The Politics of Language in African Literature.* Portsmouth, NH: Heinemann, 1986.

Ninan, Sevanti. *Headlines from the Heartland: Reinventing the Hindi Public Sphere.* New Delhi: Sage, 2007.

Orsini, Francesca. *The Hindi Public Sphere, 1920–1940: Language and Literature in the Age of Nationalism.* New Delhi: Oxford University Press, 2002.

Pamuk, Orhan. *Other Colours: Essays and a Story.* Translated by Maureen Freely. London: Faber and Faber, 2007.

Pandey, Gyanendra. *Remembering Partition: Violence, Nationalism, and History in India.* Cambridge: Cambridge University Press, 2002.

Pandolfo, Stefania. *Impasse of the Angels: Scenes from a Moroccan Space of Memory.* Chicago: University of Chicago Press, 1997.

Pollock, Sheldon. *Language of the Gods in the World of Men: Sanskrit, Culture, and Power in Premodern India.* Berkeley: University of California Press, 2006.

Rai, Alok. *Hindi Nationalism.* New Delhi: Orient Longman, 2001.

Rai, Amrit. *A House Divided: The Origin and Development of Hindi/Hindavi.* New Delhi: Oxford University Press, 1984.

Ramanujan, A.K. *The Collected Essays of A.K. Ramanujan.* Edited by Vinay Dharwardker et al. New Delhi: Oxford University Press, 1999.

Ramaswamy, Sumathi. *Passions of the Tongue: Language Devotion in Tamil India, 1891–1970.* Berkeley: University of California Press, 1997.

Rao, D.S. *Five Decades: A Short History of the Sahitya Akademi.* New Delhi: Sahitya Akademi, 2004.

Rege, Sharmila. *Writing Caste, Writing Gender: Reading Dalit Women's Testimonios.* New Delhi: Zubaan, 2006.

Report of the Official Language Commission, 1956. New Delhi: Government of India Press, 1957.
Roy, Arundhati. *The Algebra of Infinite Justice*. New Delhi: Penguin Books, 2002.
———. *The God of Small Things*. New Delhi: India Ink, 1998.
Rushdie, Salman. "Damme, This Is the Oriental Scene for You!" *New Yorker*, 23 and 30 June 1997, 50–61.
———. *Imaginary Homelands: Essays and Criticism, 1981–1991*. London: Granta Books, 1991.
———. *Midnight's Children*. New York: Penguin Books, 1981.
Rushdie, Salman, and Elizabeth West. *Mirrorwork: 50 Years of Indian Writing, 1947–1997*. New York: Henry Holt, 1997.
Said, Edward. *Beginnings: Intention and Method*. New York: Basic Books, 1975.
———. *Culture and Imperialism*. New York: Knopf, 1993.
Satchidanandan, K. *Sahitya Akademi General Information Bulletin*. New Delhi: Sahitya Akademi 2002.
Schieffelin, Bambi, Kathryn A. Woolard, and Paul Kroskrity, eds. *Language Ideologies: Practice and Theory*. Oxford: Oxford University Press, 1998.
Seth, Vikram. *Koi Accha-sa Ladka*. Translated by Gopal Gandhi. New Delhi: Vani Prakashan, 1998.
———. *A Suitable Boy*. New York: HarperCollins, 1993.
Shackle, Christopher, and Rupert Snell. *Hindi and Urdu since 1800*. SOAS South Asian Texts No. 1. London: School of Oriental and African Studies/University of London, 1990.
Shree, Geetanjali. "From the Polyphonic World of Hindi Fiction." *Caravan* 3, no. 2 (February 2011).
———. *Khali Jagah*. New Delhi: Rajkamal Prakashan, 2006.
———. *Mai*. New Delhi: Rajkamal Prakashan, 1993.
———. *Mai*. Translated by Nita Kumar. New Delhi: Kali for Women, 2000.
Shukla, Shrilal. *Raag Darbari*. New Delhi: Rajkamal Prakashan, 1968.
Singh, Khushwant. "The Romance of New Delhi." In *Khushwant Singh's India: A Mirror for Its Monsters and Monstrosities*, edited by Rahul Singh. Bombay: IBH Publishing, 1969.
———. *Train to Pakistan*. New York: Grove Press, 1956.
———. *Why I Supported the Emergency: Essays and Profiles*. Edited by Sheela Reddy. New Delhi: Penguin Books, 2009.
Sinha, Mrinalini. *Colonial Masculinity: The 'Manly Englishman' and the 'Effeminate Bengali' in the Late Nineteenth Century*. Manchester: Manchester University Press, 1995.
Slaughter, Joseph. *Human Rights, Inc: The World Novel, Narrative Form, and International Law*. New York: Fordham Press, 2007.
Spivak, Gayatri Chakrabarty. *In Other Worlds: Essays in Cultural Politics*. London: Methuen, 1987.
———. "Three Women's Texts and a Critique of Colonialism." *Critical Inquiry* 12, no. 1 (1985): 243–61.
———. "Translating into English." In *Nation, Language, and the Ethics of*

Translation, edited by Sandra Bermann and Michael Wood. Princeton: Princeton University Press, 2005.

Srinivas, M.N., et al. "The Social System of a Mysore Village." In *Village India: Studies in the Little Community,* edited by McKim Marriot. Chicago: University of Chicago Press, 1955.

Srinivasaraju, Sugata. *Keeping Faith with the Mother Tongue: The Anxieties of a Local Culture.* Bangalore: Navakarnataka, 2008.

Starke, Ulrike. *An Empire of Books: The Naval Kishore Press and the Diffusion of the Printed Word in Colonial India.* New Delhi: Permanent Black, 2007.

Stoler, Ann. *Race and the Education of Desire: Foucault's History of Sexuality and the Colonial Order of Things.* Durham, NC: Duke University Press, 1995.

Subramani. *Dauka Puraan.* New Delhi: Star Publications, 2001.

Suleri, Sara. *Meatless Days.* Chicago: University of Chicago Press, 1987.

———. *The Rhetoric of English India.* Chicago: University of Chicago Press, 1992.

Sunder Rajan, Rajeswari. "Fixing English: Nation, Language, Subject." In *The Lie of the Land: English Literary Studies in India,* edited by Rajeswari Sunder Rajan. New Delhi: Oxford University Press, 1992.

Tagore, Rabindranath. *Gora.* Translated by Sujit Mukherjee. New Delhi: Sahitya Akademi, 1998. (First pub. 1907.)

Tarlo, Emma. *Unsettling Memories: Narratives of the Emergency in Delhi.* Berkeley: University of California Press, 2003.

Trivedi, Harish. "Ahmed Ali: *Twilight in Delhi.*" In *Major Indian Novels,* edited by N.S. Pradhan. New Delhi: Arnold-Heinemann, 1985.

———. "The Progress of Hindi, Part 2: Hindi and the Nation." In *Literary Cultures in History: Reconstructions from South Asia,* edited by Sheldon Pollock. Berkeley: University of California Press, 2003.

———. "Translation as Recovery: *A Suitable Boy* as *Koi Accha-Sa Ladka.*" *Book Review* 22, no. 9 (1998): 30–31.

Valmiki, Omprakash. *Joothan: A Dalit's Life.* Translated by Arun Mukherjee. Calcutta: Samya, 2003.

Varma, Pavan. *The Great Indian Middle Class.* New Delhi: Penguin Books, 1998.

Verma, Nirmal. "Returning to One's Country." Translated by Meenakshi Mukherjee. *Vagartha* 13 (April 1976).

Viswanathan, Gauri. *Masks of Conquest: Literary Study and British Rule in India.* New Delhi: Oxford University Press, 1989.

Wakabayashi, Judy, and Rita Kothari. Introduction to *Decentering Translation Studies: India and Beyond,* edited by Judy Wakabayashi and Rita Kothari. Amsterdam: John Benjamins, 2009.

Watt, Ian P. *Rise of the Novel: Studies in Defoe, Richardson, and Fielding.* Berkeley: University of California Press, 1957.

Williams, Raymond. *The Country and the City.* New York: Oxford University Press, 1973.

Wood, James. *How Fiction Works.* London: Jonathan Cape, 2008.

Woolard, Kathryn. "Introduction: Language Ideology as a Field of Inquiry." In *Language Ideologies: Practice and Theory*, edited by Bambi B. Schieffelin, Kathryn A. Woolard, and Paul V. Kroskrity. Oxford: Oxford University Press, 1998.

Young, Robert J.C. *Postcolonialism: A Historical Introduction.* Oxford: Blackwell, 2001.

Index

TEXT
10/13 Sabon Open Type

DISPLAY
Sabon Open Type

COMPOSITOR
Modern Language Initiative

TEXT PRINTER AND BINDER
IBT Global